HOUSE OF COMMONS   SESSION 1998–99

FOREIGN AFFAIRS COMMITTEE

First Report

FOREIGN POLICY AND HUMAN RIGHTS

Volume III

Appendices to the
Minutes of Evidence

Ordered by The House of Commons *to be printed*
10 December 1998

LONDON: THE STATIONERY OFFICE
£15.90

HC 100–III

The Foreign Affairs Committee is appointed under Standing Order No 152 to examine the expenditure, administration and policy of the Foreign and Commonwealth Office and associated public bodies.

The Committee consists of 12 Members. It has a quorum of three. Unless the House otherwise orders, all members nominated to the Committee continue to be members of it for the remainder of the Parliament.

The Committee has power:

(a)   to send for persons, papers and records, to sit notwithstanding any adjournment of the House, to adjourn from place to place, and to report from time to time;

(b)   to appoint specialist advisers either to supply information which is not readily available or to elucidate matters of complexity within the Committee's order of reference;

(c)   to communicate to any other committee appointed under the same Standing Order (or to the European Scrutiny Committee, the Committee of Public Accounts, the Deregulation Committee or to the Environmental Audit Committee) its evidence and any other documents relating to matters of common interest;

(d)   to meet concurrently with any other such committee for the purposes of deliberating, taking evidence, or considering draft reports or with the European Scrutiny Committee or any Sub-Committee thereof for the purposes of deliberating or taking evidence.

———

The membership of the Committee since its nomination on 17 July 1997 has been as follows:

Mr Donald Anderson, *Swansea East* (Chairman)

Ms Diane Abbott, *Hackney North and Stoke Newington*
Rt Hon Mrs Virginia Bottomley, *South West Surrey*
Rt Hon Sir Peter Emery, *East Devon*
Mr Norman A Godman, *Greenock and Inverclyde*
Mr David Heath, *Somerton and Frome*

Mr Eric Illsley, *Barnsley Central*
Mr Andrew Mackinlay, *Thurrock*
Mr Ernie Ross, *Dundee West*
Mr Ted Rowlands, *Merthyr Tydfil and Rhymney*
Rt Hon Sir John Stanley, *Tonbridge and Malling*
Mr David Wilshire, *Spelthorne*

CONTENTS

Volume II

Volume III

LIST OF WITNESSES

LIST OF MEMORANDA
INCLUDED IN THE MINUTES OF EVIDENCE

Page

LIST OF APPENDICES TO THE MINUTES OF EVIDENCE

Memoranda or supplementary memoranda submitted by:

UNPUBLISHED MEMORANDA

Additional memoranda have been received by the following and have been reported to the House, but to save printing costs they have not been printed and copies have been placed in the House of Commons Library where they may be inspected by Members. Other copies are in the Record Office, House of Lords, and are available to the public for inspection. Requests for inspection should be addressed to the Record Office, House of Lords, London, SW1. (Tel 071-219 3074). Hours of inspection are from 9.30 am to 5.30 pm on Mondays to Fridays.

1. Burma Action Group UK

2. Foreign Secretary: Letters to Rt Hon Virginia Bottomley MP and to Rt Hon Sir Peter Emery MP, regarding the human rights situation in Kenya

3. Ghana Human Rights Committee.

4. Group of Flemish Socialists in the Belgian Houses of Parliament

5. International Confederation of Free Trade Unions

6. Kenya High Commission, London

7. Dr Akin Kumoluyi, Association of Nigeria Abroad

8. Kurdistan opposition groups: joint submission

9. Medical Foundation: Responsibility for Human Rights Violations in Algeria

10. Saferworld: The US Code of Conduct on Arms Trade

11. Shell International Limited

12. Yemeni Human Rights Organisation (Europe) : copy of letter sent to Mr Isaac Bitter, Secretary, UN Centre for Human Rights, August 1997

APPENDICES TO THE MINUTES OF EVIDENCE

TAKEN BEFORE THE FOREIGN AFFAIRS COMMITTEE

APPENDIX 1

Memorandum submitted by the Director, Local Government International Bureau

As Director of the Local Government International Bureau, (the European and international arm of the Local Government Association) I am writing in relation to the inquiry into foreign policy and human rights conducted by the Foreign Affairs Committee.

In response to the Committee's terms of reference requesting an assessment of "the extent to which such policy can be effective in preventing or remedying human rights abuses", we believe that the UK government's international human rights obligations can best be implemented *when local government in both this and the foreign country plays a critical role.*

We believe that:

(1) Democratic local government is a crucial instrument for the promotion and protection of human rights.

(2) There is a growing recognition of the importance of local self-government, not only as a principle but also as an emerging right in itself. (Our briefing on "The Emerging Right to Democratic Local Self Government' is attached [*not printed*].)"

It is increasingly recognised that effective local government has the potential to:

— Dilute the possibility of an abuse of power by national authorities.

— Empower local people to hold local representatives accountable.

— Enable minorities to be represented.

Moreover, it is precisely through democratic local government that many of the economic and social rights in addition to the civil and political rights set out in various Charters of human rights and the relevant UN Covenants are most effectively delivered. This is evidenced by the fast-growing success of the European Charter of Local Self-Government, now signed by the UK, and further by the African Commonwealth Heads of Government who have recently recognised that "effective elected local government is an important foundation for democracy."

The Local Government International Bureau therefore urges the Foreign Affairs Committee to recognise the crucial role of local and regional government in its assessment of the effectiveness of the Government's policy on implementing human rights objectives.

Amongst other matters, we believe that a strong decentralised co-operation component of the Department for International Development's policies and programmes is an important means of promoting human rights in a global context.

We would of course be pleased to develop the above points and arguments.

October 1997

APPENDIX 2

Memorandum submitted by TAPOL, The Indonesia Human Rights Campaign

1. This memorandum is provided by TAPOL, the Indonesia Human Rights Campaign, for consideration by the Foreign Affairs Committee in relation to its inquiry into foreign policy and human rights, which has the following terms of reference:

To examine how the Government implements its human rights objectives when formulating and executing foreign policy, both bilaterally and multilaterally, and to assess the extent to which such policy can be effective in preventing or remedying human rights abuses.

2. TAPOL was set up in the UK in 1973, and it has been campaigning since then against human rights abuses in Indonesia ("TAPOL" means "political prisoner" in Indonesian). It has also, since 1975, campaigned for self-determination for East Timor. TAPOL's objectives include the publishing of authoritative information on the human rights situation in Indonesia and East Timor. TAPOL is regularly consulted by MPs and the Foreign Office recently followed TAPOL's advice on which human rights NGOs the Foreign Secretary should meet during his visit to Indonesia in August 1997 (see below).

3. In order to draw conclusions and make recommendations about the formulation and execution of foreign policy and human rights, this memorandum considers two key initiatives taken by the British Government (HMG) since 1 May 1997. They are:

(a) the introduction and application of new arms export licencing criteria;

(b) the promotion of human rights by the Foreign Secretary during his visit to Indonesia from 29 to 30 August 1997.

Although these two initiatives are discussed in relation to Indonesia and East Timor, their implications extend to foreign policy and human rights in general.

I. HUMAN RIGHTS AT THE HEART OF FOREIGN POLICY

4. HMG's human rights objectives have been set out in numerous policy statements made before and after the election. In its election manifesto, the Labour Party pledged to "make the protection and promotion of human rights a central part of our foreign policy" and not to "permit the sale of arms to regimes that might use them for internal repression". The ethical approach to foreign policy was confirmed by the Foreign Secretary when he launched the Foreign and Commonwealth Office's Mission Statement on 12 May:

> Our foreign policy must have an ethical dimension and must support the demand of other people for the democratic rights on which we insist for ourselves. The Labour Government will put human rights at the heart of our foreign policy and will publish an annual report on our work in promoting human rights abroad

5. In a speech entitled *Human Rights into a New Century* on 17 July, the Foreign Secretary announced 12 policies that would put into effect HMG's commitment to human rights. In particular, he pledged that "Britain will support measures within the international community to express our condemnation of those regimes who grotesquely violate human rights and repeatedly fail to respond to demand for an improvement in standards", and stated that the "review of Government criteria for the licensing of weapons for export . . . will give effect to Labour's policy commitment that we will not supply equipment or weapons that might be used for internal repression." He further committed HMG to "publish an Annual Report on our activities in the promotion of human rights. That will provide an incentive for those of us in government with a checklist by which you can judge our performance and encourage us to even higher levels of achievement." This latter commitment is considered briefly at the end of this memorandum.

II. ARMS EXPORT CONTROLS

6. The new arms export licencing criteria announced by the Foreign Secretary on 28 July have proved disappointing both in terms of their content and application. The decision, announced at the same time, that the Labour Government would not revoke licences granted by the previous administration—including licences for the export to Indonesia of Hawk aircraft, armoured vehicles and water cannon—and the recent granting of new licences for Indonesia are worrying signs that there is a considerable gap between policy and practice. There is clear evidence that British equipment has been used for internal repression in Indonesia, and water cannon in particular have been used since the Labour Government came to power.[1]

7. Although the new criteria give "full weight" to the UK's national interests, they require HMG only to "take into account" respect for human rights. This could result in greater weight being given to commercial relations with a recipient country and to what is regarded as the UK's national interest in maintaining a strong arms industry (which Ministers have repeatedly emphasised) than to a recipient country's human rights record. *A human-rights-centred foreign policy should give full and prior weight to human rights concerns.*

8. The new criteria state that export licences will not be issued "if there is a *clearly identifiable* risk that the proposed export might be used for internal repression". This includes "Equipment where there is *clear* evidence of the recent use of similar equipment for internal repression" and "Equipment which has *obvious* application for internal repression, in cases where the recipient country has a *significant and continuing* record of such repression". [All emphasis added.] But the criteria allow exports to a country with a record of repression if "the end-use of the equipment is judged to be legitimate, such as the protection of members of the security forces from violence".

9. There is an apparent shift in emphasis in that licences will not now be granted where equipment *might be used* for internal repression, whereas previously, they would not be granted if the equipment was *likely to be used* for internal repression. However, the criteria are still interpreted subjectively by Ministers and officials who are apparently under pressure to ensure that the arms industry is not damaged (see below). The loopholes and qualifications referred to and emphasised in the previous two paragraphs allow the criteria to be interpreted with considerable flexibility.

---

[1] A BBC World Service TV news report on 20 May 1997 shows a British water cannon being used to break up a demonstration by the United Democratic Party (PPP) in the build up to the Indonesian elections on 29 May. The report shows security forces wearing gas masks and civilians rubbing their eyes and putting their hands over their mouths, indicating that chemicals, possibly including CS gas, were added to the water sprayed by the cannon. The Conservative administration stated that the use of chemicals or dyes with the water cannon is totally unacceptable. The Foreign Secretary's office has a video of this news report.

10.   There are no guidelines to indicate how evidence is to be obtained and risks assessed. In June 1997, TAPOL sent to the Foreign Secretary's office evidence of water cannon being used in Indonesia for internal repression (see footnote 1). The office responded with a letter which referred to the evidence as "allegations", which would be "considered if we receive any application in future for export of similar equipment".[1] *Credible evidence of the misuse of equipment should be investigated immediately.* Delaying an investigation until a future application is received is, for obvious reasons, unsatisfactory. *There is a need for rigorous monitoring of the end use of equipment in countries where there is concern that equipment might be used for internal repression or external aggression. Furthermore, the criteria should allow HMG to ban the sale of all arms to governments, such as Indonesia, which have a persistent record of internal repression and external aggression.*

11.   It appears that the new criteria will not result in tighter controls over arms exports. The Labour Government avoided applying the criteria to the existing licences for the export to Indonesia of Hawk aircraft, armoured vehicles and water cannon by stating it would not be "realistic or practical" to revoke the licences. It is not clear what that means since TAPOL has legal advice to the effect that it would be perfectly proper for HMG to revoke the licences and the Foreign Secretary has stated that his own legal advice is "inconclusive". *These licences should be revoked immediately.*

12.   On the eve of the Labour Party Conference, the Foreign Secretary's office announced that HMG had blocked three licences (in fact four in total were refused) for the export to Indonesia of armoured vehicles and sniper rifles worth up to £1 million.[2] However on the last day of the Conference the Department of Trade and Industry revealed that it had granted 11 licences for Indonesia[3]. At least a further 44 licence applications for Indonesia were then outstanding and close to being approved. HMG will not disclose the nature of the equipment, but its value could run into hundreds of millions of pounds. Last year, arms sales, worth £438 million accounted for half the UK's total exports to Indonesia. It is understood that negotiations are taking place for the export of more Hawk aircraft, Piranha class mini-submarines and air defence systems and artillery to protect Indonesia's oil and gas industry. There is a clear risk that this equipment will be used for internal repression in Indonesia and will be used or deployed in East Timor to maintain Indonesia's illegal and brutal occupation of the territory.

13.   Following the announcement that three licences had been blocked, *The Financial Times* reported that the Prime Minister's office had written to the Foreign Secretary urging him to moderate his policy of blocking arms sales to countries accused of serious human rights violations, because of concern about its affect on the arms industry. If such pressure is being applied it is unlikely that many licences will be refused on human rights grounds. *To counter such pressure, the criteria should be independently monitored and enforced. The criteria should be embodied in legislation enforceable in the courts by interested individuals and organisations. There must be greater openness and transparency in licensing decisions and end use monitoring.*

Recommendation I

To provide for the more effective implementation of HMG's commitment to human rights in relation to arms sales, HMG should:

Set up a committee of Parliament to:

   (a) *review and further strengthen the export licencing criteria;*

   (b) *consider the introduction of independent mechanisms to ensure greater transparency and to monitor the application of the criteria to specific licencing decisions; and*

   (c) *consider ways of incorporating the criteria into legislation, to include a provision outlawing the sale of arms to countries which have a persistent record of internal repression and/or external aggression.*

Introduce measures to ensure the rigorous monitoring of the end use of equipment.

Introduce an immediate ban on all arms sales to the Indonesian regime, which is responsible for the widespread suppression of human rights and the illegal and brutal occupation of East Timor; and monitor the use of previously-exported British equipment to ensure that it is not used for internal repression in Indonesia and that it is not used or deployed in East Timor.

III.   FOREIGN SECRETARY'S VISIT TO INDONESIA

14.   The Foreign Secretary's visit to Indonesia in August 1997 provides an instructive case-study of how the Government is implementing its human rights objectives. Before the trip, the Foreign Secretary stated that "I will set out this Government's foreign policy priorities, which include a deepening of our relations across Asia

---

[1] Letter dated 29 August 1997, Private Secretary of Foreign Secretary to TAPOL.
[2] See *Cook Lays down the law on arms, The Guardian,* 26 September 1997.
[3] Letter dated 3 October 1997 to Ann Clwyd MP from Lord Clinton-Davis, Minister for Trade.

and ensuring respect for human rights."[1] Although he then made some welcome moves on East Timor during his visit, his other human rights initiatives were disappointing gestures. They are likely to be ineffective in preventing or remedying human rights abuses.

East Timor initiatives

15.   Immediately after arriving in Jarkarta, the Foreign Secretary telephoned the Nobel Peace co-laureate, Bishop Carlos Ximenes Belo, the Roman Catholic Bishop of Dili, to ask about conditions in East Timor. East Timor then dominated the Foreign Secretary's meeting with Indonesian Foreign Minister Ali Alatas and at a press conference he made a welcome point of emphasising Indonesia's breach of UN Security Council resolutions on East Timor. He also announced that Britain would propose a European Troika visit at ambassadorial level to East Timor, during the British Presidency, to "enable Europe to be more fully informed of the situation in East Timor and the views of its people".[2]

16.   Until now, EU governments have refused to send their ambassadors to East Timor since the visit of an Ambassador could be taken as recognition of Indonesian sovereignty over the territory. As the Foreign Secretary has acknowledged, *the visit must be made subject to the issue of a statement that it does not imply recognition.*

17.   It is also necessary to ensure that the mission can hear the views of the population without jeopardising people's safety. It is understood that when EU Ambassadors have been to other disputed territories, such as Kashmir and the Chittagong Hill Tracts, they were always accompanied by officials so that ordinary people would not say anything for fear of reprisals. *HMG should ensure that the mission to East Timor has its own interpreters, that it is free to visit all parts of the territory and that discussions with the public take place in private. The mission should make a public statement following its visit so that its findings can be widely disseminated.*

18.   There are other important initiatives that HMG can take on East Timor, including pressing for the implementation of the 1997 UN Commission on Human Rights resolution on East Timor, pressing for effective on-site UN monitoring, and backing the UN-mediated talks (for detailed recommendations on these initiatives, see the submission by the British Coalition on East Timor, *Promoting Human Rights through Foreign Policy: The Challenge in East Timor). In all this, HMG and the EU ambassadorial mission should not lose sight of the only genuine solution for East Timor, an act of self-determination by means of a UN-monitored referendum.*

Other initiatives

19.   During his visit, the Foreign Secretary announced a six-point human rights plan and met with representatives of four NGOs. His planned meeting with the independent trade union leader, Muchtar Pakpahan was cancelled by the Indonesian authorities.

20.   The six-point plan comprised: meetings with human rights leaders during his visit; provision of computers, software and training for the government-appointed National Human Rights Commission; an assistance package for the legal aid foundation; up to 12 scholarships in Britain for future opinion-formers; three places at Oxford University's course on international human rights law; and lectures by senior British police officers on effective and non-confrontational crowd control at demonstrations, a common cause of violence in Indonesia. It is understood that the latter initiative will consist of a series of lectures to the Indonesian police on modern policing methods to take place in Indonesia.

21.   This six-point plan is deeply flawed and of little value in the context of a foreign policy which allows arms sales to Indonesia to continue unabated. It demonstrates the inconsistencies inherent in a policy which strives to both maintain a strong arms industry and promote human rights. What, for example, is the point in lecturing Indonesian policemen on crowd control techniques at the same time as supplying them with the means (water cannon and armoured vehicles) to act violently against peaceful demonstrators?

22.   The police training programme was rejected by the NGO representatives who met the Foreign Secretary. The Indonesian Police Force is not a civilian force. It is part of the armed forces and as such, it is part of the problem, not part of the solution. HMG has already wasted over ten years training Indonesian police officers under the British aid programme without any discernible impact on their human rights record.[3] The Secretary of State for International Development has stated that her department will no longer fund training for the Indonesian police,[4] hence FCO and DFID policies on police training appear to be diametrically opposed. *Instead of providing police training, HMG should press for the Indonesian police force to be transformed into a civilian force, it should speak out in support of the right of assembly and revoke the licences for the export of repressive crowd-control equipment, such as water cannon and armoured vehicles.*

---

[1] FCO press release, 21 August. 1997.
[2] See Opening Statement by the Foreign Secretary at a press conference, Jakarta, 29 August 1997.
[3] See the National Audit Office Report, *Aid to Indonesia*, published on 29 November 1996 (HC 101 Session 1996–97).
[4] See *Leadership wins the battle over Trident missiles, The Independent*, 3 October 1997.

23.   HMG's support for the National Commission on Human Rights is misguided, since the Commission is a quasi-governmental organisation, which has proved largely ineffective at investigating and preventing human rights abuses. Commission members have shown their lack of independence by condemning foreign criticism of the Government's human rights record.

24.   The Foreign Secretary's failure to meet Muchtar Pakpahan is to be regretted. Neither the Foreign Secretary nor the British Embassy questioned the cancellation of the meeting. Pakpahan is being tried for subversion in relation to his alleged involvement in a pro-democracy demonstration on 27 July 1996 and is not being allowed to travel abroad for vital medical treatment that is unavailable in Indonesia. He has previously been detained, harassed and subjected to intimidation while carrying out legitimate trade union activities. The meeting with Pakpahan would have been the only public display of HMG's support for a victim of repression. By colluding in its cancellation, the Foreign Secretary showed how easily he could be deflected from displaying concern about human rights abuses.

25.   The Foreign Secretary's meeting with NGO representatives was originally scheduled to last half an hour, but was cut to 15 minutes (much less time than the Foreign Secretary spent with representatives of the British business community with whom he had a working breakfast). All those present urged HMG to assist and support civil society and NGOs in Indonesia, but regrettably, the Foreign Secretary made no promises. Unlike the Foreign secretary's meeting with the National Human Rights Commission, the meeting with the NGOs took place on the quiet. One of the NGO representatives commented: "Till now, the British embassy has been very conservative, showing interest only in business. When the Foreign Secretary came up with his human rights initiative, we were taken aback. But I am pessimistic. Besides doing nothing to have his meeting with Pakpahan, he gave us hardly any time and our meeting was held on the quiet. I have no reason to expect any improvement in the attitude of the British embassy on human rights and democratisation.[1]

Recommendation II

   HMG should ensure that human rights considerations are given full weight in determining overall foreign policy and that human rights concerns impact consistently on all aspects of policy; a positive human rights initiative in one area of policy must not be undermined by a negative initiative in another area. In particular, human rights concerns should not be outweighed by commercial concerns, such as those relating to the arms trade.

   HMG should: express condemnation of regimes, such as Indonesia, which persistently violate human rights; speak out about specific human rights abuses as they occur; demonstrate support for victims of repression; and seek ways of engaging more constructively and effectively with independent civil society organisations committed to greater democracy and freedom and to the realisation of all civil, political, social, cultural and economic rights. British embassies should be used as much as possible to reach out and support such organisations.

V. ANNUAL REPORT

26.   The commitment to publish an annual report detailing HMGs activities in promoting human rights is welcome, but limited. The proposed report will fail to put HMGs activities into the context of the human rights situation in the countries concerned. The report should, therefore, also provide individual country reports on human rights. Such reports would encourage a more consistent approach to the promotion of human rights and an opportunity for independent assessment of the execution of HMG policy. HMG should follow the precedent of the US State Department, which publishes annual country reports on human rights practices. These reports have been particularly critical of the record of certain countries, such as Indonesia.

Recommendation III

   HMG should, as part of its proposed annual report, publish annual country reports on human rights so that the operation of HMGs policy can be examined against its own assessment of a particular country's human rights record.

October 1997

APPENDIX 3

Supplementary Memorandum submitted by TAPOL, The Indonesia Human RightsCampaign

I heard very belatedly that your Committee will be discussing the Human Rights Report published by the Foreign and Commonwealth Office last month at a meeting on Tuesday morning. I take the liberty of drawing your attention to our views on the Report's handling of Indonesia and apologise for not having been able to do so sooner.

---

[1] Tohap Simalungkalit, acting chair of the independent trade union federation, SBSI.

It comes as a shock to us to learn that the Foreign Office has chosen Indonesia as a country with which it has entered into "constructive partnership" on the question of human rights.

For more than three decades, Indonesia under the dictatorship of General, now President Suharto, has ranked as one of the world's worst human rights violators. As he seized power in 1965–1966, Suharto presided over one of the worst massacres this century when at least half a million people were slaughtered. Ten years later, he sent in his armed forces to invade East Timor, unleashing a war that has left at least one third of the population dead.

Against such a background, it is difficult to understand how the Foreign Secretary could have given his approval to the inclusion of a photograph of him shaking hands with one of the world's most repressive dictators.

The current situation in Indonesia is one with which your Committee will be most exercised. Let me therefore summarise briefly how things stand at present:

— Since the beginning of 1998, the security forces have used massive force to prevent all public manifestations of disapproval of Suharto's appointment to a seventh term on 11 March. Public rallies and meetings were banned in the capital and at least 350 people were arrested and held for varying periods of time. Around one half are still in custody.

— Some 150 people are awaiting trial, most of whom will be charged for engaging in anti-government political activities, simply for taking part in peaceful gatherings criticising the government and calling for lower prices. All such gatherings were forcibly dispersed by the security forces.

— At least a dozen activists have gone missing since early February, kidnapped by unidentified units of the army. One of these "disappeared" re-surfaced last month. After speaking at length to the National Human Rights Commission, he left for Europe and has since testified about the torture he underwent while in incommunicado military detention. He will travel to Washington this week to testify before a congressional sub-committee about his terrible experiences. Two others who have re-surfaced, who have remained in Indonesia, are too scared to speak publicly about their experiences.

— Heavily armed security forces are being used to prevent tens of thousands of protesting students from leaving their campuses to demonstrate in favour of political and economic reforms. These demonstrations which began in early February are now occurring on a daily basis. *We are particularly concerned that British water cannon supplied to the Indonesian police have been used in many places to spray peaceful demonstrators with chemically-infused liquid. Many have fainted or vomited as a result. We have many press photographs of the water cannon in use. We see no evidence to show that the British government has sought to prevent these vehicles from being used against people exercising their legitimate right to demonstrate and protest.*

— The Indonesian government has collaborated with the Malaysian authorities to secure the enforced deportation to Indonesia of hundreds of Acehnese asylum-seekers who had reason to believe that their lives are in danger in Indonesia because of their membership of or sympathy for the Aceh Freedom Movement. At least eight were killed during the deportation from one camp and horrifying reports are now emerging of the poisoning and shooting dead of several asylum-seekers. These are matters which require the immediate attention of your Committee, especially in view of the Queen's forthcoming visit to Malaysia to open the Commonwealth Games in September.

— The fate of some 540 Acehnese who were deported to Aceh, North Sumatra, on 26 March is unknown. We have received reports of the arrest and possible torture of Acehnese during the past few weeks which we still need to verify.

— There are persistent reports of atrocities in East Timor. According to the 1997 Report of the East Timor Human Rights Centre in Melbourne, published in February this year, at least 771 East Timorese were arbitrarily detained, many of whom were tortured. The Centre recorded 52 extra-judicial killings during the year. Bishop Belo is on record as saying that during the year following his acceptance of the Nobel Peace prize in December 1996, the human rights in East Timor has continued to deteriorate.

This is not a situation that would warrant Indonesia being treated as a "partner" by a government that claims to have placed ethics at the heart of its foreign policy.

We hope that your Committee will take these matters into consideration when considering the Foreign Office report.

May 1998

APPENDIX 4

Memorandum submitted by the British Coalition on East Timor (BCET)

EXECUTIVE SUMMARY

The Labour Government's commitment to an ethical foreign policy, and some steps taken on East Timor since April 1997, bode well for the prospects of promoting human rights through foreign policy. By using his visit to Indonesia to reach out to Nobel Peace Prize laureate Bishop Belo and by noting that the Government of Indonesia remains in breach of UN Security Council resolutions on East Timor, the Foreign Secretary sent a clear signal of Britain's commitment to defending human rights and upholding international law. By instructing her department to design an NGO aid package for East Timor, the International Development Secretary indicated her desire to promote human development on the ground.

Yet these steps will not change the human rights situation in the territory, particularly if they are undermined by continued UK arms sales Indonesia. What is required, as in many other situations of persistent human rights violations, is a coherent strategy integrating the instruments at the disposal of the Government, and articulating UK leverage to the efforts of Britain's partners, in the European Union and beyond. This paper sets out the parameters of such a strategy, to inform officials who are shaping UK policy towards East Timor and contribute to the wider debate on human rights in foreign policy.

In essence, this brief argues that HMG could more effectively promote human rights by working with its partners to press for the implementation of a key provision in the resolution on East Timor passed by the UN Commission on Human Rights in 1997, and promoting the discussion of options for an on-site UN human rights presence in the UN-mediated peace talks. The paper discusses other options open for British diplomacy, including how the UK might take advantage of its Presidency of the European Union and the Asia-Europe Meeting (ASEM II) in early 1998 to engage the Government of Indonesia on East Timor issues.

The brief also examines options for the Department for International Development, namely how DFID could use its new aid package for East Timor to support human rights organisations and gender-focused work by other civil society organisations, monitor the implementation of the European Commission's East Timor aid initiative and review broader co-operation with Indonesia to ensure that no projects financed with British money actually undermine the rights of the Timorese people, including their right to self-determination. Finally, the paper highlights the enduring gap between the arms export policy announced by the Labour Government and its actual practices in this domain, and proposes unilateral and multilateral measures to effectively prevent the continued sale of arms to Indonesia that might be used for external aggression against East Timor.

The British Coalition on East Timor (BCET) is a network of UK non-governmental organisations, campaigns, local groups and individuals working for human rights, peace and self-determination in East Timor. Established in 1992 shortly after the Santa Cruz massacre, BCET organises public information events and lobbies parliamentarians, officials and decision-makers, in order to influence UK policy on East Timor.

For further information, please contact Jackie Hoskins at BCET, PO Box 2349, London E1 3HX, Tel/fax: 0181-985-1127.

Dr Stephen Baranyi is an international policy analyst based in London. BCET thanks the individuals and organisations who contributed to this paper.

INTRODUCTION

HMG commitments on human rights and on East Timor

During his visit to Indonesia at the end of August 1997, Foreign Secretary Robin Cook raised British concerns about the situation in East Timor and unveiled a package of measures intended to build a partnership with the Government of Indonesia (GoI) on human rights issues. He noted that GoI remained in breach of UN Security Council resolutions on East Timor and announced that, during the UK Presidency of the European Union in early 1998, Britain would lead a visit by a delegation of EU ambassadors to the occupied territory. He also made a well-publicised telephone call to Nobel co-laureate Monsignor Carlos Ximenes Belo, Bishop of Dili diocese, to discuss the situation in East Timor.[1]

This high-profile display of interest built on earlier actions by the Labour Government. In London, the Foreign Secretary had already met Bishop Belo and his co-laureate José Ramos-Horta who, as Special Representative of the National Council of Maubere Resistance (CNRM), is the senior diplomat of the Timorese Resistance in exile. Mr Cook assured both men of his commitment to defending the rights of the Timorese people and supporting the UN-mediated peace talks. International Development Secretary Clare Short had also met with Mr Ramos-Horta: she indicated her commitment to ensuring that no UK development co-operation programmes with Indonesia actually undermined the rights of the Timorese people, and expressed her interest in developing a special UK aid package for East Timor, channelled through NGOs and directed at civil society. For his part, Minister of State Derek Fatchett assured concerned MPs that the UK "will press the Indonesians to implement the latest UNCHR resolution" and is "also pursuing the question of a UN Human Rights Office in East Timor itself".[2]

These initial steps on East Timor clearly represent an attempt to put the new Government's "ethical foreign policy" into practice.[3] A key aspect of this approach is the tightening of controls over arms exports. In July the Government announced new guidelines to ensure that no licences would be granted for the export of arms that might be used for internal repression or external aggression. Yet critics were disappointed to learn that licences for the sale of Hawk fighter-trainer aircraft and armoured-personnel carriers to Indonesia, approved by the outgoing Conservatives, would not be revoked. On the eve of the Labour Party conference the Government publicised its decision to withhold licences for the sale of small arms to Indonesia. However, one week later MPs and NGOs were profoundly concerned to learn that 11 new licences had been approved, on the basis of the new criteria, for the sale of other weapons to Indonesia.[4]

BCET welcomes the concern of the Labour Government for human rights and East Timor. Yet we are struck by the disjunction between the initial steps taken in the areas of diplomacy and aid, and continued arms sales to Indonesia. BCET fears that continued arms sales will undermine Britain's diplomatic message and might even facilitate further grave human rights violations. *Furthermore, the steps taken and measures announced do not add up to a clear strategy to change the human rights situation on the ground: continuing along the same course might attract media coverage but will not lead to real improvements inside East Timor. This paper sets out an alternative approach, as an illustrator of how it might be possible to operationalise an ethical UK foreign policy.* Before doing so, it is necessary to briefly review the situation in East Timor.

East Timor: an overview

On 16 April 1997, the UN Commission on Human Rights adopted a resolution on East Timor by a vote of 20 to 14, with 18 abstentions. The motion expressed the international community's "deep concern" at the reports of extra-judicial executions, disappearances, torture and arbitrary detention in East Timor.[5] Unfortunately, the situation has not improved since then. In August the East Timor Human Rights Centre, which documents the situation through its contacts on the ground, reported that during the first half of 1997 there had been "a marked increase in violations, particularly extra-judicial executions, arbitrary arrests and detention, and systematic torture and ill-treatment of prisoners. It is believed that at least 707 East Timorese people were arrested and 49 killed."[6]

These violations are hardly new. Long before the massacre of over 250 Timorese civilians in the Santa Cruz cemetery in Dili in November 1991, Indonesian security forces carried out what experts have termed a "genocide", by causing the death of approximately one quarter of the 800,000 Timorese people during their occupation of East Timor from late 1975 onward. Although the authorities have attempted to normalise the situation since, severe violations persist in a context where a vast network of military, police and para-military forces covers the territory, official impunity is entrenched and the rule of law is fragile at best.[7]

It is true that the Government of Indonesia has invested huge resources in East Timor since the invasion. As in Indonesia itself, this has generated macro-economic growth but its benefits have been unevenly distributed in East Timor. One problem is that it is mainly the growing number of Indonesian settlers who make use of the Government's development programmes, including those funded by international aid agencies. The majority of Timorese do not trust, often resent and therefore do not benefit from these services. Moreover, the state-centred approach to development common throughout the Republic of Indonesia, with its pervasive involvement of Armed Forces personnel, narrows the space for genuine human development, especially in an occupied territory like East Timor.[8]

Despite huge losses, a nationalist movement has been rebuilt under the aegis of the Resistance, the CNRM. The Catholic Church plays a key role in speaking out on behalf of its people. The tension between nationalism and the brutality of Indonesian rule has fuelled membership in the Church and popular support for CNRM activities.[9] The UN Security Council has condemned the occupation, the General Assembly has asserted the right of the Timorese people to self-determination, and the UN does not recognise Indonesia's claim to sovereignty over the territory. Yet the flow of weapons to the Government of Indonesia has enabled it to keep the Resistance on the defensive in military terms. Moreover, the international community has failed to effectively support the Church's call for a genuine exercise of self-determination or the CNRM's comprehensive peace plan.[10]

The tragic character of this struggle inspired the Nobel Peace Committee to award its prize to two East Timorese in 1996. In turn, the award prompted an expression of international concern through the UN Commission on Human Rights, motivated the new UN Secretary-General to invest energy in reviving the stalemated peace talks, led to initiatives by the President of South Africa and the search for policy options in the UK. *The challenge, for the UK and others, is to turn these events into a process, weave our actions into a strategy, and help build a framework for the enjoyment of the full range of human rights in East Timor over the long run.*

Using UN human rights mechanisms

Implementing the 1997 UNCHR resolution

In addition to expressing the international community's concerns about persistent violations, the resolution on East Timor adopted by the UNCHR in April 1997 called on the Government of Indonesia to take steps to ensure full respect for human rights in the territory. In particular, the motion called on GoI to:

— "ensure the early release of East Timorese detained or convicted for political reasons . . ."

— "ensure that all East Timorese in custody are treated humanely in accordance with international standards, and that all trials in East Timor are conducted in accordance with international standards;"

— "co-operate fully with this Commission and its thematic rapporteurs and working groups, and to invite these . . . to visit East Timor, in particular the Special Rapporteur on torture, in line with the commitment undertaken to invite a thematic rapporteur in 1997;"

— "upgrade the memorandum of intent of 26 October 1994 on technical co-operation into the envisaged memorandum of understanding . . ."

— "bring about the envisaged assignment of a programme officer of the Office of the United Nations High Commissioner for Human Rights at the Jakarta office of the United Nations Development Programme . . ."

— "provide access to East Timor for human rights organisations".

This resolution provides a guide to some of the problem areas requiring immediate attention in East Timor, and highlights steps that could be taken to begin remedying the grave situation on the ground.[11] In principle, the international community should press GoI to implement all of these recommendations. European Union member states which sponsored the UNCHR resolution in 1997 (including the UK), as well as other states which voted in favour of the motion, have a particular obligation to follow through on its implementation before the 54th session of the UNCHR in March–April 1998.

Yet in the short run it may be wise to focus on provisions that have a prospect of being implemented soon. One recommendation which fits this criterion is the call for GoI to invite the Special Rapporteur on Torture to visit East Timor. In 1996 Jakarta agreed in principle to invite a UN special rapporteur to the territory. That agreement was not followed through, partly because the Government wanted to invite the Rapporteur on Religious Intolerance while Western states insisted that an expert whose brief related to the main human rights problems in East Timor, like the Rapporteur on Torture, be allowed to visit.

Although GoI rejects the 1997 resolution because it was passed against its will, the promise to invite a special rapporteur remains valid. Torture remains a grave concern in East Timor. *As such, the UK should work with its EU partners and other states to press GoI to invite the Special Rapporteur on Torture to visit East Timor in 1997 so that he can report to the UNCHR by March 1998.*

Pressing for effective on-site UN monitoring

A second provision of the 1997 UNCHR resolution which appears, on the surface, to have prospects of being implemented soon is the call for a programme officer, working for the Office of the High Commissioner for Human Rights, to be posted in the UNDP office in Jakarta and given permission to visit East Timor.

This idea has been under discussion for several years. In 1994 the Government of Indonesia and the UN Centre for Human Rights signed a Memorandum of Intent which codified an agreement, in principle, for the Centre to establish an office in Jakarta to oversee a programme of technical co-operation in the field of human rights for the Republic of Indonesia as a whole. After his visit to East Timor and Indonesia in December 1995, the UN High Commissioner for Human Rights recommended that this document be upgraded to a memorandum of understanding to allow the establishment of an office in Jakarta, with regular access to Dili and a mandate for human rights monitoring—in addition to its mandate for technical co-operation. This idea was partly enshrined in the statement on East Timor which the Chair of the UNCHR made in April 1996, though the Government of Indonesia successfully opposed the explicit mention of any mandate for on-site human rights monitoring in that declaration. Shortly after the adoption of the resolution in 1997, GoI called off further discussions with the UN regarding this mechanism.[12]

As such, there are serious difficulties with this concept. The CNRM and several respected human rights NGOs have opposed the envisaged mechanism on four grounds. First, GoI has steadfastly rejected UN proposals that this mechanism be given a mandate for human rights monitoring, namely to receive complaints from victims of human rights violations, investigate those complaints and report on a regular basis to the appropriate bodies of the UN human rights system. Yet without a mandate for rigorous and impartial monitoring, this mechanism is unlikely to have a positive impact on the human rights situation in East Timor.

Second, it is difficult to see how one programme officer could carry out real monitoring functions from a base in Jakarta, over 2,000 kilometres away from East Timor, even if (s)he had trustworthy local support staff. Third, it is widely known that the UN Development Programme, despite its experience in the area of development, does not have a track record of overseeing human rights monitoring. The UNDP's traditionally close relations with government agencies could be a major obstacle to effectiveness, particularly given the contested nature of the Indonesian state in East Timor.[13] Finally, the posting of a UN officer in Jakarta, with a mandate for East Timor, could imply recognition of Indonesia's claim to sovereignty over the disputed territory.

If HMG really wants to change the human rights situation on the ground and wishes to remain consistent with its policy of not recognising Indonesia's claim to sovereignty over East Timor, it should therefore NOT support further talks aimed at establishing an office in Jakarta with a vague mandate for access to East Timor.

There are feasible alternatives to this problematic proposal. One option is to contribute to the discussion, within the framework of the UN-mediated peace talks, of possibilities for an effective on-site UN human rights presence in the future; this possibility will be explored in the next section. The other option is to find ways of supporting the development of local NGOs that are already monitoring human rights under extremely difficult constraints; this alternative will be more fully explored in the section on development co-operation.

DIPLOMACY

Actively backing the UN-mediated talks

It is widely believed that a significant improvement of the human rights situation cannot be achieved without a political solution to the conflict. Since 1992, the main vehicle for discussing a possible solution has been the bi-annual Tripartite Talks between the foreign ministers of Indonesia and Portugal, under the auspices of the UN Secretary-General. Since 1995, these have been complemented by the All-inclusive Intra-East Timor Dialogue (AIETD), which brings together a range of Timorese opinion from the inside and the exile community. Although the AIETD generated proposals for confidence-building measures, few of these were taken up by the foreign ministers and none have yet been put into practice.[14]

The appointment of Kofi Annan as UN Secretary-General and the selection of Ambassador Jamsheed Marker as his Personal Representative on East Timor have injected fresh energy into the peace process. At the June 1997 Tripartite Talks the foreign ministers agreed to procedural changes which could open the door to substantive advances: they shifted the discussions to the senior officials level, increased their frequency and duration, and broadened the agenda to include matters related to economic development, human rights and migration. At the same time, the number of participants in the AIETD has been increased from 30 to 35, partly to broaden participation by East Timorese women and youth.

The European Union has traditionally taken a back seat to Portugal and the UN in these processes. Through its Common Position on East Timor, the EU reiterated its official support for the UN's peace-making efforts. Several EU member states, including the UK, have given financial assistance to the AIETD. The suggestion made by Foreign Secretary Cook in Jakarta, that Indonesia's standing could be enhanced by resolving the East Timor conflict in accordance with UN Security Council resolutions, was a welcomed departure from this traditional approach.

Yet the new format of the Tripartite Talks and the broader participation in the AIETD offer the UK and its EU partners fresh opportunities for creatively supporting the peace process and promoting human rights. The discussion of human rights at the senior officials level opens the door to exploring measures to facilitate the work of local human rights organisations by, for example, allowing them greater access to detainees, prisoners and their trials. Discussions could also address how the deployment of an on-site UN human rights presence, with a mandate for institutional strengthening and monitoring, could provide an impartial viewpoint and help build the mutual confidence required to resolve the conflict. With adequate technical support from the Office of the UN High Commissioner for Human Rights or NGOs, the AIETD could also address these issues and generate informed proposals for discussion in the Tripartite Talks.[15]

The UK could contribute to a deepening of dialogue on human rights by actively supporting efforts to have measures for monitoring and promoting human rights adopted, as confidence-building measures, in the peace talks. This could include urging GoI to support the discussion of such measures in the Intra-East Timorese Dialogue and to study them further in the Tripartite Talks. It could also include backing efforts, by the Office of the UN High Commissioner for Human Rights or other bodies, to explore how the UN could contribute to the search for peace by deploying an effective on-site human rights presence inside East Timor.

The EU ambassadorial mission

During his visit to Indonesia, Foreign Secretary Cook also announced that

> "Britain is now proposing to our European partners that there should be a European Troika visit at Ambassadorial level to East Timor. We would hope that such a visit could take place under the British Presidency, and would enable Europe to be more fully informed of the situation in East Timor and the views of its people."[16]

This initiative could be helpful, if the EU takes steps to ensure that the mission is not represented by the Government of Indonesia as implying recognition of its claim to sovereignty over East Timor. It is precisely to avoid extending such recognition that EU states have traditionally instructed their Jakarta-based ambassadors not to visit the territory. Clear public statements reiterating the EU's adherence to the UN position should ensure that no such interpretation is made of the EU initiative. The Foreign Secretary has acknowledged this imperative; it will be important to follow it through with appropriate actions.[17]

The foreign ministries of the Troika states should prepare a visit which enables the ambassadors to meet a range of persons, under conditions of strict confidentiality, and to travel outside Dili to see the reality of life in rural areas. They should also be prepared to make statements, to their parliaments and to the media, to inform stakeholders about their findings.[18] The participation of Austria in the Troika from January 1998 onwards increases the prospects of using the visit to enhance EU support for the AIETD, given Vienna's role in hosting the Dialogue. A visit in February could also help the EU refine its approach prior to the 54th session of the UNCHR.[19] In brief, *the UK and its EU partners should carefully manage the visit by EU ambassadors to East Timor in early 1998 to ensure that it has the intended impact on the ground and internationally.*

ASEM II

Another opportunity to promote human rights in East Timor through diplomacy is the forthcoming second Asia-Europe Meeting (ASEM II), which will be held in London on 3–4 April 1998. Although the official agenda is dominated by trade and investment matters, there will be space under the rubric of "political dialogue" to discuss East Timor, albeit obliquely, in accordance with ASEM norms. The UK should back calls to have East Timor discussed in the political dialogue.

If the East Timor peace talks have progressed and if the Government of Indonesia has taken meaningful steps to address the international community's human rights concerns, then ASEM II might be a good occasion on which to note the benefits which Asia and Europe stand to gain from making progress on human rights issues. Should the human rights situation remain as grave as it is today and if significant advances have not been made in the peace talks, then it would be counterproductive for Europe to send anything but a clear signal of concern, at the UNCHR in Geneva and at ASEM II. If a public expression of concern in London is simply not feasible, there will be plenty of opportunities for Britain and its EU partners to make their views known, at the highest levels, in private sessions. Above all, *HMG should use its position as the host of ASEM II to lead Europe in clearly reiterating the view that it is in Indonesia's interest to respect human rights and move towards a comprehensive peace in East Timor.*

DEVELOPMENT CO-OPERATION

Designing a sound UK programme for East Timor

In October 1997 the International Development Secretary announced that her Department would soon begin supporting human rights in East Timor.[20] This pledge is crucial but it will not be easy to implement.

At present there are only two East Timorese organisations carrying out independent work in the defence of civil and political rights inside East Timor: the Justice and Peace Commission of the Catholic Church discretely documents complaints of human rights violations, while a small firm of Timorese lawyers follows the treatment of detainees and prisoners, by the police and judiciary, from the standpoint of due legal process. Both organisations face constant intimidation from the Indonesian authorities. They also suffer from resource limitations which prevent them from following up on most cases of violations, extending protection to the countryside, addressing the needs of women, assisting victims of war or working on economic, social and cultural rights.

DFID should examine ways of supporting these organisations, particularly through training and capacity-building. Yet the Department should be aware that other international development agencies have also recently re-discovered East Timor and there is a danger that the absorptive capacity of local organisations could be overwhelmed by a sudden, unco-ordinated infusion of foreign funds.

As such, DFID may be tempted to channel part of its human rights funding through the Dili office of the Indonesian National Commission on Human Rights (Komnas HAM), given the new relationship which HMG is trying to build with the Commission in Indonesia. This would be a grave mistake, since the operations of Komnas HAM in East Timor are quite different from its operations elsewhere in the Republic. First, the presence of Komnas HAM, a quasi-governmental organisation, is legally contestable in East Timor. Second, the office has proven to be largely ineffective since its establishment several years ago.[21]

Given that the absorptive capacity of legitimate human rights organisations remains limited and that it would not be appropriate to fund Komnas HAM, DFID should also study how it might promote economic and social rights through human development initiatives. An East Timorese economist has suggested ways that international agencies could support participatory rural development in the territory.[22] A complementary option would be for DFID to design a programme focusing on gender: there is an urgent need to support the development of women's organisations and efforts by women to enhance their positions in mainstream institutions.[23] The absence of a meaningful gender dimension in other donors' programmes (the EC is discussed in the next section) and DFID's considerable experience in gender and development initiatives suggest that this might be a logical focus for a DFID intervention.

As such, DFID should design its aid programme for East Timor so that it reaches legitimate civil society organisations, through NGOs with a track record of working inside East Timor rather than via Indonesia government agencies. The programme should include initiatives to promote the full range of human rights, have a clear gender focus, and should involve the gradual scaling up of allocations so as not to overwhelm the absorptive capacity of local organisations.

Monitoring the EC aid package

It is essential for DFID to co-ordinate this initiative with other donors. This is particularly germane to the European Commission (EC), which is also developing a new aid package for East Timor. Historically, the EC funded no development projects in East Timor, directly or through the Government of Indonesia. Yet the EU Common Position of East Timor unveiled in June 1996 stated that the EU.

> supports all appropriate action with the objective of generally strengthening respect for human rights in East Timor and . . . improving the situation of its people, by means of the resources available to the European Union and aid for action by NGOs.[24]

On the basis of this clause, in November 1996 the EU Council asked the EC to design a multi-annual aid package for East Timor. The *sine qua non* for the package, especially from the viewpoint of the Government of Portugal, with that EC funds should be channelled exclusively to civil society and through NGOs rather than through Government of Indonesia agencies. After discretely consulting European NGOs and East Timorese leaders, the Commission decided to launch a three-year, six million ECUs (6 MECUs, or £4.1 million) programme to finance "purely humanitarian" NGO projects in three areas: public health, education and sanitation. A ceiling of one MECU was placed on individual projects. The International Committee of the Red Cross has received almost one MECU for its water sanitation scheme; several European Catholic development NGOs are applying for funds to support projects in the areas of education and health.

The parameters of the EC package look sound, but it is important to note that the EC has downplayed the links between the EU Common Position and its "humanitarian" initiative and seems to have lost sight of the CP's provision for strengthening respect for human rights by means of EU resources, ostensibly to avoid provoking GoI into denying the EC access altogether. The difficulty is that humanitarian aid will not solve East Timor's problems since these are rooted in the systematic denial of human rights, and particularly of the right to self-determination. In addition, the Commission's handling of this process has lacked transparency and accountability towards the European Parliament and member states. For example, placing a ceiling of one MECU on individual projects minimises the need to consult member states on particular funding decisions.[25]

The aim of these observations is not to fuel the fire of Euro-sceptics but rather to highlight some of the constraints which DFID will also face as it designs its own aid package. Before gaining access to East Timor, HMG will have to negotiate with the Government of Indonesia, and the International Development Secretary's promise to fund human rights projects will come under intense scrutiny. By reviewing the European Commission's experience, DFID may be able to avoid the trade-offs which the EC made to get access to East Timor. Regular exchanges of information could help both agencies avoid duplication and identify possibilities for complementary initiatives. Finally, monitoring the EC initiative should help HMG ensure that Britain gets value for its money, as a major contributor to the EC's budget, in this financially small yet politically sensitive endeavour.

On the basis of these considerations, *BCET urges HMG to monitor the progress of the European Commission's aid package in East Timor to ensure complementarity between EC and DFID actions in the territory.*

Reviewing other development co-operation programmes

The announcement by Clare Short of a new DFID aid initiative for East Timor was coupled with the promise that no new UK funding would be extended to provide training for the Indonesian National Police. This news was welcomed by MPs and NGOs who had been lobbying, for many years, against any UK aid to Government of Indonesia programmes covering East Timor. Aside from the training project with the Police, these MPs and NGOs had raised concerns about UK funding for elements of the transmigration programme through which GoI facilitates the relocation of Indonesian citizens to troublesome provinces like East Timor. In 1996, these and other elements of the UK's bilateral programme in Indonesia were pointedly criticised in a detailed study by the National Audit Office.[26]

It is essential that the International Development Secretary's promises to end UK support for any Government of Indonesia programmes covering East Timor be fully implemented. It is also important for the UK not to undertake new commitments with GoI agencies that could undermine the human rights of the Timorese people, including their right to self-determination. Any request for UK support to the Dili office of Komnas HAM would have to be examined in this light.

Foreign Secretary Cook's 29 August 1997 promise to provide UK assistance to the Indonesia National Police seems at odds with promises made by the International Development Secretary, at the Labour Party conference, to discontinue such aid. HMG should clarify its plans with regards to future training for the Indonesian National Police. Such support would be questionable because of its implications for East Timor. It is also difficult to see how UK training could have a significant impact on the human rights performance of the Indonesian National Police until the agency is separated from the Armed Forces (ABRI), and until the legislative and judicial bases for the rule of law are dramatically strengthened.

The challenge of ensuring that UK bilateral aid and EC aid strengthen rather than undermine respect for human rights in East Timor highlights the need to review other programmes that might be supported by British taxpayers. The World Bank is the biggest source of concessional financing for the Government of Indonesia's development programmes.[27] As a major shareholder in the Bank, Britain has the possibility of ensuring that the institution's funding conforms to the same criteria which DFID and the EC are devising for their own programmes. Indeed, the UK and its EU partners could utilise their directorships and other sources of influence in the agency to ensure that none of the projects funded by the World Bank in Indonesia actually undermine respect for human rights in East Timor.

Through its directorships and its role in the Consultative Group on Indonesia, the UK could work with its partners to initiate reviews of projects financed by the Asian Development Bank, the UN Development Programme and other multilateral donors in Indonesia. UN Security Council resolutions condemning Indonesia's illegal occupation fo East Timor provide a firm normative basis on which to press multilateral institutions not to fund any projects that could strengthen Indonesia's claim to sovereignty over East Timor. In sum, *BCET urges HMG to review its separate bilateral and multilateral development co-operation programmes with Indonesia to ensure that they do not include any East Timor elements, and particularly that they do not support programmes such as transmigration and training for the Indonesia National Police, which are likely to undermine the human rights of the Timorese people, including their right to self-determination.*

ARMS EXPORTS

Tightening UK arms export controls

Shortly after taking office, the Government announced that it was developing new criteria to ensure that no arms which "might be used for internal repression or external aggression" would be exported by Britain. In July 1997, Foreign Secretary Cook spelled out the details of this policy, stating that HMG:

— "will not issue an export licence if there is a clear and identifiable risk that the proposed export might be used for internal repression";

— "will not issue an export licence if there is a clearly identifiable risk that the intended recipient would use the proposed export aggressively against another country or to assert by force a territorial claim";

— would not revoke licences granted by the previous Government—including those for the export of 16 Hawk aircraft, 50 Alvis Scorpion armoured vehicles, 300 Glover Webb armoured vehicles and seven Tactica water cannons;

— would ensure greater transparency of arms export licensing decisions through the publication of an annual report on UK strategic exports.[28]

In September HMG announced that, on the basis of this policy, applications to sell armoured vehicles and sniper rifles to Indonesia were rejected. Yet an MP was informed that 11 other licences for strategic exports to Indonesia had been approved. Parliament has not yet been informed about the nature of the arms licenced for export. At least a further 44 applications are said to be pending.[29]

It is difficult to reconcile these decisions with the new policy. The move not to revoke licences issued by the previous Government is inconsistent with the policy since there is evidence that UK armoured vehicles and water cannon were used to suppress pro-democracy demonstrations in Indonesia in 1996 and 1997. The sightings of Hawk aircraft in East Timor throughout the 1980s and in 1995 suggests that these weapons might again be used for external aggression against the illegally-occupied territory, at least to intimidate the local population.[30] The decision not to revoke past licences therefore undermines the credibility of the new Government, especially since legal advice received by NGOs suggests that HMG would not have been liable to compensate firms for any losses incurred.

The absence of details on the types of arms approved for sale to Indonesia makes it hard to know with complete certainty that the new licences contravene the Government's policy, but there are reasons for strong concern. Most of the licences granted from 1993 to 1996 were for the sale of military aircraft and components, armoured vehicles, combat vessels, electronic equipment and software, small arms and protective goods.[31] Sales currently under discussion include Hawk aircraft, Piranha class mini-submarines and air defence systems to protect offshore oil assets.[32] Of these systems, only the air defence system and certain types of electronic equipment and software are unlikely to be deployed to East Timor. With regards to all other systems, there is a clear and identifiable risk that they will be deployed or used to continue to assert by force a territorial claim in East Timor, a territory whose occupation is seen as illegal by the UK.

BCET supports the call for a freeze and indeed an embargo on arms sales to the Government of Indonesia. Yet even under the Government's current policy, it should be impossible to sell such weapons to countries like Indonesia.

What could the Government do to close the gap between policy and practice? First, *HMG could tighten the application of the new policy by rejecting applications for the sale of any weapons systems that might be deployed to East Timor. This should include small arms and heavy weapons used by the ground forces stationed there, air transport and navel vessels used to ferry troops to and from East Timor, as well as fighter/trainers used for overflights.*[33]

Second, *HMG should improve mechanisms to monitor the end use of UK arms, given the doubts surrounding past end use assurances from the Government of Indonesia.* Extra resources should be assigned to tracking UK equipment that might be deployed to East Timor. Third, *new measures should be adopted to increase the accountability of licencing decisions and of end use monitoring: in addition to publishing an annual report on UK arms transfers, there should be greater scope for the judicial review of specific licencing decisions and for parliamentary discussion of end use concerns.*[34] Fourth, *Parliament should carefully examine whether the criteria set out by the Foreign Secretary are sufficiently robust to guarantee the implementation of the Government's own policy.* In sum, *HMG should tighten the application of the new arms exports policy to ensure that no licences are granted to export any weapons systems that might be used for further aggression against East Timor.*

Promoting stronger multilateral controls

One of the reasons cited for not restricting UK arms sales to Indonesia is that other suppliers will fill market niches vacated by the British. Multilateral arms export controls should be tightened to ensure that this does not transpire. An arena for immediate action in this regard is the European Union. In 1991, the European Community adopted the Common Criteria for Arms Exports, under which member states should refrain from exporting weapons which, *inter alia*, could threaten regional stability or undermine respect for human rights. These criteria have not been effective because they are too vague and are not backed up by monitoring and enforcement mechanisms. In recent years certain officials, parliamentarians and NGOs have explored the possibility of developing an EU code of conduct which would further define the Common Criteria and lead to the establishment of robust follow-up mechanisms. *BCET welcomes the promise by Foreign Secretary Cook to press for the adoption of such a code and thereby set high common standards to govern arms exports from all EU member states.*[35]

The rigorous implementation of Labour's new policy on arms exports and the adoption of an effective EU code of conduct would bring European states into line with US practice, at least on Indonesia.[36] It is essential for the UK and its EU partners not to take advantage of the markets left by the restrictive US approach. It is equally important for the EU to work with Washington to ensure that other suppliers do not exploit those opportunities. One option is to develop a robust code of conduct which renders operational the UN Security Council Guidelines for Conventional Arms Transfers, discussed but not adopted because of opposition by the People's Republic of China. Another option is to tighten and apply the "Principles Governing Conventional Arms Transfers" adopted by the Organisation for Security and Co-operation in Europe (OSCE) in 1993.

HMG should promote more robust EU arms export guidelines and the establishment of enforcement mechanisms. HMG should also work with its EU partners, the US and Russia to strengthen UN Security Council and OSCE guidelines.

SUMMARY OF RECOMMENDATIONS

In order to effectively promote human rights in East Timor, BCET urges Her Majesty's Government to formulate a coherent strategy which integrates the judicious use of UN human rights mechanisms, diplomacy, development co-operation and the rigorous restriction of arms sales.

In particular, *BCET urges HMG to:*

1. Work with its EU partners and other states to press the Government of Indonesia (GoI) to invite the Special Rapporteur on Torture to visit East Timor in 1997 so that he can report to the UN Commission on Human Rights by March 1998.

2. Actively support efforts to have measures for monitoring and promoting human rights adopted, as confidence-building measures, in the peace talks. This could include urging GoI to support the discussion of such measures in the Intra-East Timorese Dialogue and study them further in the Tripartite Talks. It could also include backing efforts, by the Office of the UN High Commissioner for Human Rights or other bodies, to explore how the UN could contribute to the search for peace by deploying an effective on-site human rights presence inside East Timor.

3.   Carefully manage the visit by EU ambassadors to East Timor in early 1998 to ensure that it has the intended impact on the ground and internationally.

4.   At ASEM II, clearly reiterate the view that it is in Indonesia's interest to respect human rights and move towards a comprehensive peace in East Timor.

5.   Design the DFID aid package for East Timor so that it reaches legitimate civil society organisations, through NGOs with a track record of working inside East Timor rather than via Indonesian government agencies. The programme should include initiatives to promote the full range of human rights, have a clear gender focus, and should involve the gradual scaling up of allocations so as not to overwhelm the absorptive capacity of local organisations.

6.   Monitor the progress of the European Commission's aid programme in East Timor to ensure complementarity between EC and DFID actions in the territory.

7.   Review its bilateral and multilateral development co-operation programmes with Indonesia to ensure that they do not include any East Timor elements, and particularly that they do not support programmes such as transmigration and training for the Indonesian National Police, which are likely to undermine the human rights of the Timorese people, including their right to self-determination.

8.   Tighten the application of the new arms export policy to ensure that no licences are granted to export any weapons systems that might be used for further aggression against East Timor.

9.   Actively collaborate with its EU partners to develop more restrictive EU arms export guidelines and establish adequate monitoring and enforcement mechanisms. Work with its EU partners, the US and other permanent members of the Security Council to strengthen UN Security Council and Organisation for Security and Co-operation in Europe guidelines for conventional arms transfers.

October 1997

REFERENCES

1.   Opening statement by the Foreign Secretary, Mr Robin Cook, at a press conference in Jakarta, Indonesia, 29 August 1997.

2.   Letter from Derek Fatchett, Minister of State, Foreign and Commonwealth Office, to Ann Clwyd MP, 29 August 1997.

3.   For a systematic analysis of Labour's commitments on East Timor before and after the election, see Paul Hainsworth, "New Labour, new codes of conduct?", paper presented at the VII Symposium on Timor of Oporto University, Oporto, Portugal, 17-20 July 1997, mimeo.

4.   *TAPOL Bulletin* 141 (July 1997), *TAPOL Bulletin* 142 (August 1997) and *TAPOL Bulletin* 143 (October 1997).

5.   For the entire text of the resolution, see *Timor Link* 30 (April 1997).

6.   East Timor Human Rights Centre, *Human Rights Deteriorate in East Timor: Bi-annual Report of Human Rights Violations in East Timor, January to July 1997* SR2/97 (Melbourne: ETHRC, August 1997), p. 1. There are credible reports that the armed forces of the Resistance (FALINTIL) have recently committed violations of international humanitarian law. See Amnesty International, "East Timor. Respect for Human Rights—The precondition for a political solution," statement before the UN Special Committee on Decolonisation, New York, 16 June 1997 (ASA 21/40/97) and Human Rights Watch/Asia, Deteriorating Human Rights in East Timor (New York: Human Right Watch, September 1997).

7.   John G Taylor, *Indonesia's Forgotten War: The Hidden History of East Timor* (London: Zed Books, 1991).

8.   Rui Augusto Gomes, "Some thoughts for alternative development assistance to East Timor," paper presented to the 8th Christian Consultation on East Timor, Lisbon, Portugal, 13-14 September 1997, mimeo.

9.   Constancio Pinto and Matthew Jardine, *East Timor's Unfinished Struggle: Inside the Timorese Resistance* (Boston: South End Press, 1997).

10.   See Catholic Institute for International Relations, *East Timor: The Continuing Betrayal* (London: CIIR, 1996) for background on the role of the Church, the CNRM peace plan and the response of the international community.

11.   See the recommendations by the Special Rapporteur on Torture (E/CN.4/1992/17/Add.1, 8 January 1992) and the Special Rapporteur on Extra–judicial, Summary or Arbitrary Executions (E/CN.4/1995/61/Add.1, 1 November 1994).

12. GoI called off discussions on the grounds that it was not bound by the 1997 resolution since it had not agreed to it. However, Jakarta has not yet implemented the agreements which it did negotiate with the UN High Commissioner for Human Rights and members of the UNCHR, including the 1996 chair's statement.

13. The Government of Indonesia has argued, in the past, that there is no need for a UN human rights presence since it has opened an office of its National Human Rights Commission (Komnas HAM) in Dili. Yet the presence of Komnas HAM, a quasi-governmental organisation, is legally contestable in East Timor. Moreover, the office has proven to be largely ineffective since its establishment several years ago. In the words of Amnesty International:

> "the particular circumstances in East Timor mean that this new office is unable to effectively . . . monitor and investigate human rights violations in East Timor. Komnas HAM Dili has not gained the trust of the East Timorese people . . . The Dili office of Komnas HAM is not known to have intervened in any incidents of arbitrary arrest, unacknowledged detention, or to have received any complaints or initiated its own investigations into the many allegations of torture and unlawful killings."

See Amnesty International, "East Timor", *op cit,* p. 3.

14. See recent issues of *Timor Link* for updates on the peace talks.

15. See also Amnesty International. "East Timor", *op cit.*

16. Opening statement by the Foreign Secretary, 29 August 1997, *op cit.*

17. Letter from Foreign Secretary Robin Cook to Carmel Budiardjo of TAPOL, The Indonesia Human Rights Campaign, 15 September 1997.

18. These concerns are not merely hypothetical. For example, previous EU ambassadorial missions, to Kashmir and to the Chittagong Hill Tracts in India, did not allow for confidential meetings with informants and did not include the sharing of findings with parliaments or the public. Letter from Lord Eric Avebury to Foreign Secretary Robin Cook, 10 September 1997.

19. This brief visit will not enable the ambassadors to rigorously investigate the human rights situation in the territory. As such, the EU should state that its visit does not negate the Government of Indonesia's obligation to allow human rights NGOs access to East Timor or the need for a UN human rights presence.

20. Reported in *The Independent,* 3 October 1997, p. 11.

21. See note 13.

22. See Rui Augusto Gomes, "Some thoughts for alternative development assistance to East Timor," *op cit,* pp. 3-4. DFID could also look at options for supporting the establishment of independent organisations specialising in the promotion of cultural rights. The proposal for the creation of a cultural centre, made by the second AIETD and further defined in the October 1997 Dialogue, could be a starting point for this endeavour. Finally, the imperative of supporting the development of civil society inside East Timor should not obscure the need to continue supporting East Timor-focused human rights work on the outside, by exiled Timorese and by respected NGOs.

23. For a study of certain aspects of the situation of women, see Miranda E Sissons, *From One Day to Another: Violations of Women's Reproductive and Sexual Rights in East Timor* (Melbourne: ETHRC, 1997).

24. Common Position 25 June 1996, No. 96/407, *Official Journal of the European Union* L168/2, 6 July 1996. For an in-depth analysis of the CP and its implementation to date, see Ellis Ward, "EU policy towards East Timor: fulfilling the potential and the Common Position," *Timor Link* 41 (October 1997).

25. One could raise other concerns about the EC initiative. In particular, the EC has provided no indication that it is attempting to build a gender dimension into this programme, either by targeting funding at East Timorese women's organisations or by ensuring that other projects truly benefit women.

26. National Audit Office, *Aid to Indonesia. Report by the Comptroller and Auditor General* (London: The Stationery Office, 29 November 1996). See also TAPOL, "Memorandum to the Department for International Development (DFID) in relation to its white paper on development and its review of the Indonesia aid programme," 14 July 1997, mimeo; and Paul Barber, *Partners in Repression. The Reality of British Aid to Indonesia* (London: TAPOL, 1995).

27. See *TAPOL Bulletin* 142 (August 1997), p. 5 for details.

28. Written answer by Secretary of State for Foreign and Commonwealth Affairs, Robin Cook, to a parliamentary question by Stephen Timms, MP, 28 July 1997.

29. *TAPOL Bulletin* 143 (October 1997), pp. 7-8.

30. Evidence for the use of UK arms in East Timor is documented in statements by José Ramos-Horta in Lisbon on 16 November 1994, by José António Amorim Dias in London on 25 July 1994, and in Hugh O'Shaughnessy, "British-made war planes menace East Timor," *The Independent*, 12 November 1995.

31. See Malcolm Chalmers, *British Arms Export Policy and Indonesia* (London: Saferworld, May 1997), Appendix 2.

32. See *TAPOL Bulletin* 143 (October 1997), p. 8.

33. Even arms that pass this test should only be sold on condition that they are not used in East Timor; contracts should explicitly provide for a cut-off of supplies and servicing if HMG receives credible reports of use in East Timor.

34. Saferworld has suggested that an inquiry should be held into the licensing of specific arms sales to Indonesia, including the Hawk aircraft, by the previous Government. See Malcolm Chalmers, *op cit,* p. 29.

35. See *Network*, a newsletter on arms export controls produced by Saferworld, for updates on efforts to promote international codes of conduct.

36. Since the Santa Cruz massacre restrictions on US arms exports to Indonesia have been steadily increased, beginning with small arms in 1994 and extending to helicopter-mounted weapons in 1995 and armoured personnel carriers in 1996. Congressional disquiet over the sale of F-16 fighters led Jakarta to withdraw its order in 1997. See *TAPOL Bulletin* 141 (July 1997), p. 15.

APPENDIX 5

Memorandum submitted by the Government of the State of Bahrain

The United Kingdom and the State of Bahrain enjoy a historical relationship of friendship and co-operation born of mutual interests and common purpose. The United Kingdom is a valued friend and major trading partner of Bahrain. Bahrain is home to some 6,000 Britons and the Government of the State of Bahrain has every intention of seeing the close links between the two countries continue and strengthen into the next millennium.

The UK's Foreign Secretary, The Rt Hon Robin Cook, MP, has announced the Government's intention to place concern for human rights at the forefront of Britain's foreign policy and relations with the international community; what has become known as "an ethical foreign policy". Whilst the Government of Bahrain welcomes this bold directive, it also recognises that the desire to promote human rights internationally has long been a priority for the United Kingdom in the modern era. Bahrain shares these concerns for an ethical dimension in world diplomacy and would like to reassure the Select Committee that Bahrain has always given the cause of human rights the appropriate and proper significance it deserves.

The Government of Bahrain wishes to draw attention to its recent experiences which provide a model for a study of human rights in both a bilateral and a multilateral context. Beginning in mid-1994, Bahrain has been subjected to a violent destabilisation campaign which, with foreign backing, has aimed to overthrow the Government of Bahrain by force and install an extremist theocratic regime. This campaign forms part of a wider policy of regional destabilisation which can be supported with evidence. The crimes by the extremists have included murder, arson, the planting of bombs and the destruction of public and private property.

The tangible effects of this campaign of terrorism have been augmented by a vicious propaganda offensive against the Bahrain Government. Whilst the situation in Bahrain is now normal and the community is recovering, this vitriolic propaganda battle continues. The Government wishes to highlight and warn of the effects that such propaganda can have.

The Bahraini community has firmly rejected the attempts by the terrorists to destroy the stability and progress of the nation. In the same manner, the international community consistently acts with one voice in condemning acts of terrorism whenever and wherever they occur. Therefore, those who seek the violent overthrow of the constitutional Bahraini Government have attempted to justify their actions by laying claim to moral arguments. The propagandists, acting for the terrorists, allege that the Government denies its citizens their civil and political rights whilst simultaneously abusing their individual rights and freedoms. This is despite the fact that the UN Human Development Index 1997 ranks Bahrain first amongst Arab nations in human development for the third consecutive year. The Government of Bahrain has consistently and positively countered such baseless allegations and has sought to expose the nature of the sources of these fabrications, explaining that their claims are neither accurate nor credible. Allegations of this sort often originate from extremist zealots outside Bahrain, acting as fronts for terrorist organisations, who have no *bona fide* interest in human rights nor any direct knowledge of the situation in Bahrain. However, this is no easy task. These propagandists are determined and committed to their violent revolutionary cause. They exist for no other purpose but to disseminate their misinformation throughout both the international and the national Bahraini community. They seek to discredit the Government, spread subversion and incite violence and sedition.

Bahrain is not alone in facing terrorism. As with all terrorist organisations throughout the world, political fronts have been established to disassociate the organisations' leaders from their criminal acts. The groups responsible for killing, inuring and terrorizing the people of Bahrain are now exception. Their political fronts have sought to legitimise their campaign by manipulation of the international human rights movement. Despite the Government's warnings, many well-meaning and respected international bodies active in the field of human rights have been duped into presenting to the world the propagandists' biased and uncompromising views.

Bahrain has observed that many in the western world are willing to give international human rights organisations *carte blanche* in their examination of countries in the developing world. It appears that these organisations have become prosecutor, judge and jury whenever allegations of human rights abuses surface. On the rare occasions that Governments are asked for their comments upon such allegations, little, if any, credence is given to their observations. The Government of Bahrain urges that a proper and balanced view is taken of Governments' comments on claims of human rights abuses. Unless a fully balanced impartial and appropriate comment is delivered, then comments by others may be viewed as an interference in the internal affairs of States concerned and, therefore, contrary to international law and custom. Despite the undoubted good intention of such proclamations to help the people of the State concerned achieve greater political and economic benefits, such comments may give the wrong signal to terrorists and will merely serve to give them comfort and encouragement.

There is also a second fundamental issue to which the Government of Bahrain wishes to draw attention: international standards of decency and normal behaviour which can, in certain circumstances, translate into international standards of human rights. However, the interpretation of these standards may differ markedly between nations, cultures and peoples. It is unacceptable for one culture to try and impose standards onto another culture which may not hold the same values or live within the same circumstances.

The international human rights framework with which the international community works today is, of course, orientated around the developed countries of the western hemisphere; i.e., those countries which were the force behind the establishment of this framework. Islamic societies and their values do not always fit hand-in-glove with the West's perception of the requirements for civil political and human rights. Because so little is understood of the Islamic religion outside the Muslim world, and because of the West's historical suspicions of Islam, more often that not, conflicts arise over the interpretations of international standards; the issue of democracy is a case in point.

Bahrain can describe itself as a democratic nation. Of course, the overall structure of democracy that exists in the West does not exist in Bahrain (nor in the other Arab Gulf States) yet, the contemporary Islamic state is based on a number of restrictions designed to ensure that absolute power does not rest in the hands of the rulers. A fundamental principle of this is Shura, or consultation. The principle is enshrined in Islam through its interpretation is left open to be adapted to what suits the circumstances of the society concerned. The legitimate base for the Shura principle can be found in the Holy Qouran and the Sunna (the Prophet's teachings) and the works of the Orthodox Caliphs.

Bahrain is but a small island state with a relatively small (albeit rapidly growing) native population of approximately 370,000. Citizens enjoy direct personal access to the country's Amir and Government officials and there is widespread public discussion and deliberation on essential issues. Formal and informal systems to enable such participation have evolved through the years in line with the country's Islamic beliefs and cultures and also the aspirations of its people. The Shura Consultative Council is the latest manifestation of this evolutionary development, as is the planned Governate system presently being implemented. The Council is composed of 40 members representing a broad cross-section of the Bahraini community and includes academics, lawyers and businessmen. The Council has considerable powers to initiate and review legislation and has actively taken a lead on many contentious social and economic issues.

Other democratic institutions exist at a grass-roots level and further democratic developments can only be as a result of the will of the people of Bahrain and not forced by violence and intimidation.

The Bahrain Government is committed to the protection of the fundamental rights of its citizens. The citizens of Bahrain covet their right to live in peace and security and to go about their daily business without fear of intimidation, violence or threats to their property and belongings. The Government of Bahrain is doing its utmost to protect these rights and to guarantee its citizens an environment in which to live, work and prosper whilst fulfilling their maximum potential. Bahrain is facing attacks on these rights and freedoms from extremists who have no desire to see the advancement and development of the Bahraini people. Unless there is security and stability in the society then individual rights are denied and freedoms restricted: not by the Government but by the terrorists who cause the fear and the suffering. The Government is, of course, aware of the underlying social and economic pressures and is making strenuous efforts to address them in a sensitive and even-handed manner. Simultaneously, the Government is controlling the situation only through its regular police force and the strict application of the rule of law whilst balancing the rights and freedoms of the individual. These are not human rights concerns but issues of good governance.

In summary, the Government of Bahrain asks you to consider the following when examining how the UK should best implement its foreign policy objectives:

(1) Terrorists throughout the world will seek to manipulate issues of human rights through propaganda: and

(2) Developing societies can only be granted their basic civil, political, social and economic rights if they are guaranteed a secure, peaceful and stable environment free of violence and intimidation.

October 1997

APPENDIX 6

Memorandum submitted by Saferworld

1. INTRODUCTION

1.1 This submission focuses specifically on human rights policy with regard to arms exports and military equipment transfers. There are many other aspects of international human rights policy which will be covered in the submissions of other individuals and organisations. The purpose of this submission is to demonstrate the links between irresponsible arms exports and military transfers and the violation of human rights, and to suggest some concrete proposals for more effective controls.

1.2 *Saferworld's recommendations relate to five areas:*
— tougher criteria over arms exports in respect of human rights and internal repression;
— improved parliamentary accountability and transparency to enable effective monitoring and debate of impact of arms exports on human rights;
— support for a restrictive European Code of Conduct on arms sales which includes clear criteria on human rights and consultation mechanisms to avoid undercutting;
— commitment to wider and more effective international controls over arms exports;
— improved end-use provisions to ensure that equipment exported will not be used to abuse human rights.

2. THE HUMAN RIGHTS CASE FOR TIGHTER CONTROLS OVER THE EXPORT OF ARMS AND MILITARY TECHNOLOGY

2.1 *In the past, arms and military equipment exported from the UK have been used to abuse human rights.* Two recent examples are the export of leg-irons to Saudi Arabia, used to shackle prisoners in Saudi jails, and the export of armoured vehicles and water cannon to Indonesia, used by the regime in Jakarta for internal repression against peaceful demonstrators.

2.2 *More generally, arms exports to military regimes can be interpreted by the regimes in question as tacit support for their repressive policies.* Conversely, tighter controls over arms sales to repressive regimes can be a powerful signal of international disapproval. The international community has arms embargoes on China, Iraq and Nigeria—in large part because of their record on human rights.

2.3 *Irresponsible arms transfers can fuel, exacerbate and prolong armed conflicts—conflicts in which human rights are violated and abused.* It is British armed forces which are often expected to respond to such conflicts through contributions to international peacekeeping missions. Indiscriminate arms transfers can also strengthen the hand of future enemies. For example, the UK was involved in the 1980s, along with a number of other states, in supplying military technology to Saddam Hussein's Iraq, and thereby strengthening the Iraqi war machine. UK and Allied forces then faced this war machine during the Gulf War of 1991.

2.4 *The Scott Report revealed serious deficiencies in the system of parliamentary scrutiny over arms exports.* It is very unlikely that serious policy mistakes, such as the export of military equipment to Iraq in the late 1980s, would have occurred had there been in existence a proper system of parliamentary accountability and transparency. Establishing such a system is the best way to avoid future policy errors comparable to the arms-to-Iraq scandal and, therefore, to ensure that arms transfers do not contribute to human rights abuses.

3. CURRENT UK POLICY

3.1 On July 28, the Government announced the conclusions of its review of arms export guidelines. While the new guidelines contain some positive changes, there are also some disappointing qualifications. While the Government is unlikely to revise these guidelines in the short-term, if it is to effectively implement its human rights objectives, it is essential that it adopts the most restrictive interpretation of its new criteria when judging individual arms export licences. It is also crucial to introduce greater parliamentary scrutiny and accountability in respect of arms export policy.

3.2 We are also conscious that the Government is engaged in another review: the DTI review of strategic export controls. This is an ongoing consultative process, begun under the previous government as a response to the Scott Report, which is considering the whole legislative basis controlling the export of strategic goods and assessing whether there is a need for new primary legislation governing arms exports. This review offers the possibility for a further toughening of the Government's approach to arms exports and military transfers.

SAFERWORLD'S RECOMMENDATIONS

4. HUMAN RIGHTS GUIDELINES

4.1 On human rights, the new guidelines state that *"The Government will take into account respect for human rights and fundamental freedoms in the recipient country."* They go on to state that *"The Government will not issue an export licence if there is a clearly identifiable risk that the proposed export might be used for internal repression."* The guidelines state that a licence should be refused where *"there is clear evidence of the recent use of similar equipment for internal repression by the proposed end-user. . .or where there is reason to believe that the equipment will be diverted from its stated end-use or end-user and used for internal repression."*

4.2 Saferworld believes that these guidelines, as drafted, leave a wide degree of discretion and are open to considerable subjective interpretation. This has been borne out by the disclosure (9 October 1997) of the recent granting of licences for the export of ammunition, bombs and surveillance equipment to Indonesia. There are surely reasonable grounds for concern that a repressive regime might use this equipment for repression.

4.3 *Saferworld believes that greater emphasis should be placed on the potential use of equipment and the definition of "use in internal repression" should be broadened to include deployments designed to intimidate or threaten civilians.*

4.4 The new guidelines are also seriously flawed where they state that licences will not be granted for the export of equipment which has an obvious application for internal repression in cases where the recipient has *"a significant and continuing record of such repression unless the end-use of the equipment is judged to be legitimate, such as protection of members of the security forces from violence."* Judgments regarding the legitimacy of the use of force for internal security in countries with a record of internal repression are likely to be fraught with difficulties, and should not therefore be attempted.

4.5 *Saferworld believes that in states with a history of internal repression there should be presumption that the use of force in internal security is likely to be illegitimate, and exports to such regimes, of equipment which might be used for internal repression, should be proscribed.*

5. TRANSPARENCY AND PARLIAMENTARY SCRUTINY

Annual Report

5.1 The new Government is committed to publishing "an Annual Report on strategic exports" which *"will set out the total value of defence exports to each country, list by country of destination the number of items delivered in each equipment category and give details of export licences granted and refused".*

5.2 *Saferworld believes that this Report should include all military, security and police (MSP) equipment as well as dual-use goods intended for MSP end-use. The categories listed should be sufficiently narrow so that it is clear which types of equipment have actually been licensed for export. At present the DTI categories are so broad that ML10 covers both parachutes and combat aircraft. And the Annual Report should be the subject of a full Parliamentary debate.*

Prior notification

5.3 *Although an essential element of accountability, an Annual report on its own is insufficient. In addition, Saferworld proposes that the Government produce a register of all proposed exports to sensitive destinations, in advance of the granting of licences. This register should contain details of where a similar prospective export has been refused by another EU Member State.*

5.4 There are precedents for this from other countries. In Sweden, the government presents to Parliament a detailed annual report of arms exports from the previous year including: the value of exports; a breakdown of exports on a regional basis; and information on licensed production agreements. Sweden also has a system of confidential pre-notification of proposed arms exports to a parliamentary committee. This committee has the right to raise questions and objections about any proposed sale.

5.5 In the United States, there is pre-notification of all Government-negotiated defence exports over $7.5 million. This pre-notification occurs on a classified basis to a Senate Committee. Committee members have the right to raise objections to contracts. In addition, the full session of Congress is given 30 days prior to notification before a licence is granted for the export of major defence equipment over $14 million. The US administration also now produces a detailed annual report covering all transfers of arms and military assistance.

5.6 *Saferworld recommends that a register of licences be set before Parliament to enable it to measure prospective exports against the criteria set out in the Code of Conduct. At a minimum this register should be set before the Foreign Affairs Select Committee so that any concerns can be properly debated in advance. If there is any question that an export might be used to abuse human rights, the licence should be denied.*

6. EUROPEAN CODE OF CONDUCT

Guidelines

6.1 If a more restrictive British approach to arms exports is not to be undermined by the actions of other countries, it is essential that tighter controls are introduced internationally. The Government is committed to working for a European Code of Conduct *"setting high common standards governing arms exports from all EU countries"*. And the Government has said that an EU Code will be a priority for the British Presidency of the EU.

6.2 Saferworld believes that if the European Code of Conduct is to be effective, and not simply rationalise existing positions, the human rights guideliens need to be as prescriptive as possible. The precise circumstances in which an export licence should be denied on human rights grounds need to be spelt out (cf. Section 4 above)

Transparency

6.3 The above recommendations on transparency and accountability for the UK should also be extended to the EU level. EU Member States should publish a register of all arms exports from the EU. This European Register on Arms Exports should be debated by the European Parliament.

Consultation

6.4 The mechanisms for consultation and implementation of the Code are also crucial. This has three key components: (a) provisions for notifications of transfers and denials, (b) a no-undercutting rule, and (c) a list of sensitive destinations:

  (a) *Denial notification*—Denial notification will be an essential part of ensuring the rigorous implementation of the provisions of the Code of Conduct. Denials should contain information regarding the designation of the arms/technologies denied and information regarding the prospective end-user as well as the country destination.

  (b) *No undercutting*—In order to ensure that there is a levelling up of controls, and not a watering down to the lowest level through constant undercutting, the Member states should adopt a "no-undercutting without serious and in-depth discussion" rule. This would mean that once one member state has denied an export licence, any other member state which is seriously considering granting the same licence should give 30 days advance notification of an intention to undercut. During this 30-day period the member state which wants to undercut should engage in serious and effective multilateral consultations with all other member states. This process would allow the member states to constantly refine their policy towards the common list of sensitive and proscribed destinations and end-users (see below).

  (c) *Sensitive destinations and prior notification*—The EU member states should agree a list of sensitive destinations which sets out: (i) those sensitive destinations which would be embargoed for all exports of arms etc., (ii) those sensitive destinations to which exports of arms etc., should be subject to prior notification amongst the member states, (iii) those countries to which export should take place at national discretion.

7. END-USE PROVISIONS

7.1 Prioritising human rights objectives also requires a strengthening of end-use procedures for arms exports and military transfers. Current procedures for establishing and monitoring end-use within the EU are woefully inadequate. The use of false end-use certificates is not uncommon, and there is little, in current certification requirements, which would prevent irresponsible end-users from using arms for proscribed purposes. Recent high-profile cases in the UK, including Mil-Tec (where arms were sold to the former Rwandan government) and BMARC where naval cannon were re-exported from Singapore to Iran) show how easy it is for unscrupulous exporters and traffickers to abuse end-use certification. Across the fifteen EU states, a variety of end-use systems are in operation, and very few member states have follow-up mechanisms to ensure that, once exported, arms remain with the stated end-user.

7.2 *Saferworld recommends that end-use procedures be strengthened and made uniform across the EU. The best system would be one where the end-use agreement had the status of a legally binding contract. It should include a clause which would lead to the immediate termination of the contract if the goods are found to have been used for proscribed purposes, including the abuse of human rights. A system of follow-up checks should also be provided for within the contract. This is essential to ensure that exported goods remain with their stated end-user and are not diverted for proscribed purposes, or re-exported. The requisite checks could be carried out by consular officials based in the country destination.*

8.   WIDER INTERNATIONAL CONTROLS

8.1   More effective international controls also require tighter controls within the US, the UN and the Wassenaar Arrangement (the 33 member arms export control organisation, which is the successor to COCOM). In the United States, a code of conduct passed the House of Representatives on June 10, and is now being discussed by a Senate/House conference committee. With the EU and US together responsible for over 80 per cent of the arms trade, success in the Code initiatives on both sides of the Atlantic would put the EU and US in a strong position to develop the Wassenaar Arrangement. The Wassenaar Arrangement is crucial because it is the only conventional arms control regime which includes Russia.

8.2   It is also essential that tighter controls apply world-wide. A Group of seven Nobel Peace Prize Winners, led by Dr Oscar Arias, former President of Costa Rica, launched an initiative for an International Code of Conduct in New York in May. The aim is to introduce it to the 1998 UN General Assembly and to establish an international legal convention governing conventional arms transfers—similar to the Ottawa Process, currently being pursued by the Canadian Government on landmines.

8.3   *Saferworld recommends that the British Government should support the initiative to establish an international Code of Conduct and use its influence to press for tighter controls over arms exports and military transfers within the context of the Wassenaar Agreement.*

October 1997

APPENDIX 7

Memorandum submitted by the Centre for International Human Rights Enforcement

1.   A series of Euro-Mediterranean Association Agreements are currently in various stages of negotiation by the Commission and conclusion by the European Council with non-EU states in the Mediterranean region, including Egypt, Morocco, Tunisia, Israel, Lebanon, Jordan, and an Interim Agreement with the PLO. All the Agreements include a standard Article 2, which reads as follows:

> "Relations between the Parties, as well as all the provisions of the Agreement itself, shall be based on respect for human rights and democratic principles, which guides their internal and international policy and constitutes an essential element of this Agreement."

This is known as the "essential elements clause" of the Association Agreements. A further article provides that either party may take *"appropriate measures"* if they consider the other party has failed to fulfill an obligation under the Agreement. Particular attention is given to *"cases of special urgency"* which as defined by the European Commission mean *"a material breach of the Agreement by one of the Parties, [including] violation of essential elements of the Agreement."* Systematic disrespect for human rights thus constitutes a material breach of the Agreement and may give rise to reactive measures under the Agreement, which may involve suspension of some or all of the provisions of the Agreement.

The inclusion of these clauses in the Association Agreements, which cover trade and political relations between the states involved, represents a major piece of multilateral policy regarding the relation of human rights and democracy to foreign relations. Each Association Agreement must be assented to not only by the European Parliament but also, because of the political content, by the national parliaments of each EU Member State. Human rights organisations based in the region, international human rights organisations, and national development agencies and peace groups have paid considerable attention to the implications of the human rights clause, as have members of parliament in a number of EU states including the UK. It is likely that questions of implementation, monitoring and reporting in light of the clause will be raised during the upcoming UK's Presidency of the European Union and that the human rights commitments made by the current Government will give rise to expectations that Britain will take a leading role in these matters. All of this renders the human rights content of the Association Agreements particularly deserving of scrutiny by the Foreign Affairs Committee during its current inquiry.

2.   The current submission is presented as a cover note to two attached documents which deal specifically with the EU-Israel Association Agreement, assented to by both Houses on 19th February this year. This submission summarises the human rights-related undertakings made during the passage of the Israel Agreement through the Commons (at the Second Standing Committee on Delegated Legislation). The points made deal also with the relation of human rights protection to the Middle East peace process. Although the specific interventions and examples are drawn from the discussion of the Israel Agreement, clarifications made regarding the Agreement's human rights content are more generally pertinent to all the Euro-Mediterranean Association

Agreements, which as noted above contain the identical Article 2 (above) and include provision for "appropriate measures" to be taken in case of breach.

3.   The two attached documents [*not printed*] were prepared earlier this year by the Centre for International Human Rights Enforcement, a small specialised Palestinian human rights organisation based in Ramallah in the West Bank. The first document is a letter co-signed by nine Palestinian human rights organisations in the West Bank and Gaza Strip and sent to the British Consul-General, Mr Richard Dalton, in January 1997. The letter was sent in response to certain remarks by the then Foreign Secretary, Mr Malcolm Rifkind, which had given rise to concerns among these groups "that the British Government gives no serious weight to the human rights provisions of the [EU-Israel] Association Agreement" and that it was "inviting Parliament to disregard, and thus weaken, the one element of the Association Agreement most relevant to protecting the peace process from collapse over the coming months and years" (that is, the human rights clause). The letter identified a number of illegal practices by the Israeli government that the human rights groups were hoping could be restrained by the Association Agreement, and sought clarification that these and other illegal practices, should they continue after ratification of the Agreement, would constitute material breaches of the Association Agreement for the purposes of Article 2 and Article 79 (the article providing for "appropriate measures" to be taken in case of breach).

The second document is a Memorandum entitled *Implementing Human Rights Conditionality in the EU-Israel Association Agreement*. This Memorandum considered the role of national parliaments in rendering the Association Agreement more effective in restraining Israel's human rights abuses and violations of international law, and identified it as "an opportunity to close the gap between the quality of EU policy declarations [on human rights and international law] and its policy credibility in the region."

4.   During the course of the Agreement's passage through Parliament, considerable interest was demonstrated in the implications of its human rights content in light of continuing Israeli governmental policies and practices that have long been held illegal by Britain and its EU partners. In response, the then government made a number of clarifications.

(a)   generally, that assent to the EU-Israel Association Agreement did not imply acceptance by the Government or by Parliament of Israel's current standard of human rights practice, nor indeed of Israel's conduct under certain key provisions of the existing EU-Israel Interim Agreement on trade and trade-related matters.

(b)   on the relationship between Article 2 and Article 76 (the "state security clause", see attached letter to Mr. Dalton [*not printed*]), the Government clarified that "measures taken under article 76 would need to be consistent with international law, including human rights."

(c)   on the implications for the operation of the Agreement of breaches of Article 2, the then Foreign Office Minister Jeremy Hanley stated that:

"A break of human rights [. . .] would be material breach of the Agreement. As human rights issues fall within the competence of member states, a decision to suspend or withdraw from the agreement on such a ground would involve the member states deciding by unanimity. A fundamental breach would require unanimity, but I believe that the Commission would probably decide that something on the trade side would be decided by majority . . ."

(Second Standing Committee on Delegated Legislation, Wednesday 19 February 1997, c.22).

(d)   On the need to set up an adequate monitoring and reporting system to scrutinize implementation of the human rights content of the Agreement, both the Government and the Opposition at the time gave commitments to follow-up:

"Mr Hanley: It is vital to ensure that monitoring is as effective as possible. The human rights provisions of the Association Agreement reinforce that requirement. I shall raise the issue of official monitoring with those who will examine monitoring and decide how a mechanism can be established."

(Second Standing Committee on Delegated Legislation, Wednesday 19 February 1997. c6).

"Mr Fatchett: We have always said that human rights will be an important element of the foreign policy of a Labour Government. That commitment applies to these trade arrangements. I have already been vigilant in ensuring that we will push the monitoring process. Europe needs a much more effective monitoring mechanism to ensure that the parts of the agreement dealing with human rights are properly implemented." (above ref. c.9).

5.   During the debate in the Standing Committee, a number of specific practices and policies of the Israeli government were raised as matters for concern by the then Foreign Affairs Minister and by other Members. These included the extended closure of the Occupied Territories and the restrictions on movement of people and goods; settlements, and in particular the construction and expansion of settlements round East Jerusalem and discriminatory policies on residency rights and building permits for Palestinians in the city; torture; the use of force in South Lebanon.

6.   One very important point that was not clarified by the Government during the Standing Committee debate concerns what standards are to be understood as referred to in the phrase "respect for human rights". In particular,

it was not clarified that the phrase includes not only the terms of international human rights law but also of international humanitarian law, which protects fundamental human rights during times of war, civil strife and belligerent occupation. This point needs to be clarified not only in light of the law and in the interests of consistency, but to allow the Agreements fuller potential as an instrument helping to protect human rights in the region.

7.   The manner of implementation of the human rights clause will be a matter of interest to a number of domestic, regional and international constituencies as well as to the governments of those states concluding Association Agreements with the EU. It is particularly important that the UK and its European partners equip themselves to respond to this interest with clarity and adequate transparency, and that they avoid any appearance of having recourse to the human rights content of the Agreements on the basis purely, or even largely, of short-term political expediency. It is crucial to make clear the UK's commitment, together with its EU partners, to basing the application of the human rights-related provision of the Israel Agreement—and the other Association Agreements—on the non-selective application of the standards and duties placed upon states by the existing instruments of international human rights and humanitarian law by which they are bound. In the absence of a coherent policy in these regards, and without a transparent and politically independent monitoring and reporting mechanism, the human rights clause is unlikely to function as an effective instrument for helping to prevent or remedy human rights abuses.

8.   In light of the terms of reference of its inquiry, the Committee may wish to:

(1)   Clarify for the record that the phrase "respect for human rights" in Article 2 of the Euro-Mediterranean Association Agreements, includes the duties and standards embodied in the instruments of international human rights and humanitarian treaty law by which the Parties to the Agreements are bound;

(2)   Consider to what extent there already exists a coherent strategy for the non-selective and effective implementation of the human rights content of the Euro-Mediterranean Association Agreements, what input the Government has had or intends to have in this regard, and what further information might be required to assist in the formulation of such a strategy for the more effective prevention of human rights abuses;

(3)   Consider to what extent progress has been made on the establishment of a politically independent, adequately transparent monitoring and reporting mechanism for the EU-Israel Association Agreement in light of the specific undertakings made in this regard, bearing in mind the desirability of building into this framework the participation of human rights organisations, development agencies and other groups on the ground in the region with first-hand knowledge of the human rights situation.

October 1997

APPENDIX 8

Memorandum submitted by Professor Ken Booth, Department of International Politics, University of Wales, Aberystwyth

Thank you for your letter of 20 November 1997 asking me for my views. I was sorry that previous commitment prevented me from giving oral evidence.

I am sure that the Foreign Affairs Committee is extremely busy, with more than enough to read. Consequently I will keep my remarks brief. I enclose a CV, as suggested in your "Guide", together with 15 copies of a draft article I was commissioned to write for *The Times Higher* two months ago (an editorially shortened version appeared on 7 November 1997 under the title "Exporting ethics in place of arms") [*not printed*]. I had been asked to write mainly about the relationship between the arms trade and human rights policy.

Arising out of the article I would emphasise the following points for consideration by the Foreign Affairs Committee.

1.   *There can be no question about the importance of human rights in British foreign policy.*

—   They are important in themselves (in what they say about us as a civilized society).

—   Successive British governments have committed the country to agreements such as the Universal Declaration, the Helsinki Final Act etc., while the present government has made a specific commitment to make Britain "once again a force for good in the world".

2.   *"Morality"/"Ethics"/"Human Rights" are not optional extras in British foreign policy.*

The British government does not have a choice between pursuing an "ethical" foreign policy or a "pragmatic" or "prudent" one. The only choice it has is between different sets of ethical principles that deliver different ethical consequences. "Pragmatism" in foreign policy is based on a set of distinct value preferences which can have distinct consequences in terms of good and ill in peoples's lives.

3. *There are convincing sets of arguments against those who would oppose making human rights more central in British foreign policy on the grounds of naivety and self-interest*

— The old argument that to stop arms sales on human rights grounds risks a loss of influence with a foreign government should be put into the context of the instability of politics in many regions, such that today's oppressed opposition is likely to be tomorrow's government.

— The real fear about loss of jobs and profits needs to be set against the possibility and desirability of people finding alternative forms of employment to the deadly business of landmines, riot control gear etc., and of recognising the dubious economics (subsidies, escalating costs etc.,) of the armaments business.

— If other countries pick up lost contracts, so be it. Is it not better that we subsidise the production of what people need (ODA has often had a different perspective on what Third World governments spend on armaments to that of the salesmen of MOD)?

4. *The British government has to determine priorities in terms of being a "force for good"*

If it overstretches itself it may end up achieving nothing. The priority areas identified in the accompanying article point to:

— The importance of more transparency in the process of foreign policy making.

— Refusing to sell arms to oppressive regimes for internal repression.

— The desirability of acting multilaterally (but in the forefront, not using multilateralism as a shield for inaction).

— Working towards eliminating weapons of mass destruction.

— Making the promotion of economic justice globally more of a priority.

— Showing the seriousness of Britain's commitments to human rights by improving our treatment of asylum seekers, refugees etc.

5. *A human rights policy should be applied equally, as between "friends", "associates", "enemies" etc.*

If it is applied selectively, it will show that Britain is merely acting self-interestedly, and not *out of respect for* the principles of human rights. How the government expresses its displeasure might differ (a quiet word to a friendly government as opposed to a commercial contract not "honoured" when a foreign government blatantly dishonours human rights) but the principle must be universal, if it is to mean anything.

6. *There is public support*

In the areas of foreign policy discussed above there will always be grey areas in which reasonable people can disagree, but the difficulty of drawing lines should not be used as an excuse for not trying, especially after public scrutiny and more transparent processes, and in the light of public support for tougher laws on the arms trade. The title of the original draft of the article (changed by *The Higher*) was deliberately provocative in order to confront readers with the fact that we often *know* what the human rights consequences of our policies are, but prefer to look away. For the most part we are not wicked accomplices in a deadly trade with oppressive consequences for other humans, but we are *knowing* accomplices, unwilling to face up to the inconveniences of acting more decisively in this situation. Consequently, this is an area where leadership from the top could have both support at home and positive impact on the lives of suffering people elsewhere.

January 1998

APPENDIX 9

Memorandum submitted by Lord Avebury

WORK OF THE THEMATIC RAPPORTEURS OF THE UN CENTRE FOR HUMAN RIGHTS

1. The UN Human Rights Commission has appointed Rapporteurs who deal with human rights in particular countries (e.g., Iraq, Myanmar), and Thematic Rapporteurs and Working Groups, dealing with particular categories of human rights abuses such as violence against women, or extrajudicial executions. The Thematic Rapporteurs undertake missions to countries which may or may not be dealt with simultaneously by country Rapporteurs. For instance, in the case of Iran, where there is a country Rapporteur, the Rapporteurs on Religious Intolerance and on Freedom of Expression have also been there recently. A list of documents presented to the 53rd Session of the Human Rights Commission by the Thematic Rapporteurs and Working Groups is attached.

2.   When the Thematic Rapporteurs and Working Groups consider that a visit to any country is desirable, they ask the government to invite them, and they only proceed with the visit if agreement can be reached on both the principle and the modalities. This means that a country usually escapes detailed examination by a Thematic Rapporteur if it ignores the request for an invitation, or agrees in principle but creates difficulties about the modalities. For example, the Rapporteur on Extrajudicial, Arbitrary and Summary Executions, M Bacre Waly Ndiaye, in his most recently published report E/CN.4/1997/60/Add.1 of December 23, 1996, writes:

> The Special Rapporteur hopes that the commitment to openness, transparency and full co-operation, expressed by the Government in a letter dated 22 November 1995, will lead to the extension of an invitation to the Special Rapporteur to visit India in the near future.

3.   There was one case in the last Session of an investigation conducted by Thematic Rapporteurs without the consent of the state concerned. This was the study on Nigeria, conducted by the Special Rapporteurs on Extrajudicial, Summary or Arbitrary Executions, and on the Independence of Judges and Lawyers, which had been commissioned at the 52nd Session of the Commission. This means that the consent of the state concerned is not a sine qua non for such investigations.

4.   It has been suggested to Mrs Mary Robinson, UN High Commissioner for Human Rights, that the Special Rapporteurs and Working Groups should have the power to conduct special investigations of urgent country situations *suo moto*, whether or not the state concerned is willing to facilitate arrangements for a visit. This would enable them to make an analysis of material already published in the media, and by international human rights organisations such as Amnesty International and Human Rights Watch, together with any evidence available from exiles or even in some cases, informants within the country, and to report their findings to the following meeting of the Commission.

5.   In particular, this would enable the Commission, when it meets on March 16 to have an evaluation of the appalling massacres in Algeria. M Pierre Sané, the Secretary General of Amnesty International, felt that the situation there was so serious that he asked for a special session of the Human Rights Commission to examine the massacres, but this may not have been feasible for practical reasons. The next best thing would be to ensure that when the Commission does meet on March 18, it has before it an analysis by its own Special Rapporteur.

6.   Such an extension of the mandate of the Special Rapporteurs and Working Groups would have resource implications which are difficult to predict in advance, and all the staff are working at full stretch already. It is important that the budgetary problems of the UN Centre for Human Rights are relieved, and that their accounting system is improved so as to show clearly how much is spent by each of the Special Rapporteurs and Working Groups. In recent years, new mandates have been created without any corresponding increase in the total budget, and the result has been that some of the mechanisms (e.g., the Working Group on Arbitrary Detentions) have been unable to look in detail at human rights abuses drawn to their attention. If all the countries which have been required to issue invitations were suddenly to comply, the Centre would be unable to deal with the workload.

7.   No list is available of the countries which have been asked for invitations, and the date on which the request was first made. It is therefore not possible to see at a glance which countries are not co-operating with the human rights mechanisms. If the Human Rights Centre were to publish a note before every Session, listing the date of each outstanding request for a visit, and the comment by the Rapporteur or Working Group, it would focus attention on the need to secure better co-operation with the Centre by member states.

January 1998

APPENDIX 10

Memorandum submitted by Redress

Thank you for your letter dated 19 December 1997, inviting Redress to submit a memorandum to the Foreign Affairs Committee in connection with its inquiry into the field of foreign policy and human rights.

Redress welcomes this inquiry and the efforts made by the Committee to solicit evidence, and will be pleased to respond to your request.

Redress is a London based organisation established in 1992 which works in the UK and internationally to promote the right of torture survivors to reparation and to help individual torture survivors to seek redress.

We would like to draw the Committee's attention to the following:

1.   INVOLVEMENT OF BRITISH COMPANIES IN SUPPLYING INSTRUMENTS OF TORTURE TO FOREIGN GOVERNMENTS

Redress is concerned at the involvement of British companies in supplying instruments which can be used for torture to regimes around the world which practice torture. Although Britain has imposed controls on the manufacture and export of equipment such as electroshock weapons, this has not prevented British companies from trading in goods which can and are used for torture abroad. This was demonstrated, for instance, by the

Channel 4 Dispatches 1995 programme "The Torture Trail", which exposed the willingness of two British companies to supply electroshock equipment.

Of particular concern to Redress is a gap in the law which allows trans-shipment. This occurs when a British company brokers a deal for the transfer of goods between second and third countries which, if the goods had come physically within British jurisdiction, would attract legal control. In a response to a consultation document of the Department of Trade and Industry on Strategic Export Controls dated July 1996, Redress called for the law to be changed so as to close this gap. A copy of this response, dated 31st October 1996, is enclosed.— *not printed.*]

In this document, Redress also urged the Government to introduce greater accountability in this trade:

> "Redress supports the need for new primary legislation in the UK for a new Regulatory Body to control the transfer of equipment, personnel, training, expertise, technology, advice or any services to governments or other persons which on a balance of probabilities may be found to contribute to torture and human rights violations. Further we believe in the need for total transparency in the governing of such transfers, a code of conduct for transfers and a formal, written procedure for the granting of export licences."

Redress believes that the above measures are important for implementing the Foreign Secretary's pledge in his statement, "Human Rights into a New Century" of 17 July 1997 to refuse to supply equipment and weapons with which regimes deny their people human rights and to review licensing procedures.

2. LACK OF PROTECTION FOR BRITISH NATIONALS TORTURED ABROAD

Redress provides legal advice and assistance to torture survivors, including British nationals tortured abroad, on legal remedies. All too often, British nationals feel that their government has not done enough to protect them and help them to seek redress. In a recent publication "Torture in Saudi Arabia: No protection, No redress", which is enclosed, in addition to a separate copy of the relevant section of Chapter VIII, Redress and the Parliamentary Human Rights Group concluded that:

> " . . . there has been little demonstrable commitment to protect individual British citizens who may be at risk from ill-treatment and torture in Saudi Arabia or to take action that would assist them while in detention or secure redress after their release".

One of the recommendations of the report, directed towards the British Government, is to:

> "Extend diplomatic protection to its nationals who allege torture or ill-treatment abroad".

Redress appreciates the opportunity to participate in the inquiry, and is ready to be of further assistance.

January 1998

APPENDIX 11

Memorandum submitted by the British Helsinki Human Rights Group

The British Helsinki Human Rights Group is a charity under British law. It was established in 1992 by a group of trustees previously active in helping dissidents in the former Soviet Bloc and numbers academics, lawyers, doctors and journalists among its active members. In that time it has also published 16 reports on democracy and human rights.

Over the past five years the BHHRG has tried to concentrate on mainstream human rights concerns, i.e., free elections, democratic institutions, media freedom, fair trials and prison conditions. Many of the groups concerned with human rights in the post-Soviet world concentrate their efforts on minority issues which are fashionable in the West, where general rights are guaranteed, but which may seem irrelevant or even counter-productive in the former Soviet bloc.

In the past five years a number of problems have presented themselves to the Group's rapporteurs on a regular basis. As the present government is committed to putting human rights at the centre of its foreign policy agenda we would like to make the following suggestions to the Foreign Affairs Committee which might aid and abet that process.

INTRODUCTION

As a registered charity the BHHRG is unable to lobby or make suggestions of a political nature. At the same time, it would be naive to pretend that political and strategic issues cannot ever shape a government's approach to human rights. To a certain extent policy made towards the countries of the former Soviet bloc was bound to be something of a lurch into the unknown. Although there have been improvements in the field of human rights in some countries of the Eastern bloc in this period there is still much to be done. And, in some cases, the policy of Western governments has actually made things worse.

1. WESTERN GOVERNMENTS AND ELECTIONS IN THE FORMER EASTERN BLOC

During the 1990s governments in the US and EU became closely involved in monitoring elections to test the democratic credentials in the CIS and Eastern Europe. Much of this monitoring was done through organizations like the OSCE and the Council of Europe which though nominally independent naturally reflect the views of member nations.

The BHHRG has also monitored over 30 elections in the same period and has often come to different conclusions than these bodies.

As the decade has progressed it seems that elections monitoring has become more and more a tool of foreign policy and less an objective analysis of the proceedings themselves. It has become increasingly evident that flaws in the election process are glaringly overlooked in some places and heightened in others.

The following are some of the most blatant:

1.1. *Russia (1993): Parliamentary elections and Constitutional referendum.* Observers overlooked evidence that the constitutional referendum had failed to garner sufficient votes to become law. This was revealed by the Russians themselves three months after the poll.

1.2 *Presidential elections in Azerbaijan (1993),* parliamentary elections (1995): In the former election an observer from this Group had a vote cast in his name. The parliamentary elections (where few people bothered to vote) were criticized but there was no major scandal of a type that occurred in

1.3 *Albania (1996): After the parliamentary elections in May it was revealed that key members of the OSCE observer group had connections with the Socialist Party (ex-CP). The Socialists won repeat elections held in June 1997.*

1.4 *Montenegro* (October, 1997): the whole election process was under the control of one party. Despite being constantly referred to as the "opposition" (in a strikingly Orwellian fashion) this party controlled all the apparatus of state; it manned the election commissions and prevented free access to the local media. In the second round on 19 October 30,000 extra names had been added to the voting register. As it was widely accepted that the West wanted a particular result in Montenegro no monitoring of the media took place and despite widespread dissatisfaction the election was passed as free and fair.

1.5 In neighbouring *Serbia* (1997) however, an election that was no worse and in some respects much better was condemned even *before* it took place.

There are many more examples of the arbitrariness of the international community in its attitude to election monitoring. BHHRG publications deal with these examples and many more.

1.6 *Why does it matter?*

The use of election monitoring to further foreign policy initiatives by Western governments is a worrying development. For one thing, it is an inaccurate representation of the facts, which cannot be justified. However, the main reason for reflecting on this policy is that it has served to alienate large numbers of people in the CIS, Eastern Europe and the Balkans from the West.

Whereas once upon a time the people in the Soviet Union revered countries like Great Britain and the United States for their democratic institutions and freedoms they are now disillusioned and angry. An anti-Western mood is emerging that did not exist before 1989. Such views have been expressed on numerous occasions to members of the BHHRG—from respected dissidents like Paruir Hairikien in Armenia to ordinary people many of whose daily lives have failed to improve since the end of Communism and who perhaps expected more from the West. Demonstrators in Podgorica (Montenegro) carried banners blaming the United States for what they regarded as rigged elections in the republic.

2. A CONFLICT BETWEEN COMMERCIAL INTERESTS AND HUMAN RIGHTS

Perceived commercial interests are, no doubt, one of the reasons why human rights abuses in certain countries are overlooked. The corollary of this is that other countries with no commercial clout are bullied and singled out for criticism.

2.1 For example, official corruption, media harassment, random arrests and poverty in oil-rich Azerbaijan are ignored in foreign office briefings and guidelines. And because neighbouring Georgia is building a pipe-line to transport oil to the Black Sea its own heavy-handed treatment of dissidents as well as the appalling conditions in its prisons for ordinary inmates is ignored.

2.2   On the other hand, Belarus which has little commercial potential for the West is criticized harshly even though human rights are no less respected and in most cases much better than in the Caucasian republics. There are no political prisoners and penal institutions are of a relatively high standard for the region.

2.3   A delicate area but one worthy of reflection is the way that members of the foreign service are able to leave or retire from their posts and "go native". In countries like Russia and Ukraine which are rampant with corruption such career moves could be potentially threatening to national and commercial interests. It also means that diplomats are potentially sources for blackmail, if only to promote the interests of a particular company, bank or government.

3.   MINORITY RIGHTS

While strongly supporting a commitment to protect vulnerable minorities the BHHRG feels that there has been a tendency for Western governments to get bogged down by the demands of minority groups without always appreciating that their demands can sometimes cloak political aims and ambitions.

3.1   For example, in post-independence Moldova the perceived abuse of the rights of the minority Russian and Gagauz population was basically a ruse to destroy a separate Moldovan/Romanian identity. Since the short, bloody war between Chisinau and separatists in Transdniestr (1992) minority problems in Moldova have significantly abated.

3.2   Similarly, the small Lachen minority began to agitate in the winter of 1993 in the months preceding Abulfaz Elchibey's removal from power in a coup but it has not been heard from since.

3.3   Complaints about their treatment from Russians in the Baltic States and Hungarians in Romania and Slovakia ebb and flow according to the manoeuverings in local politics as much as anything else.

3.4   As there are so many problems for the majority populations in post-Communist countries the demands of minorities should be kept firmly within proper parameters. Often the international community makes demands on small, poor countries in the treatment of their minorities (providing education and reading materials, for example) that they cannot, at the moment anyway, find the resources to fully comply with.

January 1998

APPENDIX 12

Memorandum submitted by the Movement for the Survival of the Ogoni People (MOSOP)

OGONI: THE NIGHTMARE CONTINUES

INTRODUCTION

The situation of human rights in Nigeria is dismal, yet nowhere is the situation as frightening as in Ogoni especially since 1993, when under the aegis of the Movement for the Survival of the Ogoni People (MOSOP), Ogoni campaigns for human and environmental rights became internationalised. This worsening human rights situation in Ogoni, however, did not seem to make sufficient impression on the international community, including the United Nations until the brutal execution of Ken Saro-Wiwa and eight other MOSOP activists in November 1995.

Since the executions which attracted world wide condemnations, the human rights situation in Ogoni has been documented as worsening. In spite of increases in the level of human rights abuses in Ogoni after the execution of the Ogoni nine, the short span of international attention has failed to give the Ogoni situation its deserved focus and attention. The Ogoni people have been the special target of repression by the military regime for two main reasons: (i) confronted with a well organised and disciplined non-violent democratic mass movement by the Ogoni people, first of its kind in our part of the world, the military regime, in alliance with Shell oil company, is determined to use the Ogoni as a frightening deterrent to other opposition groups who may want to organise like the Ogoni people. (ii) the government here seem to hold the Ogoni people responsible for what has happened to its international image following the execution of the Ogoni leader and activists.

This deteriorating level of human rights abuses in Ogoni takes the form of torture, rape, murder, arbitrary detention and military raids on Ogoni villages, which together with the environmental devastation by Shell oil company is driving the Ogoni people to extinction. Things have now reached a point where the military now confiscate the bodies of those they kill and refuse the possibility of burial with the result that people who are now shot by the soldiers now avoid the hospitals as a result of the fear that they could die there and have their bodies confiscated. The following are some of the instances of human abuses recorded in Ogoni.

1. CONTINUED DETENTION OF THE OGONI NINE (9) CORPSES

The United Nations fact finding mission to Nigeria in April 1996 came to the conclusion that the trial, sentence and execution of Ken Saro-Wiwa and eight other Ogoni activists violated both Nigerian and international covenants to which Nigeria is a signatory. It then recommended, amongst other things, that:

> "in the case of the trials of Ken Saro-Wiwa and others, the Government of Nigeria should consider establishing a panel of eminent jurists, nominated by the Chief Justice of Nigeria, to establish the modalities to determine who and to what extent financial relief could be accorded to the dependants of the families of the deceased."

Not only has the Nigerian regime ignored this recommendation by the UN team, it continues to detain the corpses of the executed activists. As if this were not callous enough, the regime has outlawed any form of mourning for the executed activists to the extent that mere mention of the name of Ken Saro-Wiwa or possession of his books attracts instant detention. For instance on 26 August 1997, Major Obi Umahi, commander of the Internal Security Task Force (the special military Task Force set up specifically for the pacification of the Ogoni people with headquarters at Kpor in the Gokana local government area of Ogoni) impounded all Ken Saro-Wiwa's books in the stock of a book vendor displayed for sale at the entrance of the state secretariat complex; the books included: *On a darkling plain; Sozaboy; Genocide in Nigeria; the Ogoni Tragedy; Ogoni Today and Tomorrow; Ogoni Bill of Rights; First Letter to Ogoni Youths; Second Letter to Ogoni Youths; A Forest of Flowers and Similia*, amongst others. In addition the vendor was arrested and forced to deny newspaper reports of the seizure whilst the Port Harcourt correspondent of the Punch and Vanguard newspapers that carried the story were tortured and detained.

2. MILITARY OCCUPATION

Before the executions, the Nigerian military regime constituted a special military Task Force drawn from the Army, Air Force, Navy and the notoriously brutal and undisciplined unit of the police called the Police Mobile Force, a.k.a.—"Kill and Go" for the specific purpose of suppressing opposition from the Ogoni people. Although the Task Force, which is not backed up by any law, is called the Rivers State Internal Security Task Force, it takes orders directly from the Presidency in Abuja.

The Internal Security Task Force is the instrument primarily responsible for all sorts of human rights abuses in Ogoni. Thus whilst the police and State Security operatives arrest and detain people in other parts of the country, this military Task Force, whose former head, Major (now Lt. Col.) Paul Okuntimu once boasted on national television of having used three only out of the well over 200 ways he knew of killing on the Ogoni people, roam wild in Ogoni, occasionally launching military raids on villages, impounding food items including domestic animals and other property from their owners. For instance, during the 6 December 1997 State Assembly(s) elections as in the others in the series of the charade of a Transition Programme, whilst the police were used in most other parts of the country, in Ogoni it was troops of the Internal Security that were mainly used.

The terrorism which the Task Force inflicts on the Ogoni people, especially those suspected of being MOSOP sympathisers and activists, is all pervading making it impossible for people to lead some semblance of normal lives in their homes as other Nigerians. The roadblocks mounted by the Task Force increased from eight to 12 as at August 1997, making it practically difficult to travel in Ogoni without harassment, extortion, threat of and actual arrest and at times arbitrary execution. These roadblocks which continue to be fearsome centres for the commission of all forms of human rights violence including rape of women, arbitrary arrests and executions, extortion are usually dismounted during the government programmed and guided visits by some foreign visitors.

The Task Force maintains several secret detention centres, which are more or less concentration camps, within and outside Ogoni, the most notorious of which are located at Kpor, Bori, Eleme, Afam. Those detained at these detention centres, which are mostly toilets and stores of disused public buildings, are kept completely incommunicado and could be kept for periods up to a year without charges and can only be released on the orders of the military Task Force commander, Major Obi Abel Umahi, who although a smooth operator, surpasses his predecessor in brutality.

3. DETENTIONS WITHOUT TRIAL: THE OGONI TWENTY (20)

On 20 September 1995, the federal Attorney General of Nigeria brought charge No. OCDT/PH/PH/3/95 against 19 MOSOP activists before the same Tribunal that sentenced Ken Saro-Wiwa and the others. That charge which is exactly the same as the one against Ken and the others is based on the same evidence of the same suborned witnesses that were used in the Saro-Wiwa trial. In an effort to give a "judicial" face to their continued detention, they were arraigned on a holding murder charge before a magistrate, with clearly no jurisdiction over the matter, and they were remanded in prison custody.

One of the detainees, Mr Clement Tusima had earlier died in detention, having been denied medical attention. The corpse of the said Tusima has not been released to his family till now.

To the remaining 19 against whom similar charges were brought before that same gravely flawed Tribunal, was added a 20th person, Nkale Beete in March 1997, and together they are now commonly referred to as the Ogoni 20.

The appalling conditions under which the Ogoni 20 are detained has led to two of them virtually losing their sight as a result of certain chemicals and substances sprayed on their eyes during interrogation, while the 20th person, Nkale Beete lost his finger in the course of the torture he received. In February 1997, one of them— Bariture Lebe was bitten by a snake in his prison cell and denied adequate medical attention for "security reasons".

The government has consistently and stoutly stalled legal proceedings brought for the bail of these detainees arguing that only the Tribunal that tried and sentenced Saro-Wiwa and the others, and not the High Court, have jurisdiction over the matter including their bail application. On 23 July 1997, the High Court decided that it had jurisdiction over the bail application and the government appealed against that decision and at the same time applied for a stay of the bail application pending the determination of their appeal. Even the application for stay has not yet been heard because of incessant applications for adjournments, and they are invariably always granted the indulgence. This stalling tactics forced the Ogoni detainees in August to embark on hunger strike *"to protest against our apparent conviction to the indignity of a slow and painful death without any trial since 1994 by the power that be and her accomplice—Shell oil company."*

The toll that their continued detention without trial under inhuman conditions has taken on their health is best captured in their own words. In a letter smuggled from prison dated 20 August 1977, they stated:

"Our health condition here is best described as "an existence on borrowed time" as our health conditions are deteriorating by every passing day. Our health continues to be a victim of an interplay of the vicious effects of a horrible, overcrowded and unsanitary prison conditions as we have to go to toilet as well as eat on the same filthy floor that we sleep on.

For now, Messrs John Banatu, Godwin Ghodor are having serious chest pains with blood stained spectrum: Mr. Blessing Israel and Friday Gburama have serious internal pain at point of surgical operation, dizziness etc. Adam Kaa has developed hernia at the right groin region; Messrs Samson Ntignee and Benjamin Kabari have serious waist and perennial stomach pains, dizziness as well as declining sights: Messrs Popgbara Zorzor, Baribuma Kumanwe are having progressive sight decline with Mr Babina Vizor virtually blind. Kaghar Basseh, numbness of hands and legs and migraine, Samuel Asiga seriously asthmatic; Paul Dekor—pneumonia, constant urination. Ngbaa Baovi virtually blind; Messrs Monsi and Doghala—serious pulmonary problem, while Nasikpo Nyuieda has a growing lipoma on both knee joints. Some of the manifestations are beyond our descriptions."

It has to be pointed out that on occasions that their illnesses were aggravated to the extent that they were rushed to the hospital, they were against medical advice, denied admission or proper treatment.

The case of Nyieda Nasikpo deteriorated to the situation that he is currently admitted for surgical operations at the University of Port Harcourt Teaching Hospital and even then he has virtually been abandoned there due to non availability of what is required for his surgical operation.

Apart from the health problems, the government has on two occasions arranged programmed window-dressing visits by teams from the African Commission of Human and People's Rights and the National Human Rights Commission to the Ogoni detainees.

4. EXTRA-JUDICIAL EXECUTIONS AND ARBITRARY DETENTIONS

Since November 1995, a total of 45 persons in Ogoni have either been extra-judicially executed or are unaccounted for, 345 others detained arbitrarily whilst 36 people are nursing various degrees of gun shot wounds and yet another 130 others have injuries inflicted on them by soldiers through gun butts, electric cable whips and other instruments of torture. As at the end of November 1997 we had 30 MOSOP activists detained at various detention centres created by the Internal Security Task Force within and outside Ogoni.

Since December 1997, a major crackdown on Ogoni people began with the arrest and detention of 15 people and climaxed with the brutal repression to stop the peaceful celebration of Ogoni Day on January 4 1998. A total of 40 persons were arrested, a woman shot in the stomach when troops shot into a crowd of peaceful demonstrators, whilst churches were dispersed with gun shots. Two of the detainees—Batom Mitee, younger brother of the MOSOP acting President, Ledum Mitee, and Tombari Gioro were so brutally tortured that eye witnesses fear their chances of survival unless they were accorded urgent medical attention, which has not been provided to our knowledge, and the whereabouts of these two activists remain unknown since January 7. The detailed Press Release on this current event is sent herewith [*not printed*].

5. DENIAL OF FREEDOM OF MOVEMENT AND INFORMATION

Ogoni remains the only part of Nigeria where special permission is required before any foreign or local journalist and visitor can go, and even then under the guidance of government officials and the Internal Security Task Force. The only people allowed access to Ogoni are those either sponsored by Shell Oil company or on arranged visits by the government, but on those occasions, Ogonis, except stage managed audiences, are prevented from talking with the visitors except on pain of serious reprisals. Some instances of recorded incidents in this respect include the following:

In January 1996 Paul Adams, the Nigerian correspondent of the London Financial Times was arrested basically for entering Ogoni without permission and later charged to Court for being in possession of a MOSOP press statement.

In February 1996, the African-American Nation of Islam leader, Louis Farakhan, visited Ogoni on the invitation and under the guide of the government soldiers arrested, tortured and detained 15 Ogoni people who dared to speak to the visitor on the true state of things in Ogoni. One of the victims of this incident lost his left eye as a result of injuries he sustained from the torture in the hands of the soldiers that raided his home a day after the visit.

The Ogoni people also suffered very serious reprisals following the United Nations Fact Finding team's visit in April 1996. A total of 87 persons were arrested, tortured and detained for turning out to speak with the Team. Two of the victims of this reprisal including 60 year old madam Korsi, died as a result of injuries sustained from torture she received for refusing to move from her house for imposters.

In August 1996, 15 Ogonis were arrested and detained on the allegation that they were holding consultations with a view to planning to meet with a delegation of the Commonwealth Ministerial Action Group (CMAG) expected to visit Nigeria then.

On 26 August 1997, the commander of the Internal Security Task Force, Major Obi Umahi, impounded 120 copies of books written by the late Ken Saro-Wiwa from an Ogoni vendor in Port Harcourt. Two journalists that reported the incident were tortured and detained. It could be recalled that shortly after the hanging of Ken Saro-Wiwa and others on 10 November 1995, his book, *A Forest of Flowers*, was dropped from the West African Examination Council reading list of Literature in English.

6. DENIAL OF FREEDOM OF ASSEMBLY AND WORSHIP

Since the execution of the Ogoni 9, an order banning the mourning or remembrance of the Ogoni 9 in particular has been enforced with ruthless abandon. For that purpose any person dressed in black in Ogoni is publicly stripped, arrested and detained.

The sacredness of religion has not prevented the soldiers from visiting the church in Ogoni with its doses of bizarre and traumatic experiences. Ministers are often harassed, intimidated and detained on allegations that they were using the pulpit to mobilise people and praying for the repose of the souls of the executed Ogoni 9 and others killed by the soldiers. Plainclothes security men are posted to churches, to monitor what the ministers are preaching especially during period close to the anniversary of the execution of the Ogoni 9. In Ogoni today, public church ceremonies including conventions and harvest thanksgiving services, are prohibited except with prior permission of the Internal Security Task Force. For instance, in December 1996, a planned Conference for Baptist Churches in Rivers State was disallowed in Ogoni, even with the plea of officials of the Nigerian Baptist Convention whilst the annual Conventions of several other churches have similarly been refused for two years running now.

In some instances, gun shots were fired into church sessions by the soldiers to disperse worshippers. On Sunday 4 January 1998, the congregations of the Assemblies of God Church at Bori and Boue were fired on and dispersed by troops of the Internal Security Task Force, whilst a funeral service at Kaani was similarly dispersed and the chief mourner arrested.

The ban on gatherings and assembly in Ogoni is not restricted to church ceremonies alone. Burial ceremonies, cultural celebrations and performances are also affected. In 1997 alone a total of 15 burial ceremonies were dispersed by gun shots for failure to obtain prior permission from, and payment of some extortionist fees to the soldiers.

Furthermore, on 1 November 1996, soldiers stopped the New Yam festival celebrations in Kegbara Dere whilst on 23 April 1997, soldiers desecrated the Ogoni sacred *Amanikpo* shrine, tearing open the shrine blinds, arrested and tortured the shrine priests and made away with the shrine's antique puppet masquerades.

7. PROBLEM OF REFUGEES AND DISPLACED PERSONS

A direct consequence of the brutal repression in Ogoni is that many MOSOP activists have been forced to flee to neighbouring West African countries, notably Benin, Ghana, Togo and Ivory Coast, where they have now been granted refugee status by the United Nations High Commission for Refugees (UNHCR) in those countries. As at September 1997, there were 1,100 Ogoni refugees living under pitiable conditions in refugee camps in those countries. Even in such circumstances, the Ogoni refugees have not been spared the repression as attempts have been made by Nigerian security agents to kidnap Ogoni refugees across the Nigerian border, in clear breach of international law. This situation of insecurity of Ogoni refugees has deteriorated further with the saturation of Nigerian troops and security agents of the West African sub region on "peace missions". So brazen have been the Nigerian regime's efforts to get at the Ogoni refugees that they formally requested the UNHCR in those countries to furnish the respective Nigerian missions there with the names of the Ogoni refugees under UNHCR protection.

It is important to stress that the fact of presence of this number of refugees is testimony to the state of human rights in Ogoni, for nowhere else in Nigeria do we have this concentration of refugees from one single ethnic group. We strongly suggest a visit to the camp particularly the *Come* camp in Benin Republic as interviews with the refugees will provide first hand account of the instances of human rights abuses.

Apart from the refugees, there are in Ogoni today not less than 200,000 displaced persons whose villages, communities, settlements and houses were destroyed by military raids.

CONCLUSION AND RECOMMENDATIONS

The ethical foreign policy of this government cannot be more challenged and tested than by the Nigerian situation. This is not only because of the historical links that exists between both countries but also because of the position Nigeria occupies not only in the West African sub-region, but in Africa as a whole. Any major crises in Nigeria or even the attitude of the British government to developments there will have major impact on the continent.

Although the European Union has put in place certain measures in the wake of the execution of Ken Saro-Wiwa and other Ogoni activists in our view those measures failed to have their desired impact because they were limited in scope and also because they were not tied to any benchmarks.

There is unimpeachable evidence that the human rights situation in Nigeria is deteriorating considerably. Evidence also exists that the so called transition programme of the Abacha regime is a dubious sham programmed to fail or at best replace the military uniform of the arch dictator with a civilian dress.

The British, more than most other Western countries is better placed to appreciate the Nigerian situation. The British should be able to see though the peace-keeping posturing which the regime uses to deflect international attention and censure. What should be most clear is that the force which the regime is using ostensibly to install democracy in West Africa to the baffling admiration of not a few, is the same force with which democracy and human rights are stymied at home.

It is our recommendation that the British ethical foreign policy should express itself in the Nigerian case by fashioning a series of measures tied to a set of benchmarks and incrementally implemented bilaterally and through the EU, Commonwealth and the UN. This will have the advantage of making monitoring of developments easier as well as providing clear indicators for measuring progress or otherwise.

There is no doubt that Ogoni has become the metaphor for human rights abuses in Nigeria today and it is therefore important that any serious effort at improving the situation of human rights in the country must see the Ogoni situation as the mirror of the overall human rights situation in Nigeria.

We therefore request that your report should highlight this fact and to maintain that the British foreign policy should view and strive for the improvement of the human rights situation in Ogoni and Nigeria in general as well as to secure genuine democratic and due processes as important benchmarks which must be tied to a set of incremental sanctions.

The benchmarks should include:
— release of the bodies of the Ogoni 9 for proper burial and payment of compensation in line with UN team's recommendations;
— release of political prisoners including Chief M. K. O. Abiola, Rtd. General Obasanjo, Frank Kokori and others;
— release of the Ogoni 20, Batom Mitee and other victims of the military brutalities in Ogoni;
— cessation of the military occupation of Ogoni;
— repeal of all decrees and laws curtailing due process and fundamental rights;
— genuine efforts at national reconciliation through the setting up of a national government headed by Chief Abiola which will be charged with the primary responsibility of convening of a sovereign national conference to patch the wounds of the past and decide on the way forward.

A troubling development of the past has been that even where, as we have pointed out, there exists unimpeachable evidence of the deterioration in the situation, the limited measures that were put in place have been progressively watered down thereby sending a rather wrong message to the dictatorship.

It is our view that incremental measures including, but not limited to:
— downgrading of diplomatic missions and contacts;
— total ban on all sporting and cultural links;
— freeze on financial assets and bank accounts of members of the regime, their families and collaborators;

    — ban on export of support equipment for the oil industry;

    — ban on air links;

should be imposed and tied to the compliance with the above benchmarks within a stated period of not more than three months at a time.

The Ogoni people led by MOSOP, especially, and the other Nigerian pro-democracy groups have continued to bear the brunt of the escalating state of repression in the country perpetrated by the military regime of General Sani Abacha. In spite of these the groups have managed to keep up the struggle for democracy and human rights, albeit under rather tough circumstances.

If the hope of restoration of democracy is to be kept alive, then the British Government should lead in stepping up assistance to civil society through groups engaged in facilitating genuine transition to democracy and human rights. It makes sense that assistance which Nigeria lost or should lose from the international community on account of its dismal human rights records and bad governance should be channelled to alleviating the agonies and strengthening the work of the victims of the repression.

January 1998

APPENDIX 13

Memorandum submitted by The Co-operative Bank

1. INTRODUCTION

1.1   In this submission the Co-operative Bank would like to focus on the areas where we believe Government could encourage business to address human rights issues more proactively. We do not believe that the Bank is in a position to comment more broadly on Government policy as we do not generally take specific stances on these issues.

1.2   The Bank recommendations cover three key areas:

    — The Government should encourage British companies, including financial institutions, to draw up ethical codes of conducts, which incorporate policy on human rights, in consultation with key stakeholder groups, including employees and customers.

    — Furthermore, the Government should continue to facilitate through programmes such as the Ethical Trading Initiative, the development of common standards on corporate human rights policies and verification of performance against these policies.

    — British-based financial institutions should not provide financial services to companies involved in the repression trade. Nor should they provide financial services to any regime which oppresses human rights.

2. BACKGROUND ON THE CO-OPERATIVE BANK

2.1   The Co-operative Bank is the only high street bank which offers its customers the opportunity to determine how their money should and should not be used. We have carried out two major consultation exercises with our customers over the last five years and their views have been used as the basis for our thirteen point ethical policy. The Bank currently has almost £3 billion in customer deposits which is only lent to organisations that do not conflict with these ethical standards. It should also be noted that there are occasions where the Bank makes decisions on specific business involving ethical issues not included in this policy.

2.2   The ethical policy addresses human rights issues in two specific statements:

    (1) *The Co-operative Bank will not invest in or supply financial services to any regime or organisation which oppresses the human spirit, takes away the rights of individuals or manufactures any instrument of torture.*

This policy statement was backed by 88 per cent of customer respondents in our first consultation exercise, increasing to 96 per cent in our second consultation exercise. Out of fourteen policy statements, it is one that receives the greatest customer support.

    (2) *The Co-operative Bank will not finance or any way facilitate the manufacture or sale of weapons to any country which has an oppressive regime.*

This policy statement was backed by 86 per cent of customer respondents in our first consultation exercise, increasing to 95 per cent in our second consultation exercise.

2.3 All organisations that wish to use the financial services of The Co-operative Bank are rigorously scrutinised using the research services of a number of specialist agencies to ensure that they, their subsidiaries or parent companies, and suppliers, are not involved in any way with the repression of human rights.

2.4 The Bank policies and practices on human rights are made with reference to the Universal Declaration of Human Rights and the relevant conventions of the International Labour Organisation. These include Convention 98—The Right to Organise and Collective Bargaining 1949. Convention 29—Forced Labour 1930. Convention 106—Abolition of Forced Labour 1957. Convention 100—Equal Remuneration Convention 1951. Convention 111—Discrimination (Employment and Occupational Convention) 1958. Convention 138—Minimum Age Convention 1973.

2.5 The involvement of British companies in developing countries, particularly those defined as oppressive regimes, has increasingly focused the public's mind on whether the goods and services they are purchasing have been produced and traded under fair and decent conditions. The public now realises that just because a company's activities in Britain do not infringe human rights, its activities in other countries, or those of its suppliers, may.

2.6 A number of well-respected British companies have been criticised in the media for their alleged involvement with oppressive regimes. Of particular concern have been allegations that these businesses have colluded with regimes in facilitating human rights abuses or have failed to use their influence to positively influence the regime. Other well-respected companies have been criticised for insufficient scrutiny of their supply chains. For example, allegations have been made by the charity, Christian Aid, that sports goods sold in the UK may have been produced using child labour.

3. CONSULTING CORPORATE STAKEHOLDERS ON HUMAN RIGHTS POLICIES

3.1 The Co-operative Bank believes that commercial organisations have a purpose beyond mere profit. This means recognising that they have responsibilities towards all stakeholders who are involved in their business beyond the traditional responsibility to the shareholder. As a result, the Bank believes that companies should consider the views of their stakeholder groups in setting corporate policy on ethical issues.

3.2 Evidence shows that the British public are deeply concerned about human rights issues and are opposed to any corporate activity which facilitates human rights abuses. For example, a research survey, carried out by The Co-operative Bank among the general public, asked respondents to say spontaneously which business activities they were *most concerned* about their bank investing in. One in four mentioned the export of armaments to oppressive regimes as a specific area they are concerned about their bank investing in, while 12 per cent expressed concern about their bank investing in countries who abuse human rights.

3.3 Currently very few British companies, including financial institutions, give their stakeholders, including customers, shareholders, employees and other interested groups, a real say in their policies on human rights. *The Co-operative Bank believes that companies, particularly financial institutions, should regularly consult these stakeholders on their ethical policies including human rights. They should also provide more comprehensive information on their performance against these human rights policies, for example, in their Annual Reports. If possible, performance should also be monitored and verified independently.*

3.4 The Committee will note that in recent years there has been mounting concern over disruption of Annual General Meetings by small groups of shareholders who are objecting to companies' ethical performance particularly over human rights issues. Individual protesters have also sought to take the law into their own hands damaging the property of companies which they allege are facilitating human rights abuses. Shareholders have placed resolutions at AGMs addressing human rights issues. *The Bank believes that increasing debate and even physical confrontation at AGMs indicates that current processes of consultation on human rights policies, as well as performance, are inadequate in many companies. Hence, we believe there is a strong case for the Government encouraging businesses to embrace best practice in terms of setting ethical policies concerning human rights, in consultation with interested stakeholders, and monitoring performance against these policies.*

3.5 The Co-operative Bank believes that financial institutions should lead the way in consulting stakeholders, particularly customers, on human rights policies. For example, a Co-operative Bank survey demonstrates that consultation with bank customers would be popular. The survey revealed that 72 per cent of respondents believed that banks should consult customers as to how they invest customers' money. Furthermore 68 per cent thought it was important that banks have a clear policy, from an ethical or environmental point of view, on how and where they invest customers' money.

3.6 The Co-operative Bank notes the growth of the ethical investment market which now accounts for £1.6 billion funds (this figure does not include the Bank's deposits) as an example of how investment companies can be made accountable to the values of their customers. We also welcome the campaign launched by War on Want which urges holders of occupational pensions to encourage their pension funds to sign up to the "Invest in Freedom Charter" which sets out how to use the power of investment to achieve social ends. The charter commits fund managers to pressing firms in which they own shares to agree basic standards of employment for their workforce. The charter is based around the seven key International Labour Organisation conventions.

3.7   *We believe that the Government should investigate the possibility of launching an Ethical Finance Initiative that seeks to inform pension fund holders and other customers of financial institutions of the opportunities available to them to influence investment policies to take account of human rights considerations. It should also seek to promote best practice among financial institutions on consultation of stakeholders.*

3.8   The Co-operative Bank also believes that proactively offering customers the opportunity to invest ethically is also important. In addition to the Bank's ethical policy. the Co-operative Bank's Financial Advisers currently give customers a form to fill out specifying their financial needs including whether they are interested in investing ethically. *The Co-operative Bank believes that the PIA should consider compelling financial advisers to ask customers about their ethical concerns, including human rights issues, as a routine part of their attempt to "know their customers", understand their financial needs and offer suitable advice.*

4.   DEVELOPING SUPPLY CHAIN BEST PRACTICE

4.1   The Co-operative Bank believes that it is essential that the British Government assists companies in developing the best practical ways of ensuring that their suppliers, particularly in the developing world, meet strict standards designed to protect the basic rights of their employees. We therefore welcome the launch of the Ethical Trading Initiative by major companies, aid agencies, campaigning organisations, trade unions and the Government. This is an important step in providing British companies with this expertise. Developing common standards for codes of conduct and verification systems is essential if we are to ensure that the basic rights of employees are respected.

4.2   It should be noted that The Co-operative Wholesale Society, who are our parent company, are members of the Ethical Trading Initiative.

4.3   Currently the initiative is focused on retailers in the UK because it aims to ensure that goods for sale in high street shops meet strict ethical standards. However, business and Government both purchase a huge amount of goods and services for internal use. *The Government could therefore examine ways in which it could encourage the business sector to develop ethical policies to ensure these suppliers meet acceptable international labour standards and other specified human rights standards. As a major purchaser of products and services itself, the Government also has considerable market power to influence companies.*

4.4   It should also be noted that a number of charities have developed specific codes of conduct which cover employment standards for toy manufacturers (World Development Movement), clothing (Oxfam), and sports goods providers (Christian Aid). Christian Aid has also run a campaign focused on supermarkets and has produced an ethical ranking of supermarkets. The Fairtrade Foundation has established a trade mark to draw consumers attention to fair trade products which empower disadvantaged producers in the developing world.

4.5   The development of voluntary codes of conducts and verification standards are an important step in increasing company best practice over human rights. The development of the Fairtrade mark is also a good example of how consumers can be informed of the ethical standards of the product. *The Government has an important role to play in ensuring that codes of conduct and verification procedures meet common standards. It also needs to ensure that there is not unnecessary duplication in the labelling of products or services which comply with ethical standards set out in codes of conduct. It is essential that customers can have access to clear and transparent information on the ethical soundness of their products or services. The market for green consumer goods was damaged because many manufacturers started to make claims which were neither accurate or viable.*

5.   THE FINANCING OF ARMS, AND MILITARY SECURITY AND POLICE EQUIPMENT, TO OPPRESSIVE REGIMES.

5.1   The Bank's ethical policy specifically addresses the provision of financial services to regimes or organisations involved in or facilitating the abuse of human rights.

5.2   As Britain is one of the largest suppliers of arms in the world, inevitably financial institutions in the UK play an important role in providing services to arms companies and exporters of military security and police (MSP) goods and services. There is concern about the potential use of such arms and MSP goods and services exported from the UK, by governments which have committed serious human rights abuses.

5.3   The World Development Movement has revealed in its report "From High Street to Battlefield: UK Banks and the Arms Trade" the alleged level of involvement of different banks in the export of arms to oppressive regimes.

5.4   The Co-operative Bank believes that in view of the British public's concern over human rights issues, banks need strong policies and screening procedures to ensure that they are not supplying financial services to companies involved in providing arms, or military security and police equipment, to oppressive regimes. It is also necessary that banks have sufficiently robust procedures to ensure that they are not providing financial services to companies who are using diversionary routes via third-party countries to avoid arms embargoes on specific countries.

5.5 *Many banks claim to be guided by the policies of Her Majesty's Government. Although the British Government has a central role to play in controlling arms exports, The Co-operative Bank believes that financial institutions should always be prepared to act beyond the letter of the law, particularly where their customers have set out clear ethical concerns in such areas as the repression trade.*

5.6 *We recognise that the Government has an important role to play in ensuring that arms control policy is sufficiently robust in this country to prevent banks facilitating the trade in arms, or military security and police equipment, to oppressive regimes. We believe that the Bank's ethical policy statements quoted earlier in this memorandum set an important benchmark for Government policy. We welcome the launch of the Government's Ethical Foreign Policy which addresses many of the issues about which our customers are so deeply concerned.*

January 1998

APPENDIX 14

Memorandum submitted by the Campaign Against Arms Trade

1. The Campaign Against Arms Trade (CAAT) is opposed to all military exports, but recognises that, despite its negative effects on human rights, security and the economy, the arms trade will not end overnight. As an interim measure, therefore, CAAT is seeking an export licensing policy with an emphasis on restraint, especially on exports to governments which violate human rights or to countries in areas of conflict. It is against this background that CAAT welcomed, with reservations, Foreign Secretary Robin Cook's announcement in May 1997 that he would pursue an "ethical foreign policy" with human rights at its heart. Action by the Government, as well as rhetoric, is needed before CAAT can truly praise the "ethical foreign policy".

2. Military equipment constitutes a special category of goods and technology since it is designed for the use or threat of force. Sometimes the equipment supplied contributes directly to repression as, for example, when UK-made armoured water cannons were used by the Indonesian authorities to intimidate those taking part in pro-democracy demonstrations in June 1996. However, even if the equipment is not used, its sale conveys a message of international acceptance and respectability to the recipient government, and undermines those working for democracy and justice.

3. The Conservative government appeared to accept this argument when few sales were likely and imposed complete or partial embargoes on the sale of military equipment to China, Burma and Nigeria. However, it ignored human rights considerations when big orders were at stake, and consequently the UK continued to arm Indonesia and Saudi Arabia. So far, the Labour government seems to be doing likewise.

LICENSING DECISIONS AND THE ETHICAL FOREIGN POLICY

4. The new arms export criteria were unveiled by Robin Cook at the end of July 1997, and introduced a tougher test on human rights. An export licence will now be refused if the equipment might be used for internal repression; previously it had to be shown that the equipment was likely to be so used. However, at the time of writing, nearly six months later, there is no indication that, in practice, this change of wording has made any difference to the pattern of licences accepted and refused.

NEW LICENCES TO INDONESIA AND TURKEY

5. Both Indonesia and Turkey have appalling records on human rights. The Indonesian government, which seized power in 1965 in a bloody coup, has behaved brutally towards its own citizens, as well as invading East Timor in 1975. It has remained in occupation of the latter ever since, and a third of East Timor's inhabitants, about 200,000 people, have died as a result. The Turkish government has waged what could be described as a war on the Kurdish people living in the south-east. The tables below show the numbers of licences granted, by category, for six-month periods during the Conservative and Labour governments.

Indonesia

	January to June 1996		May to November 1997	
	Granted	Refused	Granted	Refused
Small arms, machine guns and accessories—ML1 (Military List classification)	—	2	—	2
Large calibre armament or weapons (e.g., guns, howitzers, mortars)—ML2	2	—	—	—
Bombs, torpedoes, missiles, mines—ML4	—	—	2	—
Fire control systems (e.g., weapons sights, bombing computers, target range finding)—ML5	1	—	1	—

	January to June 1996 Granted	Refused	May to November 1997 Granted	Refused
Vehicles including tanks and armoured vehicles—ML6	3	—	—	1
Toxicological agents, riot control agents—ML7	2	—	1	—
Aircraft—ML10	18	—	5	—
Electronic equipment specially designed for military use—ML11	6	—	11	—
Armoured goods including body armour—ML13	2	—	1	—
Specialist equipment for military training—ML14	—	—	1	1
Imaging or countermeasure equipment—ML15	4	—	—	—
Specially designed military software—ML24	2	—	—	—
Apparatus specially designed for handling, detecting, etc., improvised explosive devices—PL5006 (Police List classification)	1	—	—	—
Equipment designed for the development of goods in Group 1—PL5017	2	—	—	—
Smooth bore weapons, not covered by ML1—PL5018	—	1	—	—
Totals	**43**	**3**	**22**	**4**

Turkey

	January to June 1996 Granted	Refused	May to November 1997 Granted	Refused
Small arms, machine guns and accessories—ML1 (Military List classification)	23	—	11	1
Large calibre armament or weapons (e.g, guns, howitzers, mortars)—ML2	1	—	9	—
Ammunition—ML3	—	—	5	—
Bombs, torpedoes, missiles, mines—ML4	7	—	2	—
Fire control systems (e.g., weapons sights, bombing computers, target range finding)—ML5	2	—	1	—
Vehicles including tanks and armoured vehicles—ML6	1	1	2	—
Toxicological agents, riot control agents—ML7	—	—	1	—
Combatant vessels—ML9	2	—	4	—
Aircraft—ML10	7	—	7	—
Electronic equipment specially designed for military use—ML11	6	—	26	—
Specialist equipment for military training—ML14	—	—	2	—
Imaging or countermeasure equipment—ML15	1	—	—	—
Forging, castings military list goods—ML16	—	—	1	—
Equipment and technology for the production of military list goods—ML18	—	—	1	—
Equipment designed for the development of goods in Group 1—PL5017	1	—	—	—
Smooth bore weapons, not covered by ML1—PL5018	7	—	—	—
Ammunition for goods specified in PL5018—PL5021	5	—	—	—
Totals	**63**	**1**	**72**	**1**

(a) 1996 figures cover the period 1 January to 30 June inclusive, the latest in a set of regular lists published by the Department of Trade and Industry.

(b) 1997 figures cover the period 2 May to 13 November in the case of Indonesia (*Hansard,* 2 December 1997), and from 2 May to 5 November in the case of Turkey (*Hansard,* 11 December 1997.

6.   The Department of Trade and Industry announced (Lords Hansard, 30 October 1997) problems with its export licensing statistics which it is trying to resolve. In particular, it appears that exports may not have been logged under the correct heading. Also, it is taking longer for decisions on export licence applications to be made, and on 13 November 1997 65 licence applications were pending with respect to Indonesia. In the case of Turkey, 71 licences were awaiting a decision on 5 November 1997. (Hansard, 10 December 1997, 11 December 1997 and 22 December 1997)

7.   A longer time span and accurate statistics will be necessary for a meaningful comparison, but during both of the six-month periods, one towards the end of the Conservative government and the other at the beginning of Labour's, most licences for military exports have been granted, and just a handful refused. Certainly, with the information currently available, there is no evidence of an immediate effect of the new criteria announced on 28 July 1997 on whether export licence applications have been granted or refused.

LICENCES GRANTED BY THE CONSERVATIVE GOVERNMENT AND STILL EXTANT

8.   In November 1996, the then President of the Board of Trade, Ian Lang, announced that he had issued licences for the export to Indonesia of 16 Hawk aircraft. These have a range of capabilities, including ground attack. (Hansard 21 November 1996 and 16 December 1996) A few weeks later, in December 1996, Mr Lang,

announced that he had issued export licences to Alvis 50 Scorpion armoured vehicles, plus associated equipment, including ammunition. This was the second of an expected three orders, the first having been placed in early 1996. Mr Lang's December announcement also covered an export licence, given to Procurement Services International Ltd, for 300 armoured vehicles, including seven Tactica water cannon. (*Hansard,* 9 December 1996, 13 January 1997 and 23 January 1997)

9.   UK-manufactured armoured vehicles, supplied in the 1960's, were used against students protesting over bus fare increases in South Sulawesi in April 1996. Three students died as the vehicles entered their campus. The Foreign Office expressed its concern about this to the Indonesian authorities, which punished six junior officers for using excessive force. Their trail, and the punishment meted out, was not related to the use of the vehicles. The senior officers in charge of the operation were not charged or punished. Pictures recently smuggled out of Indonesia by human rights campaigners show Tactica water cannon in use in Bandung, in June 1996, against people protesting at the deaths of the South Sulawesi students. Descriptions from eye-witnesses indicate that a tear gas was used in the water cannon.

10.   The Government has, as mentioned above, said it will not issue licences for the export of any equipment which is likely to be used for internal repression. Since both armoured vehicles and water cannon were so used in 1996, and there have been many reports that Hawk aircraft have been used to intimidate the citizens of East Timor, CAAT believes the "ethical foreign policy" failed its first test when, on 28 July 1998, the Labour government announced it would not revoke the licences for the export of Hawk aircraft and armoured vehicles to Indonesia.

11.   The Government argued it would not have been practical to revoke the 20,000 licences that were valid and in force at the time of its election. Surely, though, a new government is not elected to be bound by the policies of its predecessor. It cannot have been impossible to look again at some of the extant licences, and to have considered them against the "ethical foreign policy".

12.   Another issue raised by the Government was that of compensation to the arms companies. CAAT and a number of other organisations sought legal advice and this was quite clear: the Government would not be liable to pay compensation if the licences were revoked. CAAT understands that the Government's own legal advice was not conclusive one way or the other. However, if the Labour government really wanted to put human rights at the centre of its foreign policy, it should have been prepared to fight any compensation claim through the courts. It should have imposed an embargo on the export of all military, security and police equipment, including those already licensed, to the murderous Suharto regime.

THE INFLUENCE OF ARMS EXPORTS

13.   The argument is sometimes advanced that selling military equipment gives the UK influence over the purchaser. The evidence does not support this. For example, there is no indication that the Indonesian government has listened to UK protests over its continuing occupation of East Timor. The converse, the influence a major arms purchaser has over the UK authorities, has however, been demonstrated by the attempt by Saudi Arabia, in 1996, to have the dissident, Mohammed al-Mas'ari, deported from the UK. Further back in time, in 1980, the UK government had to grovel to placate members of the Saudi Royal family to save arms deals following the showing of the "Death of a Princess" television programme.

CO-ORDINATION WITH THE MINISTRY OF DEFENCE

14.   The UK's military and security policy is, theoretically, foreign policy led. If, therefore, human rights are to be at the centre of foreign policy, it appears to CAAT to be inconsistent with this that the Ministry of Defence's Defence Export Services Organisation maintains offices promoting arms sales in countries such as Saudi Arabia, Turkey, and Indonesia, or that members of the military from these countries are trained by the members of the UK armed forces, or at military establishments in the UK.

MERCENARIES

15.   The provision of mercenaries has major implications for human rights. A number of mercenary companies are run from the UK, often set up by former UK armed forces personnel. Two such companies are Saladin Security and Defence Services Ltd. According to *The Guardian* of 8 September 1997, the former's contracts have included counterinsurgency work in Sri Lanka and security training in the Middle East, while the "list of countries the DSL has worked in . . . can read like Amnesty International's top 40 of unpleasant regimes".

16.   Furthermore, there is concern that, on occasions, multi-national companies exploiting natural resources overseas, are using mercenaries to keep those opposed to their actions in check. For example, according to Granada Television's "World in Action—BP's Secret Soldiers" (30 June 1997), BP hired DSL to protect its Colombian oil operations, into which it has sunk over £1 billion.

17.   In December 1989, the United Nations General Assembly, recognising the problem, unanimously adopted an International Convention against the Recruitment, Use, Financing and Training of Mercenaries, but the UK has not yet signed this. A government intent on pursuing an "ethical foreign policy" should make action against mercenaries a priority.

DEMOCRACY, OPENNESS AND PUBLIC DEBATE IN THE UK

18. Documents released at the beginning of 1998 under the 30-year rule revealed that, in 1967, the Wilson government had used the RAF to deliver ammunition to Israel on the eve of the Six Day War, and had seriously considered striking a £100 million naval arms deal with South Africa despite the United Nations embargo on the Apartheid regime there. The Israeli deliveries took place in great secrecy, while in the latter case the reason the split Cabinet finally decided against the deal was that it would risk outraging party supporters and the public. (*Independent, Times* and *Guardian,* all 1 January 1998). The decisions in both cases appear to depend on whether, or not, the public is likely to find out about the deal. CAAT does not think this is a good basis for decision-making. There is, surely, something profoundly unhealthy about an area of policy which governments feel that they need to keep secret from parliament and the people in order to pursue it.

19. The Government has said that it will report annually to Parliament on the state of strategic export controls and their application. This is welcome, but it will still not allow the public and MPs the chance for debate before the equipment is exported. A register of licence applications is needed to rectify this lack of information. Parliamentary and public debate can help reinforce human rights concerns, and if human rights are really at the centre of foreign policy, openness must take precedence over "commercial confidentiality". While this is often used as the justification for keeping information about military exports secret, it is the public, rather than a rival company or government, that is likely be kept in the dark by the prevailing secrecy. Much, if not all, of the information that would be in a licence applications register is, almost certainly, already known by those attending trade exhibitions or competing for contracts.

ECONOMICS OF THE ARMS TRADE

20. Military exports are often justified by suggesting that there is a choice to be made between jobs in the UK and human rights overseas. CAAT believes, however, that economic considerations reinforce, rather than undermine, the ethical and political case for scaling down the UK's commitment to arms exports.

21. The Al Yamamah arms deal with Saudi Arabia is the UK's biggest-ever. The human rights record of the government, under King Fahd, is far from exemplary, and public executions are commonplace. An autocratic government of this type is, however, vulnerable to cataclysmic change in a way that democracies, perhaps, are not. As was demonstrated by the overthrow of the Shah of Iran in 1979, an incoming government getting rid of a despotic leader is likely to cancel arms deals, seeing them as having supported the previous regime.

22. Furthermore, there is a growing body of academic research (notably that of Professor Paul Dunne at the University of Middlesex's Business School and of Dr Neil Cooper of the University of Plymouth) which suggests Government support for military exports has been shown to represent a subsidy of around £12,500 a year for every job dependent on military exports. This subsidy includes assistance with promotion thorough the Defence Export Services Organisation, financial underwriting by the Export Credits Guarantee Department, and the help with research and development costs.

23. All the evidence indicates that investment in civil manufacturing creates more employment per pound because of the massive research and development and capital costs associated with military production. Far from increasing employment, military exports create unemployment by depriving other sectors of Government support.

24. CAAT, therefore, believes that there are sound economic reasons, as well as ethical ones, for refraining from selling military equipment to governments which violate human rights. There is no choice to be made between ethics and jobs.

INTERNATIONAL ACTION

25. Another argument, sometimes used in support of military exports, is that if the UK acts unilaterally, then another supplier will take its place. This justification, that "if you don't do it, someone else will", would not be acceptable for other ethical issues, and should not be for a government espousing an "ethical foreign policy". It would be excellent if the UK government not only begins the process of disengaging from the arms sales, but encourages others to do likewise, especially as military industry is linking across state boundaries. The UK's actions should not, however, be dependent on others doing likewise. It could lead by a good example. The UK should also abide by embargoes and restrictions imposed by other states, making it clear that it will not undermine them by issuing export licences to UK companies for a similar deal.

26. The Ottawa Treaty on landmines is a good example of a case where a strong treaty has been negotiated, which some states feel unable to accept, in preference to a weak treaty acceptable to all. Those states which have not yet signed up to the Ottawa Treaty will be shamed, hopefully, by public pressure during the coming years, into joining. This may indicate a way forward for treaties on conventional arms transfers.

PROPOSALS

Lead Department

27. It should be clearly stated that the Foreign and Commonwealth Office has ultimate responsibility for military exports and related matters, and that the Ministry of Defence and the Department of Trade and Industry are subservient to it on this issue.

Equipment subject to control

28. All goods being transferred from the UK to overseas military, security or police forces or armaments-manufacturing bodies should be made subject to export licensing controls. This would include goods being transferred under Government-to-Government deals, or by the Crown Agents, and of surplus stock.

29. The goods would include, not exclusively:

— arms, ammunition, implements or munitions of war, any articles deemed capable of being converted thereinto or having a strategic or tactical value or nature;

— materials, equipment and technologies which are designed or used for the development, production or utilisation of arms, ammunition and implements of war;

— materials and equipment incorporating technology, the acquisition of which would give assistance to the development and production of arms, ammunition and implements of war and their means of utilisation or delivery;

— materials, equipment and technologies which may be used for the production of arms, ammunition or the implements of war or their means of utilisation or delivery;

— spare parts;

— items to be produced under licence in the purchasing country.

Where there is any doubt, or dispute, as to whether or not goods being purchased would be going to a military, security or police force or armaments manufacturing body, an export licence should be required.

Arms Sales, Human Rights and Areas of Tension

30. The Government should immediately stop all supplies to the military, security and police forces and to any armaments-manufacturing bodies of governments which

(a) have committed gross and systematic violations of internationally recognised human rights within the previous three years, including extrajudicial or arbitrary executions, disappearances, torture or severe mistreatment, systematic official discrimination, imprisonment, or detention on the basis of race, ethnicity, national origin, or religious or political beliefs; or have committed serious violations of the international laws of war or equivalent violations of the laws or war in internal conflicts; or are engaged in political killings resulting from a policy of repression;

(b) have not ratified the International Covenant on Civil and Political Rights and the International Covenant on Economic, Social and Cultural Rights;

(c) have not given effect to the will of the people through fair, genuine and effective elections;

(d) have not promoted civilian control of the military and security forces, or do not have civilian institutions that determine national security policy and control the operations and spending of the military, security and police forces;

(e) which are involved in armed conflict with another country, irrespective of whether war has been declared or not;

(f) which have involved in an international dispute where there is a risk of its leading to an armed conflict;

(g) which have failed to recognise the right of other UN-recognised states within the region to exist;

(h) where internal armed disturbances are taking place;

(i) which advocate national, racial or religious hatred that incites discrimination, hostility or violence, particularly if it incites individuals to overthrow other governments;

(j) which issue inflammatory propaganda in pursuit of territorial claims.

31. When one Member State of the European Union imposes an embargo on the sale of military equipment to a particular country or countries, this embargo should be observed by all Member States.

32.   Embargoes should cover all items listed in paragraphs a) to j) above, including sales under existing contracts, spare parts, production under licence in the purchasing country, advice and training.

33.   The Government should refuse entry into the UK to anyone proved to be concerned with military procurement for countries subject to an arms embargo, and expel those already operating here to a destination where their safety is ensured.

34.   Police and customs officials should give priority to ensuring that the UK is not used as a centre for the illegal supply of weaponry to countries against which an embargo has been imposed by the United Nations or the European Union.

35.   The Government should use the appropriate international fora to arrange co-operation between customs and law-enforcement agencies to combat the illegal trafficking of military equipment.

Training by the UK Armed Forces

36.   The provision of training is as much part of the arms trade as the provision of hardware, but at present there appear to be even fewer controls over training. A list of countries whose military or security personnel are being trained by the UK Armed Forces, or in Ministry of Defence (MoD) establishments will, at present be given in answer to a parliamentary question, but further information is usually not available.

37.   In cases of training of overseas military, security or police personnel by members of the UK Armed Forces or in Ministry of Defence establishments, details should be available for public inspection. The details should be lodged, one month in advance of the confirmation of an offer of training, in the library of the House of Commons and in a suitable public place.

The details given should include the:

(a)   country from which the prospective trainee comes and the military or other unit in which s/he is serving;

(b)   name(s) of trainee(s);

(c)   dates of training;

(d)   nature of training;

(e)   place/establishment of training.

Training by private companies

38.   Whilst information about training by the UK Armed Forces and in MoD establishments is sparse, details of training by private companies is virtually non-existent. Such training is just occasionally reported by the media, usually when it forms part of an equipment package. Training of overseas military, security or police personnel by private companies in the UK or by the company's personnel overseas should be subject to licence, either

(a)   as part of a licence for the supply of military equipment when training is in the use of equipment made by the company supplying the equipment;

or

(b)   a specific licence for training when this is not part of an equipment package. A detailed prospectus of training should be published in advance of the granting of such a licence.

Mercenaries

39.   The Government should immediately sign the UN International Convention against the Recruitment, Use, Financing and Training of Mercenaries. It should then introduce legislation to bring UK law in line with it so that the UK can ratify the Convention without delay.

Participation by UK citizens in overseas military industries

40. (a)   Legislation should be introduced to make Government approval a requirement before UK citizens could work for an overseas government's armaments-manufacturing body where their work is not already covered by an equipment licence or training licence.

(b)   The applications for Government approval for such work should be made in the same way, and be subject to the same considerations, as equipment export licences.

(c) Failure to obtain Government approval before working for an overseas government's armaments-manufacturing body should be made a criminal offence.

International companies and collaborative projects

41. There is an increasing tendency for companies producing military equipment in one country to collaborate with those in one or more other countries, or to come together to form international companies. This poses new problems for those seeking to control the military exports. The company law aspects of these changes have been covered by amendments to the Companies Acts, and we seek parallel legislation on the export licensing aspects.

(a) Where military equipment is made by a UK company in collaboration with an overseas company, by an overseas subsidiary of a UK company or by an overseas company in which a UK company has a participating interest of at least 20 per cent, such goods would require a UK export licence before they could be exported from the overseas country to a third country.

(b) The management and directors of any company found to be violating this regulation should be made personally liable under criminal law for such an infringement. The UK company itself could face prosecution under UK law, and could be fined, have its goods seized or assets sequestrated.

Parliamentary scrutiny

42. A register of all applications for military equipment export licences should be made available for public inspection ten working days in advance of the licence application being considered, in order to allow adequate time for comment and debate. Copies of the register should be lodged in the House of Commons' Library, in the Export Market Information Centre, on an appropriate part of the Internet, and in other suitable places for public inspection. Such a register would give details of the equipment and the contract value, including details of barter arrangements, offsets, etc., and of any financial support from the UK government. It would also give details of the equipment's proposed destination and of the user group (e.g., navy, police force), and the date of the proposed delivery.

43. A long debate on each of the thousands of licence applications made annually would not be anticipated. A register of applications like the one referred to above would, however, provide an opportunity for concerns to be raised about a particular sale before the licence was granted. It would also allow, for instance, a specialist journalist, to question a series of seemingly innocuous exports which might, for example, indicate missile proliferation. This could complement the Government's own intelligence.

44. A Military Exports Select Committee should be established in the House of Commons to monitor arms exports, government departments and companies involved in the arms exports.

45. The annual report to Parliament on the state of strategic export controls and their application would serve as the basis for an annual Parliamentary debate on the Government's progress in implementing its policy of disengagement from the arms export trade. It would not only provide a breakdown of export licences granted or refused and the reasons for the decisions reached, but also a review of the use to which equipment exported from the UK in previous years has been put, a report on progress made at international level, information about the observance and enforcement of embargoes, and a review of the controls over training by the UK Armed Forces and by private companies.

January 1998

APPENDIX 15

Memorandum submitted by the Agency for Co-operation and Research in Development (ACORD)

1. INTRODUCTION

1.1 ACORD—Agency for Co-operation and Research in Development—is a broad-based Uk consortium of 11 European and north American non governmental organisations (NGOS). Oxfam UK is the British member of the consortium. In practice, ACORD uses financial resources (currently £10 million per year approximately) provided by consortium members and other institutional funders to support 40 developmental programmes in seventeen African countries south of the Sahara. Most of the countries in which ACORD is active are in states of considerable stress, either economically, politically or both. ACORD works with displaced people, refugees and others marginalised and in situations of great poverty. The programmes aim to help such people achieve a greater degree of economic, social and political well-being than is possible without some level of external support. As such ACORD works at the grass roots level of aid and development effort in very practical ways.

However, the organisation is also active in researching the socio-political and economic context in which the poor people it supports live their lives in Africa.

1.2   ACORD's five year strategy to 2001 has been developed in consultation with its 750 African staff and the communities with whom they work. Together we identified the need to add to our traditional focus on local institution-building and the alleviation of economic poverty. These additions include the need to help people *build peace* and achieve their *basic rights*, all in the context of the achievement of equality between men and women, in its broadest societal sense.

1.3   Through the understanding gained from combining work at the "grass roots" with applied research into the forces that restrict and marginalise people's efforts to improve their status we offer a few insights into the issue before the Committee.

2.   THE LINKS BETWEEN BASIC RIGHTS, HUMAN RIGHTS, CONFLICT AND POVERTY

2.1   ACORD's programmes aim to help people achieve autonomous and sustainable livelihoods and the eventual withdrawal of the direct kind of support we provide. We are finding that otherwise in more and more places, people are not only getting poorer financially but that their rights for a share of dwindling resources, their right to participate in political processes, and their right to live their lives in a secure, healthy and sustainable environment are being increasingly eroded and denied.

2.2   While the policies advocated for appropriate action with respect to states that abuse human rights are a necessary and essential part of any powerful government's foreign policy, they are by no means sufficient. This is implicitly recognised in the new UK Government's aid policy as enunciated by the Secretary of State for International Development. The clear poverty focus of the Aid programme requires us to analyse and resolve the causes of poverty and deprivation at local, state and international levels. We cannot separate the levels conveniently and devise foreign policy on the basis of the attainment of democracy as defined in western terms— arguing and insisting on state level multi-party elections when the choices offered a beleaguered electorate are between cynical exploiters of their human condition or when recent experience shows how easy it can be to stage such an electoral scenario to legitimise autocratic/military-backed governments.

2.3   What our experience tells us is that people must be supported in achieving their right to participate in whatever institutions exist first at the grass-roots level, and then to insist in participation in ever higher levels of power and decision-making. The essential corollary for international foreign policy is to use whatever leverage exists to support only democratisation that includes genuine decentralisation of power. There are a few countries in Africa that are aiming for this style of democracy, and some of them would not be considered "democratic" in western terms, as their overall leadership may well be currently elected through a perversion of the ballot box processes. It is our experience, and many analysts support this view, that democracy in many parts of Africa is more a process of reciprocity between people with different forms of "wealth". Wealth in these terms goes beyond the economic to include solidarity, wisdom, spirituality, social well-being, peace of mind, and the capacity to maintain peace and harmony. All these are embedded in what one might call "social capital". There are no guarantees that governments resulting from national elections will support the needs of the marginalised. In the UK women, and poor men before them, did not acquire the right to vote and an eventual semblance of equality through parliamentary processes. Poor women and men in Africa are equally achieving their rights slowly through a bottom-up process of strengthening civil society.

2.4   The international and civil wars that wrack many African states in our experience have much to do with the weakness or disruption of civil society. This leads to an erosion of social/solidarity mechanisms to mediate conflict, prevent an exacerbation of the sufferings of the marginalised. The outcome is, more often than not, a polarisation of political forces between an autocratic government and an underground armed opposition where civilians become pawns and victims of the power game leading to today's horrific violence. Where they existed most of the mechanisms were local and came into play through popular demand for peace or an end to violence when it occurred. Most of today's violence is perpetrated by apparently modern leaders who have elevated themselves, even if elected according to the scenario referred to above, from the people they purport to serve. They are not products of civil society but rather of an elite often established and supported by foreign interests. Their legitimacy even when they stand for election is compromised, and their approach to maintaining power eventually includes resort to violence towards any challenger. If such a challenge comes from the legitimate representatives of society at large, then repression is extended indiscriminately to all members of that society. If civil society has not been allowed to take hold in the country, then this may boil down to a conflict between two opposed thuggeries.

2.5   Thus our evidence to the Committee is about the need to broaden any definition of human rights to start with the principle of the basic rights any individual needs to sustain her or his wealth as a member of a community. The wealth of people must not be measured only in terms of financial well being, important though that is. Democracy is much more than a question of national parliamentary elections, and may even exist in a form satisfactory to citizens without national elections but with genuine trading of wealth and participation in decision-making which is characteristic of a vibrant civil society disposing of true social capital. While the issue of overt and covert violence and torture remains a paramount concern for foreign policy, it must be recognised that many "approved democracies" have shown themselves as capable of the denial of human rights as dictatorships and oligarchies. Northern Government Foreign policy should link with a broad wealth creating (poverty eliminating) Aid programme that targets scarce finance and other measures to the building of vibrant "civil societies" that can solve problems locally. Civil societies that can influence the selection of appropriate and acceptable leadership, the resolution of differences that lead to conflict and excessive violence, and the sharing of wealth in all its forms.

2.6 Therefore emphasis should not be placed on the intermediation of international NGOs in only those cases where official channels are cut but also to complement at grass-roots level the essential move towards democracy and basic rights that FCO is better able to monitor at national level.

2.7 In conclusion concern with democracy and human rights must apply to grass roots processes as well as at national elections. Furthermore, to be credible, concern with democracy and human rights must not be selective but apply equally to friend and foe.

The ideas in this necessarily brief submission are enlarged in a number of reports and research papers of ACORD. We append as perhaps the most relevant one to the Committee's current inquiry "A DISCUSSION PAPER ON BASIC RIGHTS" [not printed]. The sections: "Implications of adopting a rights approach" and "Strategy for adopting a basic rights approach", we believe, would be helpful to the Ministry's policy makers in adding a local, civil society-focused perspective to any human rights policy. For reference we also attach a copy of ACORD's 1996 Annual Report and the Strategic Plan for 1997 to 2001 [not printed]. Together these provide an overview of the work we are doing in Africa and a statement of our intentions.

January 1998

APPENDIX 16

Memorandum submitted by the Westminster Foundation for Democracy

1. PURPOSE OF THIS SUBMISSION

1.1 The purpose of this submission by the Westminster Foundation for Democracy (WFD) is to offer information relevant to the Foreign Affairs Committee's Inquiry into ". . . how the Government implements its human rights objectives when formulating and executing foreign policy, both bilaterally and multilaterally, and. . .the extent to which such policy can be effective in preventing or remedying human rights abuses."

2. BRIEF INTRODUCTION TO THE WESTMINSTER FOUNDATION FOR DEMOCRACY

2.1 WFD's mission is articulated in its Memorandum of Association.[1] It "exists to assist, support and encourage the peaceable establishment and development of pluralistic democratic practices and political institutions overseas . . . democratic electoral process . . . the formation, organisation and management of democratic political parties." This is the purpose for which WFD was established, in the belief that democratic principles are sought by peoples throughout the world as the best means of fulfilling their aspirations for peace, justice, liberty and human rights, and in the recognition that Britain with its mature democratic government has a responsibility to promote good governance.

2.2 This mission, as successive WFD strategic plans have noted, is consistent with the policy aims of the Foreign and Commonwealth Office as expressed in its own Mission Statements and Annual Reports. At the same time, it should be noted that WFD was deliberately established with a legal personality and policy-making function independent of government, in order to enable it to work flexibly with the full range of democratic institutions and to ensure that the independence of its decision-making. This means, *inter alia*, that it may support parties or organisations opposing the government of the day in recipient countries, provided of course that these groups espouse non-violent democratic principles and work within the law of the country concerned.

2.3 WFD's budget for 1998–99 is £3 million, of which at least 85 per cent will be utilised in overseas grantmaking. Priority regions for WFD activity are Eastern and Central Europe, the Commonwealth of Independent States, and Anglophone Africa. Half of WFD's grantmaking resources are channelled through the British political parties, which in turn make grants to develop and strengthen counterpart parties overseas with which they have established links: these funds have to date been allocated among the parties according to the short money formula. The other half of WFD's grantmaking budget is utilised in grants made directly by WFD to democracy-building activities and institutions overseas, including:

(i) cross-party projects;

(ii) parliaments and other representative institutions;

(iii) election administration;

(iv) independent media;

(v) legal organisations;

---

[1] Memorandum of Association, 24 February 1992, under the Companies Act 1985; articles 3(A)(i)-(iii) and (on modalities and activities) 3(B) (i)–(iv) and 32(C) (i)–(xxi).

    (vi)   human rights groups;

    (vii)   trades unions;

    (viii)   organisations promoting women's political and civic participation; and

    (ix)   other non-governmental organisations involved in political development.

2.4   The criteria for identifying the priority regions and countries for WFD activity are need, effectiveness and interest, i.e., where the democratic development needs are greatest; where WFD resources can be most effectively used; and where there is British interest. Project selection criteria include whether the proposed project: will help develop democratic institutions, checks and balances; has a clear action plan with clear objectives and promising tangible results; and is likely to have sustainable and/or replicable effects. WFD is willing to be the first donor to a project meeting its established criteria, and to fund good projects jointly with other organisations in order to achieve a catalytic or multiplier effect with WFD resources. WFD does not fund projects of a purely educational, social, welfare or humanitarian nature, nor does it fund conferences, academic research or studies.

2.5   WFD's purpose is set out in its informational brochure (Annex 1) and elaborated in its annual strategic plans (Executive Summary from current Plan at Annex 2) [*not printed*].

3.   Relevance of WFD's work and remit to subject of the inquiry

3.1   As section 2 above makes clear, human rights have been since WFD's establishments one of the main areas in which it makes grants in support of democratisation and good governance overseas. Development of human rights organisations and promotion and protection of human rights remain a priority.

3.2   Since WFD's establishment in 1992, it has funded 65 human rights projects in 29 countries, with a total value of £403,022. This represents about 5 per cent of WFD's overall budget over six years, or 10 per cent of the grants made directly by WFD. Furthermore, human rights projects constitute a growing proportion of WFD's grants: 7.7 per cent in 1997–98 compared to 3.8 per cent 1993–94. WFD's human rights projects are currently concentrated in the CIS (11 projects over the last two years), Angolophone Africa (10), Central and Eastern Europe (6), with six further projects in the rest of the world over the same period. A full list of WFD-supported human rights projects, by region, is at Annex 3 [*not printed*].

3.3   WFD has also been able substantially to increase its impact in the human rights field as a result of a successful bid in the first round of National Lottery grants for overseas work. In 1997 WFD was awarded £496,796 by the Lottery for a three-year programme of work with four human rights partner organisations in Africa, specifically Ghana, Nigeria, Uganda and Zimbabwe, to enable them to protect and promote human rights more effectively in their countries. These lottery-funded projects represent a 41 per cent increase over the monies used for human rights projects from WFD's grant-in-aid form the FCO. Since this represents such a substantial part of WFD's current human rights project portfolio, the details may be of interest to the Committee. The business plan for the four projects is attached at Annex 4 [*not printed*].

4.   Information from WFD's experience of human rights work

4.1   Here I shall attempt to summarise what has been achieved and learned through WFD support for human rights work. Supporting documentation includes excerpts from our two most recent Annual Reports, recording projects supported that year (Annex 5) [*not printed*]; and copies of recent WFD newsletters featuring coverage of human rights projects (Annex 6) [*not printed*].

4.2   In essence, WFD has identified three key areas of concern in human rights protection:

    (i)   lack of awareness of human rights and the means available to defend them and assert individuals' rights;

    (ii)   poor or non-existent legislation guaranteeing the protection of human rights;

    (iii)   poor implementation of and/or disregard for existing human rights legislation, resulting in human rights repression and abuse.

WFD has addressed these problems by supporting indigenous organisations in order to help them:

    (i)   monitor and report on human rights, produce and distribute information, train legal workers, and campaign for human rights education and information;

    (ii)   campaign and lobby for changes in legislation and enlist the support of the international community;

    (iii)   investigate abuses, provide legal advice, represent victims in court and appeal to international tribunals.

4.3   I attach at Annex 7 [*not printed*] a final project report from a grantee, the Committee for the Defence of Human Rights in Nigeria, which is a current grantee and also a partner in the Lottery-funded project. This report well illustrates: the impact of our funding in terms of cases contested and remedies sought; the importance of WFD's institutional, practical and, not least, moral support to those struggling for human rights in difficult conditions; the more qualitative, long-term results of their efforts; and the enormous challenges and obstacles this work frequently faces. To put this another way, the value of supporting human rights organisations is not just for the work they do but to underwrite their very continued existence as fragile beacons of hope and effort. In some of the countries we work with (e.g., Malawi), our grantee is the only broad human rights organisation in the country, and even modest results from their efforts constitute a gain for their country.

4.4   Following, in paragraphs 4.4 to 4.8, are some broader observations and lessons learned. Firstly, solidarity is in our experience an essential component of human rights work, since activists, advocates and proponents are frequently subject to marginalisation, opposition, harassment, intimidation, or worse in their own countries. Therefore, it is particularly important to develop close working relationships and maintain regular contact, by whatever means feasible, with human rights grantees and partners who are often working in vulnerable and volatile circumstances. For the same reasons it is important to have active, informative relationships with other organisations supporting human rights work. WFD prides itself on cultivating these in its work in a range of sectors, but arguably they are most vital to our human rights projects. A list of organisations active in human rights with which WFD has links (other than grantees, listed at Annex 3) is at Annex 8 [*not printed*].

4.5   Proving the impact of one's work in this field can be exceedingly challenging. This is true of support to good governance and democratisation in general, where the results materialise only over the long run, are highly qualitative in nature, are the product of multiple and complex inputs and interactions, and where claiming "credit" for results can be tenuous at best. In the human rights field, there can be very tangible, concrete, quantifiable project results, e.gs., legislation promulgated, detainees released, cases won or dropped, lawyers trained. But these may not be the most meaningful indicators. What ultimately matters more is whether the human rights climate as a whole improves, whether the powerful respect the rights of the powerless and the dissenting, and these latter live in security and without fear. These are better measures of the ultimate effect of our work.

4.6   WFD's democratisation remit is very clearly in the political and civic arena, rather than the socio-economic sphere. This does not make us, or other organisations with a similar focus, blind to the important debates and realities concerning the "indivisibility" of human rights. For example, in several countries of the former Soviet Union, there is now at least some measure of multi-party democracy, and thus greater popular enjoyment of "third-generation" political human rights; yet economic liberalisation has been so unregulated that the basic needs of marginalised groups, including the elderly, the unemployed, and the disabled, who formerly enjoyed some minimal welfare "safety-net", now go unmet, and their "first-generation" socio-economic right are violated. While organisational remit must of necessity exclude some causes in order to focus on others, they operate at times like a medical specialist permitted to treat a disease in one part of the patient's body, but not to palliate or treat the side-effects arising elsewhere.

4.7   As new needs emerge, there should be a structured way for organisational remits to expand or evolve to respond to them. For example, and related to the points in paragraph 4.6 above, it is becoming clear that in many countries, growing corruption and the lack of both governmental, political and corporate transparency and accountability are not only a problem in their own right, but also threaten to undermine some of the gains of support to human rights, democracy and good governance of recent years. Should new organisations in the UK and elsewhere be created to respond to these needs, should existing organisations adapt themselves in order to address them or can partnerships and collaborations among current players suffice to muster a suitable response?

4.8   Just as the family of rights are connected in theory and practice, the components in the good governance equation are also interconnected. The nine main sectors of WFD's good governance and democratisation work are listed in paragraph 2.3 above. Because our remit allows us to support work in such a diverse range of sectors we tend to nurture and witness the relationships between them in the countries we work in, and even within specific WFD projects. For example a current WFD-funded project run by a Bulgarian independent broadcaster, to educate people about their human rights, spans two or three of these related areas. However, these connections are as often serendipitous as deliberate. Many organisations which have a remit to work only in human rights may be missing valuable opportunities for linkage and synergy. In our view the good governance agenda does not divide neatly into discrete compartments and may even suffer from being addressed in this manner.

5.   RECOMMENDATIONS AND CONCLUSIONS FOR THE CONSIDERATION OF THE COMMITTEE

5.1   Arising from paragraph 4.5 above a series of workshops or a consultative process could usefully be established, with the purpose of identifying meaningful evaluation methods and indicators for assessing the results of British efforts in the human rights field, not only by governmental agencies but also by NGOs, advocacy groups, public bodies and the academic and journalistic communities. Representatives of all such organisations could be invited to participate in the workshops or consultations.

5.2   Arising from paragraph 4.6 above, the time may be right to revisit the rather compartmentalised way in which human rights work is sometimes structured (both within government and among the non-governmental community), in order to minimise the fragmentation of effort and result. The realisation is currently gaining currency, that the democratisation efforts of the last half-decade may have focussed too heavily on multipartyism and electoral democracy, at the expense perhaps of constitutionalism and liberal democracy. This suggests a need to strengthen the legal, constitutional and human rights components of the complex good governance equation, but in a structured and holistic way. Certainly any reprioritisation of efforts will have implications for British human rights work.

5.3   Development approaches wax and wane in popularity, and it would seem that the doctrine of "political conditionality"—making aid dependent on democratic and governmental good behaviour—favoured in the last five years may already be on the wane. WFD was never an instrument of conditionality, but rather, crudely put, a means for British governmental money to "do good by stealth" in human rights, and other sectors, through an arms-length, quasi-non-governmental modus operandi and legal personality. Perhaps there is scope for more intensive use of such approaches.

5.4   Finally, the debate about the precise causal link, if any, between democracy (however defined) and economic development (simplistically defined as growth) rages on, but what has emerged with greater clarity (e.g., in the recent OECD/DAC Development Co-operation Report) is that some of the poorest countries in socio-economic terms are those with exceptionally bad government or in some cases no effective government at all. Therefore both the political and the socio-economic rationale for a continued high priority on human rights work are compelling. Since human rights remain a crucial part of good governance, and especially if political conditionality is declining in favour as an instrument of foreign policy and/or of development assistance, it should be a priority to define new forms of policy leverage and develop innovative development assistance approaches, in order to keep up the human rights momentum.

February 1998

APPENDIX 17

Memorandum submitted by the World Development Movement

The World Development Movement (WDM), a membership organisation with over 20,000 supporters has developed an interest and involvement in human rights issues through its work on the arms trade and the UK aid programme. This submission to the Foreign Affairs Committee focuses on those two broad areas.

1.   ETHICAL FOREIGN POLICY AND THE ARMS TRADE

Good government, including respect for human rights was seen by the previous Government as one of the then Overseas Development Administration's (ODA) primary aims. But too often, that objective carried less weight with other ministries. The formation of the new Department for International Development (DFID) may secure greater coherence between departments and WDM welcomes the Foreign Secretary's commitment to put human rights at the forefront of foreign policy. However, we are concerned that in practice the policy will not be carried out consistently. Those countries with which Britain has a significant trade or strategic relationship will be treated more leniently than other countries, thus bringing this welcome objective into disrepute.

The aspect of Britain's relationship with other countries which most clearly highlights the priority which is given to human rights is the sale of arms and torture equipment to undemocratic regimes and governments with poor human rights records. This can, therefore be seen as the key indicator of the British Government's willingness to stand by its commitment to both human rights and good governance principles.

1.1   *Arms sales to Indonesia*

Two-thirds of Britain's arms exports are to the Middle East and Asia[1] regions of considerable strategic importance and tension. Many of the regimes in those regions have governments which have limited respect for human rights. But, for organisations such as WDM the Government's willingness to continue with its predecessor's policy of arming Indonesia can be seen as *the* test of its approach to human rights.

The reason for the emphasis on Indonesia is that it is an authoritarian state which does not have territorial disputes with neighbouring countries. Yet it has become a significant buyer of weapons and equipment from Britain. Only one-third of the Indonesian military is engaged in traditional military duties, the rest are in units which function alongside the civilian administration throughout the country. So, Indonesia's arms purchases are most likely to be used for internal repression in East Timor, West Papua (Iran Jaya), against political opponents, labour activists and, at the moment, in riot control as people feel the force of the country's economic crisis.

---

[1] UK Defence Statistics 1997, Ministry of Defence.

The Foreign Secretary has announced that Britain *"will not supply equipment or weapons that might be used for internal repression"*.[1] But, since that statement, although a few export licenses have been refused other licenses for equipment have been issued and many more licenses are pending.[2] This indicates that although additional checks have been built into the monitoring system, the overall objective of maintaining Britain's commercial and foreign influence has retained its primacy.

The continuing level of arms exports to Indonesia can only be seen as a very disappointing outcome of the new Government's foreign policy review, especially as even the previous Government acknowledged that Indonesia had an unsatisfactory human rights record. The recently published Public Accounts Committee report on Aid to Indonesia quotes Ministers' concerns as including *"extra-judicial killing; the suppression of political opposition; restraints on the freedom of speech, on freedom of assembly and on freedom of association; a lack of progress towards democratic institutions; and a high level of corruption."*[3]

1.2 *A European Code of Conduct on arms exports*

Arms sales to any regime can almost always be justified by: referring to Article 51 of the United Nations Charter on the right to self-defence; to employment in Britain; and most often because if we do not sell then others will do so and Britain will then lose other trading contracts with that country.

Partly to counter this last point, the British Government is attempting, during its Presidency of the European Union, to negotiate a European code of conduct on the arms trade. But, as the Committee may be aware, the Foreign Secretary's proposal has received a less than positive welcome from NGOs. A coalition of NGOs, including WDM have developed a similar code which brings together various voluntary criteria European Union Governments adopted at the 1991 Luxembourg and 1992 Lisbon Councils, the guidelines agreed by the Permanent Five Members of the UN Security Council in 1991 and the OSCE Principles agreed in 1993.

However, the code of conduct the Government is now proposing agreement is set at the lowest common denominator and it is still only voluntary. Any code with no legal backing will mean that commercial and strategic concerns are still likely to prevail over concerns about the use of European weapons and equipment for internal repression and respect for human rights.

So, although there has been a welcome change of rhetoric on arms exports, more needs to be done to ensure that European weapons and torture equipment are not used to enable undemocratic regimes to suppress opposition—whether in Indonesia or other states whose human rights records have led to sanctions including, China, Burma, Zambia and Kenya.

Ultimately, unless the Government alters the fundamental basis of its arms export policy *"to encourage the sale of UK defence equipment unless there are compelling reasons for not doing so"*[4] then the Government's commitment to putting human rights at the forefront of foreign policy will be fatally undermined.

2. AID FOR POLICE TRAINING AND HUMAN RIGHTS

In his "Human Rights into a new century" speech in July 1997 the Foreign Secretary, Robin Cook, announced that he was inviting views on how the UK Military Training Assistance Scheme could "better support our human rights objectives". In particular he proposed that resources could be *"transferred to support work in encouraging better standards of police training and raising levels of jurisprudence."*

2.1 *Police training in Indonesia*

Since the adoption of "good government" as one of the Government's main overseas development objectives in 1990, the ODA (now DFID), has increased its financial support for police training projects. Support for police training programmes in Indonesia and Nigeria formed part of WDM's submission to the National Audit Office (NAO) and Public Accounts Committee Inquiries into Aid to Indonesia.[5]

The Indonesian programme in particular gives grounds for concern that providing support for police training in countries with dubious human rights records will do little to meet the Foreign Secretary's objectives. The NAO report revealed that the development objectives for the £1.8 million programme included encouraging *"the Indonesian Police towards the concept and organisation of community policing in terms of improved human*

[1] Human Rights Into A New Century, July 1997.

[2] *Hansard*, 22 December 1997, col. 509.

[3] Committee of Public Accounts–Overseas Development Administration: Aid to Indonesia, December 1997, para 5, p. vii.

[4] Export Licence and Arms Working Party (MoD Form 680) Applications: Guidance for Desk Officers, non-proliferation Department, July 1994.

[5] Aid to Indonesia, National Audit Office, HC 101 Session 1996–97, The Stationery Office, 29 November 1996 and Public Accounts Committee, 17 December 1997.

[6] Aid to Indonesia, National Audit Office, p. 36.

[7] Aid to Indonesia, National Audit Office, para 3.15.

rights."[1] But it found that one of the few positive outcomes of the project was improved *"procedures and practices in the issue of vehicle and driving licences in East Java".*[2]

The Public Accounts Committee concludes that the developmental benefits *"would have been more effectively realised had the project's objectives been expressed in terms of addressing human rights issues instead of focusing on the improvement of the Indonesian police force's management capacity.*[3] That is not surprising as the ODA "specifically excluded references to human rights from the project memorandum agreed with Indonesia and did not include human rights in the proposed training programme."[4]

In evidence to the NAO on the police training project in Indonesia,[5] WDM cited evidence from Ann Clwyd MP that an Indonesian police officer who received training in Britain was alleged to be responsible for severe human rights abuses in East Timor, following the Dili massacre, and in Jakarta.[6] WDM also noted that Ann Clwyd, MP had questioned whether funding police training in Indonesia was an effective use of the aid programme.

WDM has also drawn attention to the inefficiency of £1.3 million spent on aid for police training in Nigeria which began in 1991. That programme continued despite the coup which brought General Abacha to power, until November 1995 when the project came to an end just as Nigeria was expelled from the Commonwealth following the hanging of Ken Saro-Wiwa and the other Ogoni activists. The Nigerian programme was described to WDM by an official at the Foreign and Commonwealth Office as a "vain attempt" to introduce British policing standards.

The record of these two programmes indicates that Ann Clwyd's question must be asked of any police training in countries with repressive regimes whatever the source of funding, as it seems unlikely that it will do anything to promote greater respect for human rights.

2.2 *Aid funding for police training and human rights*

Post 1990, funding for police training through the ODA/DFID increased substantially with the British Government's commitment to "good government". Funding for human rights projects also began, but they were few and far between. A list of police training and human rights projects of over £100,000 between 1989 and 1995 provided by the then ODA's statistics department, shows 30 countries receiving police training projects worth over £32 million. By comparison, just over £7 million had been spent on six human rights projects, over half of which went on a large programme in South Africa.

3. CONCLUSION AND RECOMMENDATIONS

The initial evidence is that simply shifting funding from military training to police training and making stronger statements on human rights issues will do little to improve human rights in countries with oppressive regimes. Indeed providing the most up-to-date riot control equipment and funds for police training are more likely to strengthen the control of an existing regime rather than stimulate the desired improvements in respect of human rights.

So, WDM would recommend that in order to implement its human rights objectives, the Government should look to providing much more support to human rights organisations and other NGO's working to strengthen civil society in developing countries and should stop all arms sales and aid to the police in repressive regimes. These measures will increase the likelihood that Britain's foreign policy can, as the Committee set out in its original brief *"be effective in preventing or remedying human rights abuses."*

February 1998

APPENDIX 18

Memorandum submitted by John F Kerry, United States Senator

I applaud the progress made by the European Union toward agreement on an EU-wide Code of Conduct on arms sales. I welcome the lead taken by the UK and French governments in establishing this as an important issue, and understand that their joint Code proposal has now been discussed by all 15 Member States. As an advocate of the Code of Conduct in the United States, I sincerely hope that this activity will mark the start of a global process of increased restraint in arms sales.

---

[1] Aid to Indonesia, National Audit Office, p. 36.
[2] Aid to Indonesia, National Audit Office, para 3.15.
[3] Overseas Development Administration: Aid to Indonesia, Public Accounts Committee, p. xi.
[4] Aid to Indonesia, National Audit Office para 25.
[5] Evidence to the National Audit Office on Aid to Indonesia and Police Training, WDM December 1995.
[6] British Aid to Indonesia: The continuing Scandal, Ann Clwyd MP, September 1995.

In the United States, efforts are being made in both the Senate and the House of Representatives to pass legislation to stop arms transfers to internal repressors and external aggressors. It is of inestimable importance for the EU States to seize the opportunity to establish a similar Code in Europe. Together the United States and the EU account for approximately 80 per cent of the global arms trade. Consequently, we have a special responsibility to lead the world in this effort. The adoption of Codes of Conduct on both sides of the Atlantic would serve this aim.

Success in the European Union would provide an important stimulus to our efforts in the United States. As you may be aware, last summer the House of Representatives passed a Code of Conduct amendment offered by Representatives Cynthia McKinney and Dana Rohrabacher. The similar legislation I introduced in the Senate has already secured considerable support.

In supporting these items of legislation, many members of Congress were reassured by the developing support for a similar Code in the EU. Transatlantic co-operation to control the arms trade is essential to overcome the oft-cited argument "If we don't sell arms, someone else will". It is crucial that parliamentarians and governments working towards Codes of Conduct on both sides of the Atlantic seek to develop closer links to reinforce their respective efforts to control the arms trade.

The Senate Code legislation includes an expanded section calling for increased multilateral co-operation on arms transfer restraint. Increased dialogue between the United States and the European Union on the Codes of Conduct could facilitate progress on multilateral arms restraint and transparency within the Wassenaar Arrangement. Moreover, the adoption of responsible US and EU Codes would serve to encourage progress toward agreement on an International Code of Conduct as advocated by a commission of Nobel Laureates including Oscar Arias, Jose Ramos-Horta, Elie Wiesel, and the Dalai Lama. I understand that members of the commission have already had a number of encouraging meetings with several EU Foreign and Development Ministers.

I urge you to do everything possible to translate the welcome UK/French proposal into an effective Code that limits the supply of arms to dictators and oppressive regimes, and that incorporates strong multilateral consultation mechanisms. My fellow Code supporters and I look forward to these leadership steps being taken by the governments of the European Union, and we pledge our continuing efforts to secure enactment of a United States Code and to stimulate actions by the Executive Branch of the United States Government to pursue multilateral arms sales Code of Conduct agreements.

March 1998

APPENDIX 19

Memorandum submitted by the Save the Children Fund

1. INTRODUCTION

Save the Children's long and distinguished history has been built on the belief that children have rights and that societies have an obligation to respect and encourage the realisation of those rights. Save the Children's programmes are driven by the determination to demonstrate ways in which their rights can be realised, while also playing a major role in working for their wider recognition. In legal terms the latter has been largely achieved by the almost universal ratification of the UN Convention on the Rights of the Child (CRC), which now covers 90 per cent of the world's children. Together with other UN conventions and regional and national legislation, the CRC provides a firm basis for taking action on behalf of all children and young people in all countries and in all circumstances. The focus now is on observation of the CRC through implementation and greater awareness.

Save the Children believes that society has an obligation to satisfy the fundamental needs of children and to provide assistance for their protection and development. The added value that a children's rights perspective brings is a concern for the totality of children's rights (economic, social, civil, political and cultural), a focus on children's strengths as much as their dependency, and recognition of the role of the family, community and governments in working to secure children's rights. Most importantly, the over-riding importance of considering the best interests of children in any decision affecting them is established.

2. CHILDREN WITHIN A BROADER HUMAN RIGHTS FRAMEWORK

Save the Children believes that if UK Foreign Policy is to genuinely have human rights objectives, a top priority, not only in terms of rhetoric but also in terms of action, must be the rights of children. It is worth bearing in mind that human rights are also about:

— ensuring that all people have the opportunity to achieve their full potential, something which is particularly crucial during childhood;

— building a society which is respectful of the rights of others, so beginning with children will ensure that short-termism is avoided;

— the protection of the vulnerable, so children must be among the first to be protected.

We believe there are both principled and pragmatic imperatives which demand that children's rights be prioritised. This means two things in terms of foreign policy: first, where there are specific children's issues, such as sale of children, child prostitution or child pornography these must be thematic priorities in foreign policy; secondly, in consideration of all other issues, in particular country specific issues, the situation of children must be a primary concern. Thus when investigative missions are sent to human rights crises, such as recently with Algeria or Kosovo, such missions must make an examination of the situation of children an explicit priority.

2.1 "Mainstreaming" children's rights

Traditionally, international focus on the situation of children has been seen as a foreign policy focus of the Nordic states in general and Sweden in particular. This has resulted in large amounts of expenditure on their part on child-focused projects around the world. However, it has not resulted in the "mainstreaming" of children's rights into international human rights fora. By this, we mean considering children specifically and as a priority in all discussions of specific situations which are being viewed from a human rights perspective.

For example, there has been considerable focus on issues such as child labour or sexual exploitation of children, particularly with regard to sex tourism. These are vital issues to which Save the Children has devoted a great deal of time and effort. Both are issues which specifically affect children, harming their immediate welfare as well as their long-term development. To this may be added a number of other child-specific issues, such as the use of children as soldiers, the treatment of children in prisons in certain parts of the world, and the application of the death penalty to children in countries including Bangladesh, Iran, Iraq, Nigeria, Pakistan, Saudi Arabia, the USA and Yemen.

These all constitute some of the most serious violations of human rights occurring in the world today. However, it is also important to look beyond those issues which are explicitly focused on children, and to bring in children's concerns into issues where the harm to children may be less apparent. This is the essence of mainstreaming children's rights. The following examples below illustrate how children's rights can be "mainstreamed".

Bhutanese refugees in Nepal

Save the Children has been alone in suggesting that focusing on children is an essential component of improving the situation of these refugees. Other agencies often will not take into account the difficulties faced by children, perhaps because refugee leaders are all adults. Save the Children delivers a wide range of services to these refugees, primarily focused around health care. Even without a specific child focus it is clear that children's issues are very high in the list of priorities for these refugees. With a high birth-rate there are many new born children in the camps. Many children have spent their whole lives as refugees. These children have no clear nationality, since both Bhutan and Nepal deny responsibility for them. Insecurity in the camps has led to an increase in early marriages, as parents fear for the safety and welfare of their children that goes along with a breakdown of existing social mores. Some children are married as young as 12 years old, with all the attendant health and psychological hazards. Teenagers in the camps have no prospects for the future, since Nepal does not allow refugees to work outside the camps in a bid to prevent integration. As a result they are often restless and disruptive. Any intervention in this situation needs to address both immediate needs and long-term development issues. Both these considerations require prioritising children.

Palestine

Save the Children has been concerned with the situation of Palestinian children for a considerable time. In partnership with the American Save the Children we deliver around eight million dollars worth of assistance to the West Bank and Gaza—around 30 per cent of which comes from the Department for International Development.

There has been a good deal of attention on the human rights situation that has arisen from the Arab-Israeli conflict. Specifically and most recently, there has been concern raised over an Israeli Supreme Court ruling allowing the use of "moderate physical force" in the interrogation of Palestinian prisoners, which has been interpreted by many, including two United Nations Special Rapporteurs, as in effect legalising torture.

However, from the Save the Children's perspective a far larger and more pressing issue is the effect of the conflict on children. The collapse of the Palestinian economy has led to an increase in child labour, and the poor diet as a result of lack of income has led to increases in rickets and anaemia among children. Israeli-imposed security closures of the borders between Israel and West Bank and Gaza have disrupted children's access to education and to health care. At one point a number of deaths of minors were reported as having occurred at checkpoints because these children were unable to reach hospitals as a result of security closures. The case for focusing on children on the basis of need is very strong. However, it is also essential that those interested in a lasting peace in that region ensure that Palestinian children are both protected and provided for if the seeds are not to be sown for future resentment and hostility.

Liberia

In Liberia, a country which is trying to rebuild itself after war, there are numerous development issues, and, again, considerable international aid is being made available to help with this process. Save the Children believes that it is vital to focus on children in such situations. We firmly believe that education has to be prioritised, and that the reintegration of children who were used as soldiers by warring factions is a prerequisite for future stability. These child soldiers have been taken from their families, willingly or unwillingly, and used to fight, kill and commit atrocities at the request of their military leaders. Often they were drugged, beaten, terrorised or sexually abused to instil discipline and ensure that they would obey orders without question. These children have lost out on their childhood, and know no other way of life or way of dealing with everyday conflicts other than with violence. Rehabilitation and normalisation of these children is a priority not just in terms of need, but in terms of longer-term development for Liberia as a whole.

From these examples it is apparent that there are strong arguments for prioritising children's rights on both principled grounds, thus prioritising the most vulnerable, and pragmatic grounds, thus laying the foundations for future development.

2.2   Children's lack of visibility

It is often the case that children's rights are overlooked, or at least not adequately appreciated, as a result of children in general being less 'visible' than adults. By this we mean that children are seldom perceived to be relevant social actors in a particular country, and have less opportunity to make their concerns heard, and as a result these concerns can have very low visibility.

Save the Children has evidence of state-sponsored torture of children in a number of country situations. Torture of children occurs both within and outside of prisons. It is used primarily as a means of social control. This may be to control the activities of children, as in torture of street children to encourage them to leave a particular area, as seen in some countries in South America. Often it is a method of terrorising their parents, families or communities. For example, in 1994 in Kuwait the 15-year-old son of a political dissident was arrested and later left unconscious outside his family's home. His body was marked with electrical burns. During detention the son was questioned about his father's political involvement. In another example in Bahrain in January 1998, 22 minors were arrested and detained incommunicado, beaten and held until wanted persons gave themselves up. Evidence available to Save the Children indicates that the torture of children is alarmingly widespread, yet the popular perception of the phenomenon is that it is more commonly practised against adults who are considered to be political dissidents or journalists. When a well-known activist is detained and tortured it is particularly conspicuous and normally provokes a response even at an international level. The same is not true of children. This demonstrates the general phenomenon of children's lack of visibility. This has to be addressed by a corresponding determination to highlight children's issues in both thematic and geographical human rights matters.

2.3   Children's rights as a vehicle for broader human rights concerns

In our experience children's rights can be used as an approach to open doors to negotiations which might otherwise be considered politically sensitive. Human rights are usually considered *de facto* "political", largely because they have often been used, or abused, to make political points. Save the Children welcomes the Foreign Office's consideration of the human rights record of China as an example of a more politically sensitive way of addressing international human rights concerns in a non-confrontational way.

In contrast with this, raising children's issues can seem far less threatening. This is demonstrated by the almost universal ratification of the United Nations Convention on the Rights of the Child, achieved in under 10 years, as compared with the two-thirds ratification of the International Covenant on Civil and Political Rights which has taken 30 years to reach this level. As an example, Save the Children's advocacy on the subject of Palestinian children in the Occupied Territories has involved work on one of the most sensitive and politically charged contemporary international issues. NGOs working on this issue are normally considered fiercely partisan and are linked with one side or the other.

By contrast, through focusing on children's rights Save the Children has avoided this problem, and is probably the only NGO to address this issue that has good and regular relations both with the Government of Israel and with the Palestinian authority. However we are still of the view that children's rights are fundamental rather than instrumental, and we see them primarily in these terms. None the less, children's issues are seen as purely humanitarian concerns. By utilising children's rights as a vehicle for discussing broader human rights concerns, it is possible in our view to address the human rights situation in a particular country which might otherwise be closed to it.

2.4 *Children's participation*

Save the Children also believes that children's participation is an essential component of good foreign policy interventions. Although the concept of participation is usually more pertinent at a project or programme level, we are of the view that the most effective way to make any policy truly sustainable is to have full participation at all stages of design and implementation of the beneficiaries of the project or programme. Save the Children has been working with this principle for many years, in line with Article 12 of the UN Convention on the Rights of the Child, which states that children should be part of any decision-making process that affects them. This is not dissimilar to the concept of participatory rapid appraisal developed by Robert Chambers and others over the last 20 years, but with particular relevance to children. The consultative and participative methodology for children and young people is different to methods used for adults, and we have worked on a number of different initiatives to ensure that such methodologies are appropriate for children, ensuring that their needs are met and their rights are respected. Giving children access to decision-making process develops their negotiating and conflict-resolution skills, and ensures that they have a genuine sense of ownership of services or process which have a direct effect on them. We see such an approach as having added value in foreign policy considerations where children are affected.

3. IMPLEMENTATION

Save the Children is not unique among NGOs in both welcoming the Foreign Secretary's statements on ethical foreign policy, while at the same time remaining concerned that these sentiments are turned into practice and tangible policy change. We believe the following general considerations are essential to implementing human rights considerations in foreign policy.

All foreign policy necessarily entails weighing up alternatives, and making choices according to which of a set of options is most attractive in the light of the objectives that such a policy has. The UK Government's commitment to human rights means that the promotion of human rights and fundamental freedoms is one among a range of objectives. However, there are varying degrees of commitment, and it is not yet clear how much weight is placed on human rights considerations as opposed to other considerations which more clearly constitute part of the national interest. Clearly, if the UK Government places low priority on human rights considerations then its commitment is of little value.

The two key areas in terms of policy will be omission and commission. Omission will entail not doing things which, in the absence of human rights considerations, might otherwise have seemed attractive. Commission, on the other hand, will entail doing something that would otherwise seem too financially or politically costly in the absence of human rights considerations.

3.1 *Implementation through omission*

Implementation of human rights standards in foreign policy in terms of omission raises a wide range of issues. These include:

— Arms sales.

— Trade agreements and business deals.

— Strategic alliances (for military purposes).

— Rejection and lack of support for international standards in order to avoid adverse consequences for domestic policy.

The issue of arms sales is perhaps one of the more obvious acts of omission entailed by a human rights commitment in foreign policy. Save the Children would have very little to add to the concerns raised daily by other organisations that focus more specifically on the arms trade. However, we are specifically concerned with the issue of the supply of light weaponry to situations where children are being used as combatants. The ready availability of weapons which can easily be used by children is clearly a factor which encourages the use of children as soldiers. This is one of the most harmful practices which impacts directly on children's survival and development in conflict situations. A human rights-sensitive policy on arms sales needs to extend further than the current interpretation of the OSCE guidelines which preclude the export of implements which might be used for oppression or torture, or other grave violations of human rights. It must include the non-provision of light weaponry to situations where children are known to be being used as combatants.

Trade agreements and business deals all potentially support regimes which violate human rights, and an ethical foreign policy needs to appreciate and employ the potential persuasive force of trade on the behaviour if rights-disrespecting governments. For example, concerns have been raised in the UK Parliament over the EU-Israel Association Agreement (a trade agreement). While it contains a human rights conditionality clause (making it a material breach of the treaty to violate human rights standards) this does not seem to be being used appropriately to influence the Government of Israel regarding its treatment of the Palestinian population of the Occupied Territories. If human rights objectives are to be implemented, one implication is to refrain from otherwise beneficial trade agreements, bilateral or otherwise, if certain minimum human rights standards have not been met.

Much the same considerations apply to strategic alliances with countries with questionable human rights credentials. The example of Turkey is current, but hardly exclusive.

The UK has in the past failed to support the establishment of international human rights standards on the grounds that they jeopardised domestic policy. For example, the Ministry of Defence has encouraged the Foreign Office not to actively support the creation of an Optional Protocol to the Convention on the Rights of the Child on the protection of children in armed conflict, because it may well affect UK recruitment into the armed forces. The actual numbers of recruits is very small, yet until the recent change in Government the UK actually blocked changes. While it has changed its policy to one of non-obstruction it still continues to not actively support this measure.

These are all areas where a human rights consideration runs contrary to other competing considerations, or vice versa. The successful implementation of human rights objectives involves considering the "human-rights" cost of a particular course of action against other costs or benefits in such a way as to give adequate weight to these human rights objectives.

3.2 *Commission*

In terms of commission it is important to remember that there are two broad categories of human rights, both of which are equally essential to human welfare. These are civil and political rights, such as the rights to liberty and security of the person, and social, economic and cultural rights, such as the rights to food, shelter and health care.

In both of these categories the UK Government already undertakes a broad range of activities. The Department of International Development carries out work which impacts on both of these areas of human rights, as does the Foreign Office. Save the Children welcomes the recent white paper on international development, and, in particular, the specific focus on children's rights contained within it. However, the current levels of expenditure on overseas aid are not adequate, and at 0.26 per cent of GDP are a long way from the commitments made by the UK Government of 0.7 per cent GDP.

Again, there is always more that can be done in terms of applying pressure to governments with poor human rights records. However, the application of pressure always has associated costs. It is also appropriate to ask whether applying pressure is always the best way to achieve the desired results. In the case of China Save the Children agrees with the Foreign Secretary's recent course of action with regard to the China Resolution at the United Nations Commission on Human Rights. The Foreign Office will be well placed to assess what the most politic and effective approaches are to achieve a particular policy change in a foreign government. The issue is not one of capacity but of will.

Parliamentary scrutiny of executive actions can play an important role in this. It can seek to discern how high a priority human rights considerations have been in a particular course of action with regard to foreign relations. This can provide an effective mechanism for ensuring that the UK uses its capacity to promote human rights and fundamental freedoms to best effect.

4. EFFICACY

There can be little doubt that the attitudes of foreign governments can have a major effect on the behaviour of governments which do not respect the human rights of their citizens. While there are reasonable reservations which can be held over the efficacy of human rights efforts since the last World War, it would be incorrect to suggest that they have not been effective to a degree.

Similarly, the expectation of the implementation of human rights objectives in foreign policy must be that it will be effective to a degree. The United Kingdom, for a variety of reasons including military and economic strength, membership of the EU and the UN Security Council, and the Commonwealth, has the capacity to influence the behaviour of other governments, not only to change their own practices, but also to change their relations with third parties.

5. CONCLUSIONS

Save the Children believes that in order to effectively implement human rights objectives the UK Government must:

1. prioritise the rights of children;

2. achieve this in the first instance by identifying child-specific issues in all broader human rights concerns;

3. promote the participation of children in decisions which affect them;

4. give adequate weight and consistency to human rights considerations in foreign policy;

5. refrain from otherwise attractive policies on grounds of their "cost" in human rights terms;

6. undertake policies which are primarily or solely justified by human rights considerations, even where there is a high political or financial cost; and

7. ensure that this process is effective by allowing high levels of Parliamentary scrutiny of foreign policy with regard to human rights objectives.

March 1998

APPENDIX 20

Memorandum submitted by International Pen Writers in Prison Committee

INQUIRY INTO SUPPRESSION OF HUMAN RIGHTS RELATED REPORTING IN THE MEDIA

The Writers in Prison Committee of International PEN welcomes the Foreign Affairs Committee's inquiry into the suppression of human rights related media reporting. Since its inception 77 years ago, PEN has raised its concerns about the imprisonment, and in some cases, killings, of writers and journalists whose only "offence" was to bring to light abuses of human rights. This pattern of abuse continues to this day. Some current examples include:

— a total of 28 years' imprisonment served against a *Mexican* army officer, *Brigadier General Jose Gallardo Rodriguez.* Although convicted of "illicit enrichment" from and embezzlement of army property, it is widely recognised that the sentence has been levied as a means of punishment Brigadier General Gallardo for his writings in which he explicitly criticised the Mexican military of human rights abuses;

— in April this year, *Turkish* writer and human rights activist, *Edip Polat,* was sent to prison to serve a 10-month sentence for an article criticising the Turkish judicial system;

— also in *Turkey,* the playwright and human rights activist, *Esber Yagmurdereli,* was sentenced to 10 months in prison for a speech made to a human rights gathering in 1991 in which he raised the issue of the rights of Kurds in the Turkish south-east. He will also have to serve an additional 16 years in prison, the remainder of a previous sentence from which he was conditionally released in 1991. During his previous imprisonment he was considered a prisoner of conscience.

— in *China, Liu Xiaobo,* a literary critic and human rights activist, is serving a three-year "re-education through labour" term for having circulated a petition calling for free expression and the right to form opposition parties;

— a *Vietnamese* Buddhist priest, *Thich Quang Do*, is serving a four-year sentence solely for having written to protest the arrest of four aid workers who had assisted flood victims in 1993.

These cases serve to illustrate the problems faced by those who attempt to report on or comment upon human rights abuses in their countries. The Writers in Prison Committee strongly urges the Foreign Affairs Committee to raise its concerns with those governments who use imprisonment or other means to persecute those who criticise their human rights policy. Our primary aim is to gain the release of those who are detained, followed by legislative changes which would ensure that further abuses do not occur.

The Writers in Prison Committee of International PEN further urges the Foreign Affairs Committee to recommend to the British government that it supports the proposed United Nations Declaration on Human Rights Defenders with a view to eventual ratification. In the Declaration, there are numerous clauses which emphasises the role of free expression as central to the work of Human Rights Defenders in ensuring that all citizens are protected against attacks upon their internationally recognised rights.

International PEN is the leading voice of literature worldwide, bringing together poets, novelists, essayists, historians, critics, translators, editors, journalists and screenwriter. Its members are united in a common concern for the craft and art of writing and a commitment to freedom of expression through the written word. Through its Centres, PEN operates on all five continents with 130 centres in 94 countries.

Founded in London in 1921, PEN connects an international community of writers. It is a forum where writers meet freely to discuss their work. It is also a voice speaking out for writers silenced in their own countries.

The *Writers in Prison Committee* of International PEN was set up in 1960 as a result of mounting concern about attempts to silence critical voices around the world through the detention of writers. It works on behalf of all those who are detained or otherwise persecuted for their opinions expressed in writing and for writers who are under attack for their peaceful political activities or for the practice of their profession, provided that they did not use violence or advocate violence or racial hatred.

Member centres of International PEN are active in campaigning for an improvement in the conditions of persecuted writers and journalists. They send letters to the governments concerned and lobby their own governments to campaign for the release of detained writers and for investigations in cases of torture and killings. Through writing to the families, and where possible, directly to prisoners, they provide encouragement and hope.

International PEN has consultative status at the United Nations Commission of Human Rights and with UNESCO.

May 1998

APPENDIX 21

Supplementary Memorandum submitted by New Economics Foundation

Thank you for your letter of 1 May inviting us to comment on the recent publication of the FCO/DfID Annual Report on Human Rights.

Broadly we welcome both the commitment and first publication cycle of this report. It is a readable and useful document.

In the spirit of constructive criticism, there is a central question about the report which the government needs to address; namely, whether it is a celebration of what you think has been achieved, or a more rigorous, systematic, and objective report on what has happened.

These options are not, of course, mutually contradictory. The celebration of success best takes place within the context of an honest and complete record of what has, and has not, worked. Such an approach would be well received both in the UK and internationally, and set an important precedent for other governments to follow. An overly "PR" type of approach, on the other hand, also sets a precedent, but a bad one. Indeed, in the light of the move by some multinationals towards approaches to social auditing which address basic human rights issues, this latter approach will appear, and is, regressive.

The FCO/DfID has the opportunity to forge ahead in demonstrating substantive progress in its human rights related work, and transparency and accountability in its approach. This first report could set a foundation for this direction, but only if the next cycle and publication takes a more in-depth and rigorous approach. Fortunately, emerging social audit methods offer a practical route for this, and we would encourage the FCO/DfID to engage in such an approach in the future.

I hope this is some help in your evaluation and deliberations. Please do not hesitate to contact us should you want further clarification of our perspectives.

May 1998

APPENDIX 22

Memorandum submitted by Christian Aid

AN ASSESSMENT OF THE ANNUAL REPORT ON HUMAN RIGHTS APRIL 1998, FROM THE FOREIGN AND COMMONWEALTH OFFICE AND THE DEPARTMENT FOR INTERNATIONAL DEVELOPMENT

1. Christian Aid welcomes the Government's recent Annual Report on Human Rights as a valuable first step in promoting human rights observance in international relations. Christian Aid outlined its formula for a Government Annual Report on Human Rights in an earlier submission to the Committee which should be read in conjunction with the present document.[1]

2. The published Annual Report is a report on what the UK has done to further human rights observance in a number of countries and to develop international instruments rather than a comprehensive account of the

---

[1] See Ev. p. 135.

human rights situation in countries across the world as provided by the annual US Senate human rights report. Christian Aid believes the US Senate report offers a more effective model for such a report.

3. Even as an account of UK Government activity, the present Annual Report portrays human rights problems in a variety of countries in broad thematic terms with very limited accounts of UK interventions. The approach is illustrative rather than analytical and comprehensive, without detailing what important next steps need to be taken in particular countries of concern.

4. Such an approach tends to limit transparency and, in doing so, shrouds coherence, two of the government's key policy objectives in human rights and development.

5. Fore example, in the section of the report entitled *Working with the world* the account of new arms sales criteria introduced by the Government (page 35) illustrates the dangers of such a partial approach. Without a detailed accounting of export licences issued and the Parliamentary scrutiny of such processes, it is impossible to confirm that the Government has followed its own criteria, particularly on not providing arms for internal repression.

6. After recent events in Indonesia, the granting of over 50 licences for arms exports from UK in the last year has created the perception that such criteria may have been breached. A separate Annual Report on Arms Sales debated by Parliament giving detailed accounts of such export licences would provide the transparency to dispel such perceptions.

7. Likewise, the absence of detailed reporting on individual countries in the present Annual Report makes it difficult to confirm how coherent, and indeed effective, British initiatives on human rights have been in any given situation.

8. Christian Aid would prefer to see the report produced by a process closer to the present Select Committee procedures thus enabling the experience of civil society and NGOS on perceptions of human rights' observance in particular countries including the UK to be recognised and quoted.

May 1998

APPENDIX 23

Supplementary Memorandum submitted by Amnesty International

ASSESSMENT OF THE UK GOVERNMENT'S ANNUAL REPORT ON HUMAN RIGHTS

INTRODUCTION

Our overall response to the FCO/DFID "Annual Report on Human Rights" ("the report") is positive.

The publication of an annual human rights report is something we have sought from successive UK Governments.

The Report's publication reflects the Government's recognition of its responsibility under international human rights law to promote and protect human rights.

It provides a clear explanation of the Government's policy and preferred approach and of the different factors that will be balanced in making policy. It provides an accurate identification of the underlying causes of human rights violations and related problems such as conflict.

We welcome the Report's emphasis on the indivisibility and interdependence of social, economic and cultural rights as well as civil and political rights, together with its emphasis on the need for implementation of human rights standards. We also welcome the Report's emphasis on open government and constructive work with NGOs. This reflects a recognition and support for human rights defenders and civil society in general which is very important and this was positively backed up by the Foreign Secretary's recent visit to Turkish human rights defender Akin Birdal, in hospital following the attempt on Mr Birdal's life.

The report will assist Parliament in holding the Government to account and we hope and expect that Parliament will put it to good use for this purpose. There should at least be an annual debate on it in Parliament.

However, the Report is a first step, not a finished article. It has gaps and shortcomings, some of which are addressed below.

LACK OF HUMAN RIGHTS CONTEXT

The Report outlines some of the UK projects to promote human rights in various countries. However, the significance of those projects cannot be fully understood without a description of the main human rights problems in the relevant countries. While the Government has made it clear that the Report is not to replicate or provide alternative views to the US State Department's annual human rights report, a brief summary on particular countries should still be included. Such background information is an essential component of public education, which is one of the report's specified objectives.

KEEPING BRITAIN'S HOUSE IN ORDER

The report recognises that the credibility of the UK's commitment to human rights in its foreign policy will be low if human rights are not taken seriously at home. We agree that incorporation of the European Convention of Human Rights into UK law and ratification of the Additional Protocols to the Geneva Conventions are positive moves in that direction. However, there are a number of instruments which the UK has not ratified and we would like to see an explanation for this in the Report.

DEATH PENALTY

Parliament's recent decision to include Protocol 6 to the European Convention in the Human Rights Bill is a welcome addition in this trend to support for international human rights treaties, in spite of Government opposition. This development, together with the very positive decision to participate in international campaigns for abolition, provide the UK with an opportunity to act on some challenging countries such as Saudi Arabia, China, Nigeria and the USA. We hope to see such action described in these areas in subsequent Reports.

ASYLUM/DOMESTIC POLICY

The lack of any mention of asylum is a serious omission as the worldwide plight of refugees has become one of the greatest challenges in the field of human rights. It is essential that the problem is addressed both as a foreign policy and a domestic policy issue. The Government's current review of asylum procedures would be an opportunity to demonstrate that its stated commitment to human rights is integrated in all areas of policy and effects all departments equally.

MILITARY SECURITY POLICE TRANSFERS (MSP)

While a separate report will shortly be produced on the granting of licences for export of military equipment, the human rights report refers to the new arms' sales criteria and the proposed European Code of Conduct, so we will comment briefly on this here.

The Report refers to the risk of "internal repression" being amongst the UK's criteria of reasons to avoid selling weapons. The same expression is used in the text of the EU Code of Conduct finally agreed at the EU General Affairs Council. This term, is vague and is not used in international human rights law, which therefore limits the applicability of the human rights criteria. Human rights guidelines should refer explicitly to international human rights and humanitarian laws and standards.

The Report mentions that the Government will report annually to Parliament on the application of these controls. However, we remain concerned at the lack of transparency and public and Parliamentary scrutiny at both EU and UK levels which in the UK has been exacerbated by the current failings of the DTI ECLIPS computer system used to record information on licences.

DIALOGUE AND PARTNERSHIP

The policy described in the Report favours seeking long term engagement through partnership, co-operation and constructive engagement. It is argued that this is the best way to encourage reform in certain countries. The point is also made that the approach may not be feasible where states reject co-operation or lack of credibility as partners. Examples are given of Iraq and Nigeria and stronger measures have been taken against those countries.

However, more detail should be given about the criteria used to determine when constructive engagement should apply and when it should not. This should include some indication of the Government's expectations and a time frame for the process of dialogue and engagement. This will allow an assessment of its effectiveness or not. Subsequent reports should state where and why the approach has achieved success or failure.

It is important that political dialogue does not become an end in itself.

LEVERAGE/WORKING WITH OTHER GOVERNMENTS

We agree that the UK has been well placed to influence international debate and action on human rights violations. This will certainly continue while the UK is a permanent member of the Security Council, a member of the EU, a leading member of NATO and of the Commonwealth and has more or less guaranteed membership of the UN Commission on Human Rights.

The Report should contain more detail about the UK's strategy for working within these inter-governmental fora. The Report gives the impression that consensus is preferred, and that particularly within the European Union gaining a unified approach has been a priority for the Government. While this may be important, the UK must on occasion be prepared to take a lead and if necessary act alone in public defence of human rights. Our information suggests that there is frequently a willingness amongst other governments to take firm action on human rights if the lead is first given by another state.

One example is the International Criminal Court (ICC) on which the UK had adopted an increasingly positive position over the last year. With a diplomatic conference to establish the court about to start in Rome, the UK could take a firm political lead on some of the major principles of the court, in particular for an independent prosecutor and for freedom of the court from political interference. Such action would be supported by members of the Like-Minded group of countries who support the court and who have benefited from and welcomed the UK's recent membership.

The ICC is mentioned in Section 5 but the reference could be more informative and should expand on the policy. In particular it should seek to explain the UK's decision to support granting the UN Security Council the power to delay or prevent an investigation or a prosecution by the ICC.

COUNTRY CASE STUDIES

Many of the country cases provided in the Report reflect the policies discussed above. When such examples are used, human rights concerns must be used to provide some context. The following are four countries mentioned in the Report.

ALGERIA

Reference is made to the recent massacres in Algeria, which briefly put Algeria in the headlines. But there is no mention of the severe human rights abuses in Algeria during the last six years. These began when the 1992 elections were cancelled after the first round gave victory to the Islamic Salvation Front.

Amnesty International's research indicates that these abuses were not only carried out by the armed opposition groups which subsequently formed but also by Algerian Government forces. However, European governments, including the UK, have accepted the Algerian government argument that abuses are committed only—or at least predominantly—by armed groups who say they are Islamist.

When dialogue is the UK's objective, countries such as Algeria can easily satisfy the Government by committing themselves to lengthy talks, without feeling any real need to end human rights violations. The UK's own EU Presidency policy of pursuing dialogue with the Algerian government is unlikely to achieve real improvements for human rights unless there are more explicit objectives.

CHINA

Human rights dialogue with China is cited as the main objective. The Report also provides a handy, if brief, indication of the actual human rights violations and concerns which are raised with Chinese officials. Some results are claimed, such as the signing or intended signing of some key international human rights treaties and greater co-operation with UN human rights mechanisms.

The EU's failure to agree a common policy on China over recent years, resulting in the public split and no resolution at the 1997 UN Commission on Human Rights and this year's decision to take no action, sends a message to the Chinese that EU governments will not hold out for human rights improvements against political and economic pressures. Therefore, those governments which advocate dialogue—such as the UK—need to state the minimum improvements required in China's human rights record if a more critical approach is not to be taken at the 1999 Commission. It is also important that it is made clear to the Chinese that their willingness to discuss these matters, hold seminars on human rights and release a few high profile dissidents is no substitute for real, sustained improvements in human rights.

RWANDA

The Report's section on Rwanda states that the issues surrounding human rights and justice are central to reconciliation and economic development. It describes the sensitivity of the Rwandese Government which feels let down by an international community that stood by and allowed the genocide to happen.

The Government considers that support and constructive dialogue are the best ways to deal with the Rwandese Government.

The Report does not mention on-going and grave human rights violations committed by the Rwandan Patriotic Army (RPA). Having failed to take effective action during the 1994 genocide, the international community must not compound its mistake by now allowing guilt from that failure to cloud its view of current violations by the RPA. Although privately the Government says it is putting pressure on the Government of Rwanda to prevent human rights violations, it still appears reluctant to criticise human rights violations by all sides. The Report does not correct this impression. The present Rwandese government should not be allowed to excuse violations committed in its name because of either earlier violations or security problems.

INDONESIA

Recent events in Indonesia will presumably have led to a change in the UK policy from that described on page 13 of the Report. We hope this is the case.

Again constructive partnership is the Government's preferred approach. The six point plan for co-operation on human rights is described and the announcement which followed the foreign Secretary's visit—that the Troika will visit East Timor—is reiterated. Elsewhere in the Report mention is made of a resolution on East Timor by the UN Commission on Human Rights, which did not in fact happen.

The first point of the six-point plan is to support the work of Komnas HAM, the Human Rights Commission. This could be important but only if political pressure is put on the Government of Indonesia to implement Komnas HAM's recommendations.

While the announced Troika visit could be useful, its likely effectiveness is difficult to judge without any more details about how it is to be set up. For example, who will be met, how will the visit be used to obtain more information about human rights and what messages will be delivered to the Government of Indonesia? It should be made clear that the trip is not a substitute for visits by genuine human rights monitors.

Amnesty International's own reports have reflected a deteriorating human rights situation in Indonesia with increasing arrests of political activists around the election and a spate of disappearances earlier this year. Events of the last two weeks have highlighted that the situation had dramatically worsened since 1996, fuelled by unrest caused by the economic crisis in the country. However, the Government's approach (indeed that of other governments such as Australia) has not reflected this.

No mention is made in the Report about the export of arms to Indonesia, yet this has been of considerable public interest and concern in the last year, starting with the decision to honour the export licenses for armoured personnel carriers and water cannon issued under the previous government. Over 50 further export licences have been granted since. Given the controversy of such actions, the Report should make some reference to the human rights criteria applied when making these decisions, the guarantees sought from Indonesia on end use and the efforts of UK officials based in Indonesia to monitor the use of such equipment.

CHILDREN

One of the main themes of the report is children. Some of the issues are outside Amnesty International's mandate, although we support the use of a rights-based approach to tackling the grave problems outlined and the recognition that this area in particular demonstrates the indivisibility of rights.

The age of children in armed conflict is within Amnesty International's mandate, and we are calling for the minimum age of recruitment and participation to be raised to 18. A UN Working Group is negotiating a new optional protocol to the UN Convention on the Rights of the Child, which will deal with this issue. The report mentions that the Government is working for a successful conclusion of the process, but fails to state what this means. The Government has indicated to NGOs that it will not block a decision to raise the age to 18, but there seems to be conflict on this between Government departments because the UK's own minimum age of recruitment to the armed forces is 16. It therefore remains unclear what outcome the UK is working towards.

BUSINESS

We agree with the conclusion from this section of the need to include business in an integrated approach to human rights, encouraging businesses to operate ethically and transparently, and relating their activities to the human rights of the communities in which they work. However, we would like to see more detail in this section about how the Government intends to encourage businesses in this direction.

CONCLUSION

We hope that our comments will be useful to the Committee in assisting it to evaluate the Government's foreign policy on human rights as set out in the Report.

We hope that, in the longer term, these comments will also help the Government to improve that policy and improve the content of future annual human rights reports.

The first Annual Report on Human Rights is a welcome step.

Future reports will be enhanced by the inclusion of more detail on the human rights record of particular countries, and the publication of success criteria for the Government's policies with such countries. Also needed will be some indication of the mid-term goals and the Government's strategy for taking forward its human rights policy over the next few years.

Regular Parliamentary scrutiny of the Report would also be welcome.

May 1998

APPENDIX 24

Supplementary Memorandum submitted by Saferworld

THE EU CODE OF CONDUCT ON THE ARMS TRADE: FINAL ANALYSIS[1]

PREAMBLE

The EU Code of Conduct agreed by Foreign Ministers on 25 May 1998 is an important initiative in that it represents a first step towards the development of a common, responsible, approach to arms exports by the EU Member States. However the agreement fails to provide full respect for international humanitarian law and falls short of establishing adequate EU mechanisms and procedures for Member States to take co-ordinated action to effectively monitor and control transfers by the Member States and their nationals of military, paramilitary and security equipment and services.

Despite appeals from parliamentarians and non-government organisations in the EU, there is no explicit obligation to prohibit transfers to forces which would most likely use them to seriously violate international humanitarian law (which sets out the rules of war). Moreover, there are virtually no provisions to address the current deficiencies in most EU Members States' arms control regimes, such as the failure to strictly regulate international arms brokering and licensed production agreements, or to adopt rigorous systems of certifying and monitoring end-use. Finally the Code, as agreed, contains no provision for parliamentary or public scrutiny over arms exports from the EU and thus does little to foster greater transparency and accountability over the arms trade across Europe as a whole. These omissions will need to be rectified in the near future if the Code is to achieve its aims of high common standards in management of and restraint in conventional arms transfers.

THE GUIDELINES

Criterion Two: The respect of human rights in the country of final destination;

Criterion Six: The behaviour of the buyer country with regard to the international community, as regards in particular its attitude to terrorism, the nature of its alliances and respect for international law.

Promoting full respect for international humanitarian law, complimenting respect for international human rights standards, is an essential requirement for an EU Code, but the failure to do this under Criterion Two and Six could easily undermine the Code as it stands.

Under Criterion Six, Member States are only required to "take into account the record" of the "buyer country" with regard to "its compliance with its international commitments, in particular on the non-use of force, including international humanitarian law applicable to international and non-international conflicts". In other words, they may still consider that arms transfers can be authorised in spite of likely breaches of international humanitarian law because of other strategic reasons. It should be pointed out that under Article 1 of the Geneva Conventions, states have a responsibility to "respect and ensure respect" for international humanitarian law. The right to transfer arms cannot take precedence over the duty to ensure respect for such law, and this obligation should have been explicitly recognised in the Code.

Criterion Two adds to this weak formulation because the term "internal repression" is used as a summary term and defined without reference to the obligations set out in international humanitarian law—which has been primarily designed to protect those not actively participating in hostilities during both international and non-international conflicts.

---

[1] This paper was drafted by Liz Clegg, Saferworld, in consultation with representatives of Amnesty International, BASIC, Christian Aid, Oxfam UK and the World Development Movement. These organisations have differing mandates and areas of speciality and while we, individually, do not have detailed policy on all the areas covered by the Code, we can each comment on specific elements and expand on the recommendations given. Amnesty International policy does not include opposition to, or support for, comprehensive arms embargoes, arms transfers which alter a strategic military balance, or criteria to determine excessive military expenditure.

EU governments could thus claim that the Code as currently worded allows them to authorise arms transfers to recipient forces even if they are likely to commit breaches of humanitarian law in the context of an internal armed conflict. This wording may also allow governments to send arms to those forces even if they are likely to be used to abuse human rights and violate humanitarian law outside their own borders, for example, when serving in other countries or during cross border attacks on their own nationals who have fled internal fighting. Since very many of the worst atrocities and repressive acts are committed in the context of armed conflict, these are serious flaws in the wording of the Code and should be addressed as soon as possible.

The text under Criterion Two, which was bracketed in the penultimate draft, and which defines "internal repression" as "major violations of human rights and fundamental freedoms as set out in relevant international human rights instruments" and includes the risk of the diversion of the equipment for use in "internal repression", has been retained in large part and strengthened. The examples of actions which would constitute internal repression have been extended to include "torture *and other cruel, inhuman and degrading treatment or punishment, summary or arbitrary executions, disappearances, arbitrary detentions*". This particular wording is a welcome inclusion. However, the EU governments should clarify that the term "internal repression" will mean "violations of international human rights standards and/or humanitarian law".

Beyond these criticisms it should be noted that under criterion two, the clause which requires the Member States to exercise restraint when considering the export of arms to countries with a record of repression is not as restrictive as was hoped. On 25 May, the Member States were faced with a choice of two formulations: the first advocated caution—on a case by case basis, taking into account the nature of the equipment—in the export of arms to countries where human rights violations had been "established by the competent bodies of the UN, the Council of Europe or by the EU", the second, more restrictive option, advocated restraint in the export of arms in general to recipients which are guilty of serious human rights violations, however, it also implied that Member States should abstain from licensing, to such end-users, exports of equipment which has a potential for use in repression.

Unfortunately the final text of the Code incorporates the first option which is expanded to include "*special caution and vigilance* in issuing licences. . .where serious violations of human rights have been established by competent bodies of the UN, the Council of Europe or by the EU" in the recipient country. The failure of the Member States to incorporate the more restrictive option within the Code represents a missed opportunity in terms of ensuring that maximum restraint is exercised in the supply of military, paramilitary and security equipment to regimes which abuse human rights.

While acknowledging the legitimacy and authority of the judgements of "competent bodies" of the inter-governmental organisations named, it is possible that a prospective recipient may be guilty of human rights violations which, owing to their recent occurrence, or the refusal of access to investigators, have not been censured by the "competent bodies". Moreover, it is not clear which "competent bodies" are referred to, nor why the EU governments have chosen not to include, for example, the Inter-American Court of Human Rights. EU governments should clarify that the phrase "where serious violations of human rights have been established by competent bodies" will include those human rights abuses documented in reports by special rapporteur, working groups and other thematic mechanisms of the United Nations.

Also under Criterion Six it should be noted that there is still an error in section (b) of the guidelines under Criterion Six. This asserts that "Member States will take into account inter alia the record of the buyer country with regard to: . . . (b) its compliance with its international commitments, in particular on the non-use of force, including under international humanitarian law applicable to international and non-international conflicts". However, it should be noted that international humanitarian law refers to the regulation of the use of force rather than the non-use of force.

Criterion Eight:The compatibility of the arms exports with the technical and economic capacity of the recipient country, taking into account the desirability that states should achieve their legitimate needs of security and defence with the least diversion for armaments of human and economic resources.

The text under Criterion Eight now refers to EU and bilateral aid as a consideration in export licensing. A wider variety of development indices, such as figures produced by the UNDP, are also now to be included. Whilst these inclusions are to be welcomed, the text still fails to articulate how this and other considerations will affect export licensing decisions. If this criterion is to prevent the transfer of arms to where they could undermine the prospects for sustainable development or hamper the effectiveness of development programmes or reconstruction initiatives, then the Code must state clearly that the presumption will be to deny exports where there is evidence to suggest that negative effects would accrue.

OPERATIVE PROVISIONS

Consultation on undercutting

The penultimate draft of the Code of Conduct set out two alternatives for the consultation mechanisms which related to the procedures for the Member States following a decision to take up a licence which had been denied by another Member State. Unfortunately the Member States have agreed on the more limited option. This requires any Member State wishing to undercut a denial to consult with and ultimately inform only the Member State which issued the denial in the first instance. The other alternative, to inform all Member States of a decision to undercut, would have served the purposes of transparency to much greater effect.

The decision to restrict consultation and notification on undercutting to bilateral exchanges carries with it certain potential dangers. In the first instance, bilateral consultation between the Member State wishing to undercut and the Member State which issued the denial is unlikely to facilitate the development of a consistent approach towards sensitive end-users amongst the wider group of Member States. Secondly, because any decision by a Member State to go ahead and take up a licence denied by another will only be notified to the Member State issuing the denial, undercutting is likely to take place virtually in secret. If and when details of undercutting eventually emerge, the net effect could prove divisive, possibly leading to a reduction in the number of denials issued and/or an increase in undercutting.

There remains the possibility that Member States which have issued denials will seek, informally, to notify to the wider group, a decision by another Member State to undercut. Rather than relying on ad hoc procedures, however, a clear priority for the Member States in the development of the Code of Conduct should be the establishment of full multilateral consultations on undercutting before and after a decision to undercut is taken. Moreover, the Member States should agree to notify an appropriate committee of their national parliament in order that the purposes of transparency and accountability may be fully served. In view of Foreign Minister Vedrine's statement that "we shall see how to go further", progress in this area is imperative in the short term.

A Common Control List

The Operative Provisions also state that "EU Member States will work for the early adoption of a common list of military equipment covered by the Code, based on similar national and international lists". Until this process is completed, national lists will form the basis of denial notification and consultation "incorporating where appropriate elements from relevant international lists". It is unfortunate that the Member States could not agree on a common comprehensive list at the same time as the Code of Conduct. However it is essential that this process is completed without delay because some national and international control lists do not cover the full range of goods and services used in defence and law enforcement to which the Code should apply. Utilisation of national and international lists for any length of time could lead to a gap in the application of controls on the part of some Member States. The Member States should, moreover, ensure that the agreed EU Code control list contains: i) all types of major conventional weaponry, all types of small arms and light weapons, police and paramilitary equipment, military and paramilitary training equipment and services; and ii) a list of prohibited equipment—such as anti-personnel mines, death penalty equipment, leg irons, electro-shock weapons etc.— whose sole or primary practical use results in serious abuses such as breaches of humanitarian law and international human rights standards.

The Annual Report

A truly accountable system would be one which requires Member States to allow national parliaments (or committees thereof) to scrutinise proposed arms exports in advance of the granting of licences (as is the case in Sweden). In particular those licences which may be granted to countries where there are serious concerns over human rights violations, internal instability, regional or international conflict, or high military expenditure, should be scrutinised and evaluated by national parliaments.

In this regard, the provisions for an annual review which are contained within the final text of the Code fall some way short of the level of public transparency which is necessary for the proper regulation of the arms trade. In the penultimate draft two alternatives were advanced. One required the Member States to compile an annual report on their defence exports and on the implementation of the Code and, further, for a consolidated report to be provided to the Council of Ministers and the public. The second weaker option provided for an annual meeting to review the Code from which a report would be drafted for submission to the Council only.

Clearly the first option went significantly further in terms of transparency and accountability as it required the Member States to provide details of their arms exports and for some form of report to be made public.

While welcoming the decision by the Member States to undertake an annual review of the Code, it is disappointing, that the option chosen is, in fact, a watered down version of the first option. While still requiring the Member States to produce a report on their arms exports, it is stressed that this should take place in confidence. Moreover, while a consolidated report is to be produced, it appears that this will only be provided to the Council of Ministers, and not to national parliaments, the European Parliament, or the public. This is a major weakness in the Code of Conduct. The net effect of this formulation is thus to remove any reference to public or parliamentary accountability from the Code of Conduct. As such the provisions for the annual review of the Code are unlikely to facilitate achievement of the aims of "greater transparency" which are articulated so clearly in the Preamble to the Code. If the aims of transparency and accountability are to be realised, the Member States should, immediately, commit themselves to publishing their national reports on defence exports as well as the consolidated report on the implementation of the Code. This will allow post facto review of arms export policy and, as such represents a minimum standard.

LEGAL STATUS OF THE CODE

The political and legal status of the proposed EU Code will be crucial to its effective implementation. It is disappointing, therefore, that the Member States have agreed to adopt the EU Code of Conduct on Arms Exports only as a Council Declaration (under CFSP). However, this type of politically, but not judicially, binding agreement has not been sufficient to ensure a common approach amongst the Member States under the eight common criteria on conventional arms exports agreed by the Council of Ministers in 1991 and 1992.

The decision that the Code should not be legally binding upon the Member States means that the need for parliamentary scrutiny over arms exports from the EU becomes even more pressing. EU governments must be held accountable for their implementation of the Code of Conduct and, in the absence of any legal mechanism for achieving this, increases the importance of parliamentary scrutiny over EU arms exports and the need for the Council to publish the consolidated annual report (see above).

OTHER ESSENTIAL MEASURES

In spite of concerted pressure from the non-government sector, the EU Code of Conduct which was agreed by Foreign Ministers on 25 May 1998 contains no reference to the need to control the activities of international arms brokering agents, the need to control licensed production of military, paramilitary and security equipment or the need for common EU controls governing end-use. The absence of even a reference to these issues is a major disappointment. The lack of common EU controls in these areas means that inconsistencies will exist in the stringency of national controls in key areas which could serve to undermine the aims of the Code of Conduct. The Member States should, therefore, seek to address these omissions at the earliest opportunity by agreeing common EU controls on international arms brokering, on end-use certification and monitoring and on licensed production.

August 1998

APPENDIX 25

Supplementary Memorandum submitted by the World Development Movement

The World Development Movement believes that the Government should take stronger action in expressing its disapproval for those companies which either violate human rights themselves or who are implicated in the human rights abuses of repressive regimes. Some form of sanction should be used against British companies breaching the spirit of the Government's ethical foreign policy in their operations overseas.

Shell, Rio Tinto (and BP) are the three multinationals in the world who have recently proclaimed their company's support for the UN Universal Declaration of Human Rights. Yet they continue to abuse human rights.

RIO TINTO IN INDONESIA

At the Grasberg mine in Indonesia the Amungme tribe are still demanding that Rio Tinto recognise their land rights. The company is funding the expansion of this large copper and gold mine in the face of local opposition. The protests of these people who have lost their land and livelihoods has been met with repression by the Indonesian army. Just days ago, two Amungme tribal leaders were stopped at the airport and prevented from travelling to Britain where they were hoping to address shareholders at Rio Tinto's annual meeting on 13 May.

SHELL IN NIGERIA

Last month a UN report highlighted the serious human rights abuses of the Nigerian government on the Ogoni people. The report goes on to say that "the Nigerian authorities have put at SPDC's [Shell's subsidiary in Nigeria] disposal a mobile police force to suppress protests". Reference is also made to Shell's "well armed security force which is intermittently employed against [protestors]".

In response to criticism Shell has included wording on human rights in its Statement of General Business Principles and has asked for comments on its actions from the general public. However this welcome rhetoric has yet to filter down to operations on the ground. Moreover when questioned at their AGM on the UN report's call for an independent investigation they dismissed it as unnecessary.

PREMIER OIL IN BURMA

British oil company—Premier Oil—has been asked by Robin Cook not to invest in Burma, but has so far ignored the request. Premier Oil is the leading member of a consortium developing off-shore gas reserves south of Rangoon. The military regime has forced 2 million people to build the infrastructure which will be used for the pipeline. It will run through an area where 25,000 have been displaced.

Aung San Suu Kyi of the National League of Democracy has said "Premier Oil is not only supporting the government financially, it is also giving it moral support, and it is doing a great disservice to the cause of democracy. It should be ashamed of itself."

May 1998

APPENDIX 26

Memorandum submitted by The British Council

A.   BACKGROUND: THE ROLE OF THE BRITISH COUNCIL IN THE PROMOTION OF HUMAN RIGHTS

Interpretation

1. The Council's interpretation of Human Rights is broad: it acknowledges their universality; and encompasses economic, social and cultural, as well as civil and political rights.

Trends in Patterns of Assistance

2. There has been a trend in patterns of Council assistance: from activities designed to strengthen the organs of state, towards those promoting popular awareness of rights, access to justice; support for advocacy amongst groups hitherto excluded (rights of the poorest, women, children, prisoners); strengthening the independence of the judiciary; conscientisation of police and security forces through training and direct contacts with counterparts.

British Council Comparative Advantages

3. The British Council has some comparative advantages as a designer and deliverer of Human Rights-related programmes:

— a *long-established presence in 109 countries;* local knowledge built up, and long-serving locally-recruited staff in post; we have just opened an office in Bolivia.

— trust built up with a *wide range of in-country constituencies*—ministerial/governmental, academic, judicial, legal professional, civil society/NGO, English language teaching, artistic, media, diplomatic; experience indicates that many rights issues are multi-disciplinary, cross-departmental and society-wide;

— reputation as *non-confrontational, non-campaigning, independent broker* of international contacts, aimed at giving a balanced, informed view on human rights and other issues (the Council does not act as a mouthpiece for HMG policy);

— strong, well known capacities in *information provision and professional network establishment and maintenance*; libraries' doors are open to all. Information is crucial in equipping individuals and organisations with the means to argue their case peacefully and persuasively;

— access to a *wide range of UK and third countries' resource persons* with comparative international experience; the Council has just organised an International Seminar in Belfast on "Human Rights—their Protection at National Level" which attracted over 80 delegates from a wide variety of countries and featured an internationally renown group of resource persons;

— *unique profile* combining capacities in a range of activities relevant to rights agenda: arts and cultural media, English language teaching; information provision; education (management of systems and curricula); environment, public administration, social development and gender. There is no other organisation like it in the World.

British Council Human Rights Policy Guidelines

4. The Council's work in human rights is influenced by Guidelines to its Country Directors drafted by its governance and law specialists in Manchester, but refined by consultations with many partners in the UK and overseas. These Guidelines stress the following:

— identify *appropriate country and target group priorities* for British Council activities in the human rights field, in the light of a growing consensus that a balance is needed between support on the one hand to elements of states' administrative or legal apparatus to make it more responsive, and on the other to groups who champion the cause of the governed, the excluded or the oppressed;

— exploit the *potential synergies between its various sectoral activities* (e.g., arts, English language teaching, information, education, governance, social development and gender) in order to respond to needs at country level. For example, an ongoing British Council study is exploring the use of artistic and cultural media for the communication of rights-related information or for spreading awareness amongst people who for reasons of poverty, illiteracy and remoteness are not amenable to formal approaches to presentation or discussion of such material. The scope, according to the findings of the study, is huge.

— *co-operate with other international organisations. The Council liaises with the United Nations for example in many country operations, and manages projects for the World Bank and the European Commission.*

— attempt to *evaluate the impact of its human rights programmes.* This is not easy: there are conceptual problems (attribution of effects to the original initiative), and practical ones (costs of evaluation; inadequate sources of reliable information; time taken to firm conclusions; delays in feeding back conclusions into future project design).

5. These Guidelines are attached for your information, as is the leaflet for the new Council exhibition on Men, Women, Democracy and Governance [*not printed*]. This has been displayed at the UN during the last meeting of the Commission on the Status of Women and at the last meeting of the UN Commission on Human Rights in Geneva. It has attracted favourable comments in both places.

Sources of Guidance

6. Human Rights are integral to the Council's policy and practice in the field of governance. Our work in this field is guided by our Law Advisory Committee. Its members include Professor Kevin Boyle (University of Essex Human Rights Centre), Dr Vivien Stern (Secretary General of Penal Reform International), Baroness Helena Kennedy QC (prominent rights barrister and designate Chair of the British Council), and Roger Pannone (Chair of the Law Society's Human Rights Committee).

Sources of Finance for Human Rights Work

7. The Council's work in the human rights field is financed both through its Grant-in-Aid, in which case country-level activities are identified and managed by its Country Directors, and to a larger and growing extent through its management of projects financed through FCO and DFID. Proportions vary country to country and over time. Globally we spend nearly £3 million on governance and human rights activities. The Council is also to be involved in managing projects to the value of nearly one million pounds from the Projects Fund established by the FCO earlier this year: that represents over half the total value of projects approved to date.

B. COUNTRY PROFILES OF RIGHTS-RELATED WORK

Africa Group

Africa Region: One of the Council's major regional events was the recently-mounted Human Rights NGO Consultative Forum, targets at all principal Human Rights NGO's in Africa. The South African Human Rights NGO networking Consultative Forum held in November 1997 was sponsored in Johannesburg by the British Council, and organised in conjunction with the Inter-African Network for Human Rights and Development (AFRONET) and the Human Rights Institute of South Africa (HURISA). It was attended by over 20 representatives of NGO's working in the human rights field from both Francophone and Anglophone countries. It was intended to forge stronger links between them and develop a formula for closer collaboration, regular networking and information exchange in future. The Council also sponsored a facilitator from UK and several other resource persons to assist delegates formulate an agreed strategy and action plan, which were the outputs of the Forum.

Kenya: The Council participates in the Good Government Forum (chaired by the British High Commission). In collaboration with the British High Commission, the Council has supported the establishment of a Human Rights Database with professional assistance from Interrights. One very successful course of journalists in press coverage of elections has been sponsored by BC, and DFID. Also with DFID finance, it has designed an approach to building awareness of democratic rights and to enhance democratic participation through civic education theatre, delivered to audiences throughout two provinces in Kenya. This was one component of the Civil Society Programme the Council manages for DFIF. The Council manages five projects under the FCO's Human Rights Project Fund to a total value of nearly £150,000. With its grant-in-aid funds, the Council has sponsored a wide variety of Kenyan participants in international seminars, events, and courses, from broadcasting organisations, the press, universities, non-government organisations, International Commission of Jurists (Kenya Chapter), International Federation of Women Lawyers, and the Kenyan Magistrates and Judges Association.

Uganda: The Council has latterly funded a series of attachments, attendances at training programmes, and research opportunities in UK for several activists in the human rights field, from the Uganda Magistrates Association, a local Human Rights NGO, academics, and the women's lawyers foundation. It has also embarked on a project with the Refugees Studies Programme of Queen Elizabeth Hall in Oxford to address the needs and rights of refugees living in Uganda.

Middle East Group

Kuwait: The Council has used two vehicles to promote gender equality in Kuwait over the past year. It has jointly with FCO adopted a women-only policy in the selection of candidates for the Chevening scholarships awards. Health care for women has been the focus in a Council-sponsored inward visit by an Arabic-speaking doctor from the UK to the Ministry of Education's Child and Motherhood Centre.

Qatar: The Council has complemented the British Embassy's support of Westminster Foundation for Democracy input in connection with the forthcoming local municipal elections in Qatar where for the first time women will be allowed to vote and stand for election. The Council has sponsored a British academic to participate in a seminar at Qater University's faculty of Economy and Administrative Sciences on the forthcoming elections.

Israel: Gender-related activities are our principal contribution towards improved human rights in Israel. These have involved helping the highly-developed women's lobby analyst needs for access to international experience in equal opportunities, and to tackle constraints on women's participation in the labour force. A working party has been established to examine models for an Israeli Equal Opportunities Commission (of special interest is that of the UK). A study tour to the UK for legal experts on the working party is planned. The Council will sponsor several delegates to the EU/EOC/BC conference on "Mainstreaming equal opportunities in the public sector" in June. One will be the Head of the new Commission on the Status of Women in the Prime Minister's Office. Political skills training for women who were potential electoral candidates was provided by a UK consultant in late 1996: the target group were Bedouin women in the Negev.

Empowerment training was provided to 100 women middle managers in the civil service in later 1997. Both these workshops generated considerable interest in UK experience. We have delivered individual briefings on equal opportunities and managing diversity to the police force, Jerusalem Municipality, and the National Insurance Institute.

Palestine Territories: The Council manages a number of activities with local partners, which provide an opportunity for improving access and take-up by Palestinians of public services, and increased understanding and knowledge of their rights. Through its work, the Council seeks to address the specific needs of the poorest and marginalised, within the context of a rights-based approach to social development in general.

The Council has been asked to manage a £350,000 allocation for the Palestinian Rights Programme under the FCO Human Rights Project Fund. The overall aim of this proposed Programme is to assist Palestinians in achieving their human rights. The 10 projects which compose the programme—identified by the Council—are all priorities for the Palestinian people, and assist in the development of a democratic society, based on the rule of law.

The projects are expected to have a far-reaching impact on all sections of Palestinian society. Children and women will have increased their understanding of their rights. The public will be better informed and educated about human rights by the media. The projects span public sector, private sector and NGOs.

The 10 projects are:

1. Children's charter

2. Theatre in education

3. Peace Education

4. Democracy training programmes for teachers

5. Radio programme

6. Institute of Modern Media

7. Press relations

8. Citizen's Charter

9. Centre for Democracy

10. Human Rights study tour to UK

For DFID, the Council manages the Management for Government Project, aimed at strengthening the capacity of the Palestinian Authority to co-ordinate, promote and manage human resource development in the Palestinian public service. This £1 million Project is concentrating on the development of the National Centre for Public Administration, as well as the Core Group on Public Administration. Also for DFID the Council manages the Gender and Law project, aimed at improving the *de facto* and *de jure* protection of women's rights through law and social and economic policy, and increasing the effectiveness of Palestinian institutions and pressure groups working for gender equitable legislation and policy. This £750,000 Project is being implemented in partnership with Birzeit University and the Women's Centre for Legal Aid and Counselling.

We are also managing the DFID Parliamentary Library Project, aimed at establishing a parliamentary library in order to strengthen the access of Palestinian Legislative Council members to the information required to better meet the needs of the Palestinian people, particularly the poor and women. This is valued at £200,000. Also for DFID, the Council runs the Technical and Co-operation Training Programme, in which Palestinian Authority officials visit the UK to examine best practice, and to identify experience which could be applied in their own institutions.

The Council is involved in managing the major World Bank Palestinian NGO Project. This $20 million Project is managed by consortium including the British Council, the Welfare Association and the Charities Aid Foundation. The main aim of the Project is the eradication of poverty through the strengthening of Palestinian NGOs.

The Council's own Services for People Project aims to increase the access of Palestinians to public services, through information media. Its activities include training for targeted NGOs on the setting up of websites, and "English for the Internet" training. (This is valued at £25,000). The Council is also support an exhibition on human rights to mark the 50th anniversary of the Universal Declaration on Human Rights. It also provides books, videos and materials related to public sector management, human resource development, and poverty alleviation, and provides English training got Palestinian officials.

May 1998

APPENDIX 27

Memorandum submitted by CAFOD

INTRODUCTION

CAFOD is the overseas development agency of the Catholic Bishops Conference of England and Wales. Although the bulk of CAFOD's grants are made to mainstream development projects, a significant number of grants have been in countries where the Catholic Church has provided institutional support for community activists, peasant organisations and human rights groups in order to address or provide protection from human rights abuses. In some countries the Church itself has provided moral leadership in defence of human and civil rights and has itself come under sustained attack from authoritarian regimes and/or paramilitary groups. A very recent example is Bishop Juan Gerardi, Auxiliary Bishop of Guatemala City, who was bludgeoned to death on 26 April 1998, almost certainly because of his leadership of the project called "Recovery of Historical Memory" documenting atrocities and the killings of tens of thousands of Guatemalans in that country's long drawn-out internal conflict.

CAFOD is often asked by partner organisations in developing countries to raise human rights issues with the British government. They hope that CAFOD can persuade the government to provide support for particular human rights initiatives or use its influence with friendly governments or in international fora to further the cause of human rights or to protect individuals working in the field of human rights or humanitarian aid. Church-linked organisations, the Catholic Church itself and NGOs generally are frequently able to provide reliable information about the nature and scope of human rights violations and to indicate who the perpetrators are or might be. In countries where there are widespread or systematic violations of human rights, lack of security and basic freedoms becomes a development issue: people cannot meet, express opinions freely or represent their views to government. Development workers and community activists are threatened and killed.

CAFOD welcomes the Government's declared intent to develop an ethical foreign policy. To be effective such a policy would have to be applied consistently and demonstrate clearly to other governments that there cannot be "business as normal" with governments which are responsible for serious violations of human rights. It is also clearly desirable that ethical foreign policy should be agreed and implemented in a co-ordinated way by a number of governments, most obviously by members of the European Union.

CAFOD can confirm that it has found the Ministers of State at the Foreign Office dealing with areas of concern to CAFOD open to discussion and, when available, willing to hear first-hand what overseas visitors have to say.

The two examples which we put before the Committee are Sierra Leone where we believe that a political objective—the removal of an illegal government—overrode the humanitarian imperative to assist the civilian population and East Timor where we believe that HMG can do more to help bring the illegal Indonesian occupation to an end.

SIERRA LEONE

After the military coup in May 1997 which ousted the elected government of President Kabbah, the British (and US governments) cut aid to Sierra Leone and discouraged other international bodies from providing humanitarian assistance to civilians affected by the conflict. The situation of insecurity intensified in February

1998 when Armed Forces Ruling Council (AFRC) forces were expelled from Freetown by the Nigerian-led ECOMOG peacekeeping force together with troops loyal to President Kabbah. This led to generalised fighting in most areas of the country. President Kabbah returned to the capital on 10 March but looting, acts of vengeance and sabotage by AFRC supporters continued for several weeks in other areas of the country.

NGOs, such as CAFOD, are aware of the pitfalls of providing humanitarian aid in situations of conflict (complex political emergencies) and take all necessary steps to reduce the possibility of such assistance "falling into the wrong hands" and directly fuelling the war effort. The intention behind HMG's policy of cutting aid and preventing any relief supplies from entering Sierra Leone, in effect, the imposition of sanctions, has been interpreted as a deliberate attempt to prevent rebel forces gaining any advantage—material or moral—from the availability of humanitarian assistance. In Sierra Leone this had the effect of depriving the most vulnerable sectors of the civilian population of relief supplies at the time when they most needed them.

CAFOD is a signatory to the Code of Conduct for the International Red Cross and Red Crescent Movement and NGOs in Disaster Relief published in 1994 (attached). DFID will not now approve disaster relief funding for any NGO if it is not a signatory to this Code of Conduct. Other codes of conduct, such as the Joint Policy of Operation drawn up by International NGOs working in Liberia, have also been developed for specific situations. Common threads running through these codes of conduct are:

— that priority should be given to the humanitarian imperative;

— that assistance should be distributed on the basis of need alone;

— that NGOs involved in disaster response should not act as instruments of government policy.

This does not mean that NGOs can behave recklessly or turn a blind eye to the risks inherent in complex emergencies. The Joint Policy of Operation of NGOs working in Liberia explicitly states that NGOs should:

— "endeavour to do no harm through international NGO assistance to programme beneficiaries, implementing partners and programme staff: *potentially harmful effects of assistance will be minimised through a variety of key strategies such as analysis and evaluation of programmes; security risk assessments for beneficiaries and implementors; a common approach to needs assessment; targeted and monitored interventions to support and encourage research into potentially negative effects of aid; and a commitment to the sharing of information.*"

— "provide only the essential capital assets needed to address the 'agreed to' needs of the beneficiaries so that the international NGOs minimise the risk of fuelling the war in Liberia: *although levels of resources and staff will be left to the discretion of each organisation, sharing of resources and equipment will be encouraged as appropriate. operations will be decentralised to minimise potential losses of equipment and commodities. For example, cross border operations will be encouraged.*"

CAFOD does not normally employ operational staff in emergencies but works through established Catholic institutions, with local NGOs or with other international NGOs (such as the World Food Programme) working in the field of relief or development. Monitoring is, however, undertaken by people or organisations with the right skills and able to form objective judgments about the use and distribution of relief supplies. In the case of Sierra Leone, international NGOs operated from neighbouring Guinea, making quick visits into Sierra Leone when it was safe to do so. In situations of extreme insecurity, when most operational international NGOs are forced to withdraw their expatriate personnel, CAFOD has a moral obligation to support local partners who at some risk to themselves decide that they must remain in post and continue to provide humanitarian assistance. This does not excuse CAFOD from making its own risk assessment but the confidence of its partners that they can continue to provide a service to the affected population is a powerful argument in support of humanitarian assistance. In August 1997 CAFOD made a grant of £60,000 to the Diocese of Kenema for emergency feeding of infants displaced by the fighting. This grant was successfully administered by the Kenema Diocesan Development Office, the only NGO which at that time was able to reach the affected population. This grant was followed in February 1998 by a further grant of £50,000 for war-affected children and mothers. A third grant of £50,000 was made in March 1998 to Caritas Makeni in the northern Sierra Leone, again to provide immediate relief to war-affected civilians.

Assistance to partner agencies at times of extreme need enhances their credibility with the local population and enables them to play a constructive role in subsequent years both in reconstruction and in the more sensitive tasks of peace-making and reconciliation. Conversely failure to stand by the population in such emergencies may undermine the credibility of an agency when it returns and resumes its work. Many UN staff in Sierra Leone felt that UN agencies should have maintained a presence in the country instead of pulling out.

For these reasons it is regrettable that the British government imposed a blanket ban on assistance to Sierra Leone during the AFRC interlude. A more discriminating and focused policy would have increased the availability of basic supplies to the civilian population and supported those NGOs still able to work in the country.

EAST TIMOR

Very soon after the ending of Portuguese rule in East Timor in 1974, the country was occupied by Indonesia. After many years of Portuguese rule, the people of East Timor had their own cultural and religious identity—most of them are Catholics—and spoke indigenous languages or Portuguese as opposed to Bahsa Indonesia used in Indonesia. The East Timorese had hoped that decolonisation could be followed by independence. In the years of conflict during the Indonesian occupation, up to a third of East Timor's indigenous population of 650,000 have been killed. East Timor remains heavily militarised with continuing restrictions on civil liberties. The Catholic Church under the leadership of Bishop Carlos Belo, and protected to some extent by its international connections, became by default the only East Timorese institution which could speak for the East Timorese people and, with severe restrictions, discuss the future of the country from an East Timorese perspective.

CAFOD has supported the role of the Catholic Church with grants for training, capacity-building and development work which enable it to discharge the role which has been thrust upon it. Conscious of the need for better access to information and the need for skills to communicate internationally, CAFOD has given particular attention to developing the media in East Timor. We firmly believe that it is ultimately the development of a free and informed civil society in East Timor which will lead to resolution of the political problems and development of the territory.

CAFOD is a member of the British Coalition for East Timor which has been pressing for greater international awareness of and involvement in human rights issues in East Timor and debates around the political future of the country. CAFOD, together with the other members of the coalition has had good contacts with the Foreign and Commonwealth Office and the Minister of State responsible for Asia, Derek Fatchett MP, has been receptive to approaches from the Coalition. Soon after President Habibie was sworn into office, Mr Fatchett travelled to Indonesia and met the new president and also visited Xanana Gusmao—the gaoled East Timorese Leader—in prison where they held a joint press conference.

The resignation of President Suharto provides an opportunity to reopen discussions about the future of East Timor in a more receptive climate. President Habibie, however, has indicated only that he would be willing to grant East Timor "special status". This falls far short of self-determination which the East Timorese people have argued for and would not change the situation of illegal occupation by Indonesia. CAFOD hopes that HMG, together with our European partners, will continue to seek opportunities to press the issues of self-determination and human rights with the Indonesian government. The introduction of a rigorous Code of Conduct on Arms Sales, one of the early priorities of the Foreign and Commonwealth Office in the British Presidency of the EU, should reinforce the positions advanced in international fora and through direct contact with the Indonesian government.

CAFOD was disappointed that HMG, occupying the European presidency, did not seek approval for its draft resolution at 54th Session of the United Nations Commission on Human Rights held in Geneva in April 1998. The text of the draft resolution did not differ widely from last year's which called for:

(i)   full respect for the human rights and fundamental freedoms of the people of East Timor;

(ii) to ensure the early release of political prisoners and clarify further the circumstances surrounding the violent incident in Dili in November 1991;

(iii) that all trails in East Timor are conducted in accordance with international standards;

(iv) to invite the Special Rapporteur on Torture to visit East Timor; and

(v)   to provide access to East Timor for human rights organisations.

This year, however, at the eleventh hour Indonesia agreed on a Chairman's Statement which reiterated the need for further clarification of the circumstances surrounding the Dili incident of 1991. The Statement also notes that the Government of Indonesia will invite the Working Group on Arbitrary Detention to visit East Timor in advance of the 55th session of the Commission. We hope that this visit will actually take place unlike the visit of the Special Rapporteur on Torture set out in last year's Resolution. The British Government, having played a key role in negotiating this Chair's Statement now has the moral obligation to ensure that it is implemented.

The forthcoming "EU Troika" visit of ambassadors to East Timor—a British initiative—is now imminent. The ambassadors should be aware as they seek to speak to East Timorese people that those who speak out openly could face serious reprisals and that this will limit the range of opinions that will be voiced to them. Their visit will also be accompanied by an element of stage management by the Indonesian authorities. We are heartened, however, by agreement on the part of President Habibie, during his recent meeting with Bishop Belo, to confidence building measures in East Timor including the significant withdrawal of Indonesian military. The Troika should seek ways of ensuring that military withdrawal from the territory can be verified by international observers.

The meeting between Bishop Belo and President Habibie took place on 24 June. On the previous day the two Catholic Bishops of East Timor, Mgr Basilio do Nascimento—Apostolic Administrator of Bacau, and Mgr

Carlos Belo—Apostolic Administrator of Dili, issued a statement (Appendix 2, attached to this memorandum) calling on the Indonesian government to:

— guarantee the right and the freedom of movement and of settlement for East Timorese people within the territory of East Timor. This means the abolition of resettlement areas built along national highways as a counter-insurgency measure;

— to acknowledge and guarantee of the right of expression;

— to reduce the presence of military operational and territorial forces currently deployed in East Timor. The Bishops mention specific counter-insurgency units by name. The reduction of troop levels, the Bishops say, means changing the status of East Timor from a military operational to a "normal" area. President Habibie's offer a withdrawal of Indonesian troops appears at least partially to meet this demand;

— to give freedom of access to East Timor to all international organisations, including Amnesty International and the UN Commission on Human Rights;

— to permit exiles from East Timor to return freely, either to settle permanently or simply to visit;

— to permit (i.e., to remove the ban on) the teaching of the East Timorese language (Tetum) in schools and Portuguese to be taught in senior high schools and in universities.

CAFOD urges HMG to reinforce the Catholic bishops' "suggestions" in direct contacts with the Indonesian authorities and multilaterally through international bodies. It is significant and positive that for the first time for many years a space for genuine dialogue has been opened up between the Indonesian government and civil society in East Timor. Such openings, however, are fragile and need support and reinforcement from the international community if they are to lead to lasting understanding and agreement.

June 1998

APPENDIX 28

Letter to the Clerk of the Committee from Sir James Adams, Control Risks Group Limited, 30 June 1998

We spoke on the telephone on 1 June. You very kindly explained to me the interest of the Foreign Affairs Committee in Indonesia in the context of their general examination of Foreign Policy and Human Rights issues. You were also good enough to say that I might write to you to describe the service which the Control Risks Group (CRG) has been offering to business clients—British and international—operating in Indonesia. I am sorry not to have followed this up before but I have been away for much of the intervening period.

CRG is a British-based international security consultancy with four main areas of activity–*political and security assessment (Control Risks Information Services: CRIS), investigation* (mainly on behalf of corporate clients), *asset protection* and *crisis response*. We have 12 overseas offices and an annual turnover of about £20 million. A majority of the Group's shares are owned by our management and staff. We have no ties to security equipment manufacturers though we work closely with the specialist insurance underwriters at Lloyds. Since our foundation in 1975, we have operated in over 130 countries. We work to the highest ethical standards in strict conformity with the law.

CRIS—who have an in-house staff of some 20 analysts and editors and a large net-work of stringers overseas—provide a daily on-line service, devoted to the security and political risk situation in 118 countries. This is produced for a long list of corporate clients, and for a few governments and government agencies and international organisations. It is supplemented by telephonic advice which is on a round-the-clock basis in crisis situations (e.g., recently in Indonesia). CRIS also provide commissioned reports for such clients and some published material.

In the evolving Indonesian operation, our Australian office deployed experienced consultants over several months to advise our clients in Indonesia on the ground, on how best to protect personnel and other assets. Meanwhile our CRIS Asian desk here in London, aided by their stringer in Indonesia, gave political and security risk advice to numerous corporate headquarters by telephone. On 28 May we gave a presentation in the London Chamber of Commerce on the risk to business from the Indonesian crisis, to about 40 important corporate clients. I enclose as background the text of the presentation given by one of our speakers at that event as well as the text of our on-line service on Indonesia as of 30 June.

Perhaps I might also mention our recent activities in another area of current interest: the role of companies in the field of human rights in general. On 20 April, John Bray, our Principal Research Consultant, gave a presentation on the role of the Internet to the Chatham House conference on "Multinationals and Human Rights". The following day, we organised a "Human Rights Scenario Workshop" at Chatham House, as a follow-up to the main conference. The discussions revolved around a three-part scenario involving an oil company in a fictional country with a questionable human rights record. Some 20 companies, NGOs and diplomatic officials took part. We plan to follow this up with similar exercises—and analysis—both for future conferences and for individual companies.

If you think that any of the above as regards Indonesia, Human Rights or any other aspect of our services is of interest to members of the Committee, we should be happy to go into more detail. If there is any requirement for British companies to give evidence on Indonesia, e.g., on the likely impact of the current crisis on business there, we should also be very happy to contribute. (We supplied a contribution on India to the Trade and Industry Committee in 1996.)

For the sake of completeness, I should mention that in January of this year I took the liberty of writing to your Chairman, Mr Donald Anderson MP, to ask if he would like a briefing on our services. I did not receive a reply to that letter, but perhaps it should have been more properly directed to you.

APPENDIX 29

Memorandum submitted by the Defence Manufacturers Association (DMA)

THE DMA

1. The DMA is a non-profit making Trade Association representing the UK Defence Industry. It has 370 members ranging from the largest (BAe, GEC, GKN, Alvis, Vickers, Vosper Thornycroft) to many small companies including manufacturers, service providers and Defence executive agencies supplying to land, sea and air environments. Through a subsidiary (the Association of Police and Public Security Suppliers) it also represents companies (including Defence contractors) supplying to the Police, Prison Service, Customs and Excise etc. Total membership of both Associations exceeds 450.

THE UK DEFENCE INDUSTRY

2. The UK Defence Industry is a key element of the UK's Defence capability and a major creator of wealth in the economy. It has a long and successful history of providing the equipment required for the UK's Armed Forces. It offers a full product range from complete platforms (aircraft, warships and armoured fighting vehicles), through major sub-systems (communications, radar, propulsion systems, munitions) and support services (repair, spare parts, training, catering), to basic equipment (clothing, footwear, tentage, etc.).

3. The Industry, particularly in the electronics sector, enjoys a world-wide reputation for technical excellence. Consequently, as well as winning major platform orders, many of its contracts are for sub-systems and components. There are few, important Western high technology Defence programmes that do not have some level of UK sub-contractor participation. The UK has also pioneered many recent innovations, including the development of thermal imagers, simulators, and command, control and communications equipment. It is also a world leader in the development of nuclear, biological and chemical *protection* equipment. Much of this technology has dual-use application in the civilian sector.

INDUSTRY STATISTICS

4. The Industry, wholly privately owned, comprises a large number of companies involved partly or wholly in the Defence business and employing some 415,000 people. This represents around 10 per cent of the UK's total industrial manufacturing workforce and Industry accounts for about 11 per cent of the country's industrial manufacturing output. Most of the companies involved are small to medium enterprises but some are amongst Europe's largest. Ten companies were listed in the 1995 list of the "Top 100 World-wide Defence Firms", of which two were in the top 10.

5. Influenced by major cuts in national Defence spending, and the adoption by the previous Government of a policy of meeting its' equipment needs through tough, international, competitive procurement, the Defence Industry has donwnsized and become highly competitive. In the last decade it has completed a major restructuring, with the loss of over *300,000* jobs since 1980 (160,000 of these since 1988). It has also compensated by increasing, significantly, its share of the world export market.

6. Current MoD business to the Industry is about *£8 billion* per annum, with a further £1 billion given to overseas competitors.

7. Although Defence spending has reduced significantly as a proportion of GDP (down from 5.1 per cent to 3.0 per cent in 10 years), the importance of the sector for the Government cannot be overstated. The Government is its' only domestic customer. With the exception of roads, Defence procurement expenditure (at £9 billion per annum) is the only area of major capital spending left to Government large enough to impact upon the UK economy for better or worse.

EXPORTS

8.   The present Government has pledged to maintain a strong and capable Defence Industry. Defence exports are crucial to this undertaking. Defence Exports:

(a)   Reduce the cost of equipment procured for our own Armed Forces by amortising development costs across increased production quantities. The MoD also exacts a commercial exploitation levy on exports of equipment developed at the UK taxpayer's expense.

(b)   Contribute significantly to the UK balance of trade.

(c)   Account for almost 40 per cent of Defence Industry business and are, therefore, now critical to its survival, and are likely to be increasingly so in the future.

(d)   Provide employment for over 140,000 people in the UK. The remaining 275,000 Defence industry jobs not dependent directly on exports would be at risk were exports to be seriously curtailed.

(e)   Are an important instrument of Foreign policy for the Government in supporting allies, influencing other nations, helping to maintain regional stability etc.

(f)   Help to improve the prospects of achieving non-defence export sales to recipient countries

9.   The UK Government, mainly through the Defence Export Services Organisation (DESO), provides strong support for exports by identifying target markets, supporting the marketing effort, establishing essential Government to Government links and liaising with senior civil and military representatives of foreign nations' Defence establishments. DESO was established 25 years ago by Denis Healey under a previous Labour Government. The DTI also provides support, in a similar way to that provided for non-defence exports, by means of subsidies to inward and outward trade delegations and the Trade Fairs Support Scheme. They also identify priority target markets for Defence exports, interestingly not always the same as those identified by the DESO.

10.   Industry's general position, therefore, is that Defence exporting is legitimate and important business, strongly encouraged by Government and complementary to its highest priority role of supplying equipment to the UK Armed Forces. It is a national, strategic asset. That said, it fully recognises the need for control of Defence exports by Government to ensure they comply with current foreign and Defence policy aspirations, including the protection of human rights. It equally recognises that the decision to allow or refuse exports is sometimes a difficult one, needing the balance of complex factors such as treaty obligations, local external threats, regional stability, the importance of influence, the likelihood of conflict between the UK and the state concerned, relationships with third party states, intelligence advice, the nature of the recipient states Government, economic considerations, etc.

11.   Industry considers that it is not sufficiently well informed or qualified to make judgments on all these issues and whether particular exports would or would not serve the UK national interest. It, therefore, accepts the need for a system of licensing of Defence exports, whilst having reservations about the efficiency, effectiveness and fairness of the current system.

12.   Defence exports are controlled under legislation enacted in 1939 to prevent the sale of arms to Nazi Germany. Four departments of State are involved in the processing of licences. Initial application is made to the DTI, the responsible Department. Reference is then made by the DTI, at their discretion, to the FCO, MOD and the DFID. Over 1,000 licenses a month are submitted by industry and take many weeks, often months, to process. Very few are actually refused, reflecting Industry's highly responsible adherence to the issued guidelines by not making controversial applications. However, much business is lost to our competitors as a result of the uncertainties and delays inherent in the system. This has been severely exacerbated in the last year by delays consequent upon the Government's review of ethical guidelines.

13.   It is often difficult for companies to track progress on their applications. Some officials are secretive and difficult to approach, especially in the FCO, and there is sometime ignorance amongst them about the nature of the equipment involved and its intended role. Recent examples of delays or refusals include the sale of spares for British built flail vehicles used by the Canadians for *clearing* mines in Bosnia and the sale of helmets for use by UN Observers in Afghanistan. It is particularly frustrating that in these, and other cases, business is sometimes lost to competitors (including from EU countries) who do not have to seek a licence at all because their governments do not categorise such equipment as military.

14.   Industry's greatest concern in the export market is its competitiveness. Competition is tough and winning business requires protracted effort and investment. It is frustrating, after being encouraged by Government to secure a sale, to lose a contract to competitors through licence refusal or, worse, bureaucratic delay. Nations, even those ruled by questionable regimes, *will* secure Defence equipment elsewhere if we refuse to sell. Further, it is not merely a matter of the loss of individual contracts. A Defence order normally leads to long term involvement in training, spares support and maintenance. Even if regimes change, the Navies, Armies and Air Forces of a country are committed to the systems they have procured. A good example of this is perhaps that of Spain. In the mid 1960s the UK Government refused to sell naval ships to Franco. Spain went elsewhere and

bought what it needed then, and ever since, from the USA and France. Today, many years after Spain achieved democracy, there is little UK equipment in the Spanish naval inventory.

15. Industry notes the failure of even *international* embargoes to control the spread of arms. The consequence of the embargo on apartheid South Africa was for that country to develop its own, indigenous, Defence industry. It is particularly ironic that democratic South Africa, under Nelson Mandela, is now one of our most effective competitors in the world market.

16. Finally it is worth repeating that, above all, Industry seeks fairness, clarity and efficiency in the export licensing process. It believes new, primary legislation is needed, and welcomes the publication of the 1 July 1998 White Paper on Strategic Export Controls upon which it will be commenting, in detail, to the DTI in due course.

Afternote

It is appropriate, because of its topicality, to comment on the Sandline affair. Sandline are not members of the DMA and Industry notes that had Sandline, or their advisors, chosen to recommend *British* equipment a licence would have had to be applied for and, almost certainly, been refused!

July 1998

APPENDIX 30

Supplementary Memorandum by the Foreign and Commonwealth Office

1. This Memorandum responds to the Committee's request for further information contained in the Clerk of the Committee's letter of 7 October 1998. It comprises six sections corresponding to the questions asked in the letter and five annexes.

    (i) Human Rights Instruments.

    (ii) Country Human Rights Strategies.

    (iii) NGO Reports.

    (iv) Annual Report on Strategic Export Controls.

    (v) Human Rights Policy on China and Burma.

    (vi) EU and Human Rights.

Annex A   United Kingdom Reservations to the Six Core United Nations Human Rights Instruments.

Annex B   The Status of Ratification of the Six Core UN Human Rights Instruments at 15 October 1998.

Annex C   United Nations' List of Human Rights Instruments.

Annex D   List of International Labour Organisation Conventions.

Annex E   Foreign Secretary's speech on Human Rights, 16 October 1998 [*not printed*].

(i) HUMAN RIGHTS INSTRUMENTS

United Nations

2. There are six core UN human rights treaties: the International Covenant on Civil and Political Rights (ICCPR); the International Covenant on Economic, Social and Cultural Rights (ICESCR); the Convention on the Elimination of all forms of Discrimination Against Women (CEDAW); the Convention on the Rights of the Child (CRC); the Convention on the Elimination of Racial Discrimination (CERD), and the Convention Against Torture and Other Cruel, Inhuman or Degrading Torture or Punishment (CAT).

3. The United Kingdom is a state party to all six of these instruments. A list of UK reservations and declarations is at Annex A.

4. The status of ratification of the six core UN human rights instruments at 15 October is at Annex B.

5. The United Nations' List of Human Rights Instruments (December 1997) is at Annex C.

Council of Europe

6.   The six major Council of Europe human rights instruments are the Convention for the Protection of Human Rights and Fundamental Freedoms (ECHR); the European Convention for the Prevention of Torture (ECPT); the European Social Charter; the European Social Charter (Revised); the European Charter for Regional or Minority Languages, and the Framework Convention for the Protection of National Minorities.

7.   The UK has ratified the above instruments with the exception of:

EUROPEAN SOCIAL CHARTER (REVISED)

8.   The European Social Charter (Revised) was opened for signature in 1996. It takes account of developments in labour law and social policies, updating the 1961 European Social Charter, to which the UK is party.

9.   The Revised Charter is selective, and states parties choose which articles to ratify, subject to the requirement to ratify a minimum number on which parties submit to the supervisory mechanisms foreseen in the Charter.

10.   The Revised Charter has not yet entered into force. The Charter requires three ratifications for entry into force. To date, only Sweden has ratified.

11.   The UK has signed the Revised Social Charter, and is actively considering which articles it might ratify. The UK is progressing steadily towards ratification.

EUROPEAN CHARTER ON REGIONAL OR MINORITY LANGUAGES

12.   On 4 June 1998 Mr Fatchett, Minister of State, informed the House that the Government intended to sign the Council of Europe Charter for Regional or Minority Languages, which entered into force on 1 March 1998.

13.   Mr Fatchett stated that the Government further intended to specify the Scots language under the general provisions of Part II of the Charter and Welsh, Irish and Gaelic in Scotland under Part III of the Charter, in addition to considering which, if any, other languages should be bound by the general principles in Part II.

14.   Specification under Part III of the Charter requires a minimum of 35 paragraphs or sub-paragraphs to be applied to a language. The Scottish, Welsh and Northern Ireland Offices are in the process of identifying these paragraphs. Once identified, the relevant paragraphs for each language would be listed in a (FCO) Command paper and laid before both Houses (Ponsonby Procedure) prior to UK signature in Strasbourg. It is hoped to complete this exercise before the end of 1998.

15.   The UK's position on the ECHR Protocols is set out below.

International Labour Organisation

16.   There are a total of 181 ILO Conventions, of which the UK has ratified 65. A full list of the Conventions is at Annex D. The Conventions that the UK *has* ratified are highlighted (in bold type).

17.   Seven of the Conventions are regarded as "core labour standards". They are:

Convention 29 (1930): Forced Labour

Convention 87 (1948): Freedom of Association and Protection and the Right to Organise

Convention 98 (1949): The Right to Organise and Collective Bargaining

Convention 100 (1951): Equal Remuneration

Convention 105 (1957): Abolition of Forced Labour

Convention 111 (1958): Discrimination (Employment and Occupation)

Convention 138 (1973): Minimum Age

18.   The UK has ratified five of the seven key Conventions. We have not yet ratified Convention 111 (Discrimination—Employment and Occupation) and Convention 138 (Minimum Age), but the DfEE's review of the UK's position in respect of both Conventions is at an advanced stage. At the International Labour Conference in Geneva in June 1998 Mr Smith, Minister for Employment, announced, "that the UK is taking active steps towards the ratification of Convention 138 on the minimum age for admission to employment". The Government is currently examining all the issues closely in order to establish the most appropriate way forward towards ratification.

Review of UK Accession to Human Rights Instruments

19.   The Government announced on 3 July 1997 that it would review the UK's commitments under international human rights treaties. This is a wide-ranging review which is being carried out across several departments. It is now nearing completion and the Government hopes to announce the outcome before the end of the year.

20.   The review covers:

European Convention on Human Rights (ECHR):

—   whether to ratify the substantive Additional Protocols (4,6,7);

—   to examine whether the reservations and derogation to the ECHR are still valid.

International Covenant on Civil and Political Rights (ICCPR).

—   whether to ratify the Optional Protocols: on the right of individual petition and the abolition of the death penalty;

—   to examine whether the reservations and derogation are still valid.

UN Convention Against Torture and Other Cruel, Inhuman or Degrading Treatment or Punishment (CAT):

—   whether to make a declaration under Article 22 on the right of individual petition.

International Convention on the Elimination of All Forms of Racial Discrimination (CERD):

—   whether to make a declaration under Article 14 on the right of individual petition;

—   to examine whether the reservations are still valid.

The review also covers UK reservations to the Convention on the Rights of the Child, the Convention on the Elimination of all Forms of Discrimination Against Women, and the International Covenant on Economic, Social and Cultural Rights.

ECHR PROTOCOLS

21.   The White Paper "Rights Brought Home" (CM 3782) set out the position in relation to the Protocols to the ECHR. The Government is still looking at Protocol 4, but there is some progress on Protocols 6 and 7. On Protocol 6, relating to the death penalty, the House of Commons voted to add this to the Human Rights Bill and the Home Secretary has undertaken to take steps to ratify it. The Government will be introducing some technical amendments to the Bill when it comes before the House again to enable ratification to take place. The FAC will also be aware of the announcement by the Secretary of State for Defence that, in Armed Forces legislation, the use of the death penalty will be abolished in peacetime and wartime, so the Protocol will be ratified without any savings for wartime use.

22.   On Protocol 7, the White paper said that the Government would legislate to remove the obstacles to ratification when a suitable opportunity arose. The Government hopes that this will be in the next session, subject to other demands on the Parliamentary timetable.

Promotion of Human Rights Standards Overseas

23.   The Government takes every appropriate opportunity to encourage all States to accede to the six core UN human rights instruments. The Foreign Secretary announced on 16 October a specific UK lobbying campaign in respect of the UN Convention Against Torture, the least ratified of the core treaties. The text of the Foreign Secretary's speech, which includes details of other human rights initiatives, is at Annex E.

24.   States which have acceded to the core Treaties have an obligation to submit reports to UN expert committees which monitor compliance with each treaty. States' reports and the UN committees' findings and recommendations are made public. The UK regularly follows examinations of States by the UN Committees in Geneva and New York. This process can provide further information on the human rights situation in individual countries and possible areas for technical co-operation. The UK and EU may also refer to a country's specific international obligations under the core UN Treaties when carrying out individual demarches.

25.   Since 1 May 1997, three further countries have ratified ICCPR (Greece, Honduras, Monaco); two have ratified ICESCR (Monaco, Turkmenistan); two have ratified CEDAW (Burma, Turkmenistan); one has ratified CRC (Cook Islands); one has ratified CERD (Saudi Arabia), and two have ratified CAT (Krygyzstan, Saudi Arabia).

26.   In addition, three further countries have ratified the first Optional Protocol of ICCPR (Greece, Sri Lanka, Turkmenistan), and four have ratified the Second Optional Protocol (Colombia, Costa Rica, Greece, Nepal).

(ii)   HUMAN RIGHTS COUNTRY STRATEGIES

27.   In May 1997, guidance to all diplomatic posts highlighted the need for human rights to be considered a priority activity. Subsequently, certain posts, in conjunction with geographical departments, drew up individual papers to highlight particular problems and scope for UK action. Strategies were proposed for countries where human rights were generally perceived to be a significant issue, and where the UK was deemed to have instruments available to it to seek to improve the position, where possible, on the basis of partnership and co-operation.

28.   A list of countries for which strategies have so far been prepared is submitted to the Committee separately. The list does not include countries where the UK has no diplomatic representation and where scope for action may be limited to multilateral bodies in present circumstances. Strategies were also not prepared for some countries where human rights issues were already under regular consideration by Ministers.

(iii)   NGO REPORTS

29.   The Committee asked for the FCO's observations on three recent publications:

Amnesty International: "Signing up for Human Rights, the UK and International Standards". While the FCO made no specific comment in response to this report, the UK's position is set out in the April 1998 FCO/DFID Annual Report on Human Rights;

Amnesty International: "Audit of UK Foreign and Asylum Policy". Mr Lloyd, Minister of State, issued the following statement on 23 September 1998: "The Amnesty International report recognised that the Government's human rights policy represented "an important step forward from the position of previous governments and has already resulted in a series of measures which may improve human rights around the world. This is the central and welcome message of the report." He added that Government departments had worked closely and successfully together on a range of human rights initiatives. The UK-inspired EU Code of Conduct on Arms Exports was a good example;

Saferworld: "Policy and Practice, UK Arms Exports 1 May 1997—10 May 1998". The FCO issued a statement on the report on 24 June 1998:

> "Under the new criteria announced by the Government in July 1987, every application to export arms is considered on a case-by-case basis against the same tough set of tests. In particular, where there is a clearly identifiable risk of the equipment being used for internal repression, applications are refused. Since the new criteria were adopted, a number of licences have been refused which would have been approved under the previous guidelines. Contrary to suggestions in the press, no licences have been granted in breach of any international arms embargoes.

> It was never the Government's intention to create new national arms embargoes against individual destinations, but rather to ensure that every application should be individually scrutinised against the same tough criteria. The Government believes that this is the most responsible approach to arms export licensing.

> The Government recognises that the categories in the Military List are broad and that wrong conclusions can be drawn about the details of licences which have been granted. This is why it is committed to publishing an open and transparent Annual Report on Strategic Export Controls to allow public scrutiny of the application of its export licensing policy. The report will make clear what military equipment has been licensed for export on a country by country basis".

(iv)   ANNUAL REPORT ON STRATEGIC EXPORT CONTROLS

30.   This report will be published during the current Parliamentary session.

(v)   HUMAN RIGHTS POLICY ON CHINA AND BURMA

31.   The Committee asked how the Government's human rights policy had been reflected in its positions on China and Burma.

32.   We believe that it is important to address our human rights concerns in the way most likely to bring about results. This will not be the same in each case. On China, we believe that a policy of dialogue on human rights, supported by a programme of practical cooperation, is more likely to bring about positive developments than confrontation and hectoring.

33.   Following the events of Tiananmen Square in 1989, the previous government annually supported a draft resolution on China's human rights performance at the Commission on Human Rights (CHR). None of these resolutions was passed. (All but one failed even to reach a vote, being blocked by a Chinese no-action motion).

In 1997, the EU consensus on a draft resolution collapsed, but the UK supported a draft resolution tabled nationally by Denmark. That too failed.

34.   Since the election of this Government, we have established a wide-ranging human rights dialogue with China. (The EU has also been able to resume the EU/China human rights dialogue which had been suspended by China following previous EU resolutions). Through these broad and unconditional dialogues we have been pursuing the same objectives as previous CHR resolutions.

35.   These dialogues are underpinned by programmes of practical assistance which cover civil and political as well as economic and social rights. These should have a real impact on developments on the ground affecting ordinary Chinese people. We are intensifying our cooperation in such areas as legal reform.

36.   This dialogue-based policy is beginning to produce results. The Chinese have taken several positive steps e.g., signature of the ICESCR and ICCPR and a visit to China and Tibet by the UN High Commissioner for Human Rights in September 1998. These steps will help to engage China more fully with the UN's human rights machinery.

37.   In view of China's willingness to address our human rights concerns in a frank and constructive way, and the positive steps taken by them, the UK agreed with EU partners not to table or co-sponsor a resolution on China at the CHR in April 1998. Instead we will encourage further positive steps from China through dialogue and co-operation.

38.   But, as the Prime Minister demonstrated during his recent visit to China, we will continue to voice our concerns at every opportunity. During his visit, he raised human rights, including the cases of individuals and the situation in Tibet, with President Jiang Zemin and Premier Zhu Rongji. Human rights featured prominently in the Prime Minister's speech to the British Chamber of Commerce in China and he intervened personally in the case of Xu Wenli who was detained on 7 October and then released.

39.   In the case of Burma, the political and human rights situation remains appalling. In the past 16 months the Government's policy on Burma has strengthened. In June 1997, Mr Fatchett, Minister of State, announced that the Government was suspending financial support to companies for trade missions to Burma and trade promotion activities within Burma: we no longer encourage trade with or investment in Burma. In July this year, Mr Fatchett drew attention to the view of Burmese democracy leaders that it was inappropriate for tourists to visit Burma at present: he wrote to tour operator associations informing them and published a copy of his letter on the Foreign and Commonwealth Office website. The British Government has taken these measures on a national basis, but has also encouraged other EU member states to take similar national measures.

40.   The EU has had a Common Position on Burma since 1996, which includes a full-scale arms embargo; visa restrictions on members of the regime; suspension of defence links; ban on non-humanitarian aid; and a ban on high-level bilateral visits. The Government secured the renewal of this Common Position under its Presidency. The Common Position is due for renewal again by the end of October; the Government is pressing partners to do so, and to strengthen it by expanding the visa restrictions to include transit visas. Decisions will be taken at the 26 October General Affairs Council.

41.   The UK has also worked to secure strong resolutions in the United Nations General Assembly and Commission on Human Rights condemning human rights violations in Burma. The tough April 1998 UN Commission on Human Rights resolution was drafted by the UK acting as EU Presidency.

42.   The Government believes that further measures should be targeted against the Burmese authorities. It also believes that there is a case for providing assistance, consistent with the Common Position, to help disadvantaged communities in Burma directly. The Government also supports the Burma Border Consortium (BBC) which helps refugees on the Thai-Burma border (about £270,000 was allocated to the BBC in 1997–98).

(vi)   EU AND HUMAN RIGHTS

43.   The EU regularly considers the human rights situation in countries throughout the world in the relevant CFSP geographical working groups and the Human Rights Working Group. Where appropriate, the CFSP working groups may ask EU Heads of Mission to prepare reports on specific issues in individual countries. While these are mostly for internal use only, the EU also publishes the texts of public statements on human rights. Examples in 1998 include EU declarations on Nigeria, the Democratic Republic of Congo and Mexico; a declaration on the abolition of the death penalty in Estonia, and the EU's Common Position on Afghanistan.

20 October 1998

ANNEX A

United Kingdom Reservations to the Six Core United Nations Human Rights Instruments

(i)   The International Covenant on Civil and Political Rights (ICCPR).

(ii) The International Covenant on Economic Social and Cultural Rights (ICESCR).

(iii) The Convention on the Elimination of all forms of Discrimination Against Women (CEDAW).

(iv) The convention on the Rights of the Child (CRC).

(v)   The convention on the Elimination of Racial Discrimination (CERD).

(vi) The Convention Against Torture (CAT).

DECLARATIONS AND RESERVATIONS MADE BY THE UNITED KINGDOM IN RESPECT OF:

THE INTERNATIONAL COVENANT OF CIVIL AND POLITICAL RIGHTS (ICCPR)

Upon signature:

"First, the Government of the United Kingdom declare their understanding that, by virtue of Article 103 of the Charter of the United Nations, in the event of any conflict between their obligations under Article 1 of the Covenant and their obligations under the Charter (in particular, under Articles 1, 2 and 73 thereof) their obligations under the Charter shall prevail.

"Secondly, the Government of the United Kingdom declare that:

"(a) In relation to Article 14 of the Covenant, they must reserve the right not to apply, or not to apply in full, the guarantee of free legal assistance contained in sub-paragraph (d) of paragraph 3 in so far as the shortage of legal practitioners and other considerations render the application of this guarantee in British Honduras, Fiji and St Helena impossible.

"(b) In relation to Article 23 of the Covenant, they must reserve the right not to apply the first sentence of paragraph 4 in so far as it concerns any inequality which may arise from the operation of the law of domicile.

"(c) In relation to Article 25 of the Covenant, they must reserve the right not to apply:

"(i)   Sub-paragraph (b) in so far as it may require the establishment of an elected legislature in Hong Kong and the introduction of equal suffrage, as between different electoral rolls, for elections in Fiji; and

"(ii) Sub-paragraph (c) in so far as it applies to jury service in the Isle of Man and to the employment of married women in the Civil Service of Northern Ireland, Fiji, and Hong Kong.

"Lastly, the Government of the United Kingdom declare that the provisions of the Covenant shall not apply to Southern Rhodesia unless and until they inform the Secretary-General of the United Nations that they are in a position to ensure that the obligations imposed by the Covenant in respect of that territory can be fully implemented."

Upon ratification

"Firstly the Government of the United Kingdom maintain their declaration in respect of Article 1 made at the time of signature of the Covenant.

"The Government of the United Kingdom reserve the right to apply to members of and persons serving with the armed forces of the Crown and to persons lawfully detained in penal establishments of whatever character such laws and procedures as they may from time to time deem to be necessary for the preservation of service and custodial discipline and their acceptance of the provisions of the Covenant is subject to such restrictions as may for these purposes from time to time be authorised by law.

"Where at any time there is a lack of suitable prison facilities or where the mixing of adults and juveniles is deemed to be mutually beneficial, the Government of the United Kingdom reserve the right not to apply article 10(2)(b) and 10(3), so far as those provisions require juveniles who are detained to be accommodated separately from adults, and not to apply article 10(2)(a) in Gibraltar. Montserrat and the Turks and Caicos Islands in so far as it requires segregation of accused and convicted persons.

"The Government of the United Kingdom reserve the right not to apply article 11 in Jersey.

"The Government of the United Kingdom reserve the right to interpret the provision of article 12(1) relating to the territory of a State as applying separately to each of the territories comprising the United Kingdom and its dependencies.

"The Government of the United Kingdom reserve the right to continue to apply such immigration legislation governing entry into, stay in and departure from the United Kingdom as they may deem necessary from time to time and, accordingly, their acceptance of article 12(4) and of the other provisions of the Covenant is subject to the provisions of any such legislation as regards persons not at the time having the right under the law of the United Kingdom to enter and remain in the United Kingdom. The United Kingdom also reserves a similar right in regard to each of its dependent territories.

"The Government of the United Kingdom reserve the right not to apply article 13 in Hong Kong in so far as it confers a right of review of a decision to deport an alien and a right to be represented for this purpose before the competent authority.

"The Government of the United Kingdom reserve the right not to apply or not to apply in full the guarantee of free legal assistance in sub-paragraph (d) of paragraph 3 of article 14 in so far as the shortage of legal practitioners renders the application of this guarantee impossible in the British Virgin Islands, the Cayman Islands, the Falkland Islands, the Gilbert Islands, the Pitcairn Islands Group, St. Helena and Dependencies and Tuvalu.

"The Government of the United Kingdom interpret article 20 consistently with the rights conferred by articles 19 and 21 of the Covenant and having legislated in matters of practical concern in the interests of public order (ordre public) reserve the right not to introduce any further legislation. The United Kingdom also reserve a similar right in regard to each of its dependent territories.

"The Government of the United Kingdom reserve the right to postpone the application of paragraph 3 of Article 23 in regard to a small number of customary marriages in the Solomon Islands.

"The Government of the United Kingdom reserve the right to enact such nationality legislation as they may deem necessary from time to time to reserve the acquisition and possession of citizenship under such legislation to those having sufficient connection with the United Kingdom or any of its dependent territories and accordingly their acceptance of Article 24(3) and of the other provisions of the Covenant is subject to the provisions of any such legislation.

"The Government of the United Kingdom reserve the right not to apply sub-paragraph (b) of Article 25 in so far as it may require the establishment of an elected Executive or Legislative Council in Hong Kong [. . .].

"Lastly, the Government of the United Kingdom declare that the provisions of the Covenant shall not apply to Southern Rhodesia unless and until they inform the Secretary-General of the United Nations that they are in a position to ensure that the obligation imposed by the Covenant in respect of that territory can be fully implemented.

DECLARATIONS AND RESERVATIONS MADE BY THE UNITED KINGDOM IN RESPECT OF:

THE INTERNATIONAL COVENANT ON ECONOMIC, SOCIAL AND CULTURAL RIGHTS (ICESCR)

Upon signature:

"First, the Government of the United Kingdom declare their understanding that, by virtue of Article 103 of the Charter of the United Nations, in the event of any conflict between their obligations under Article 1 of the Covenant and their obligations under the Charter (in particular, under Articles 1, 2 and 73 thereof) their obligations under the Charter shall prevail.

"Secondly, the Government of the United Kingdom declare that they must reserve the right to postpone the application of sub-paragraph (a) (i) of Article 7 of the Covenant in so far as it concerns the provision of equal pay to men and women for equal work, since, while they fully accept this principle and are pledged to work towards its complete application at the earliest possible time, the problems of implementation are such that complete application cannot be guaranteed at present.

"Thirdly, the Government of the United Kingdom declare that, in relation to Article 8 of the Covenant, they must reserve the right not to apply sub-paragraph (b) of paragraph 1 in Hong Kong, in so far as it may involve the right of trade unions not engaged in the same trade or industry to establish federations or confederations.

"Lastly, the Government of the United Kingdom declare that the provisions of the Covenant shall not apply to Southern Rhodesia unless and until they inform the Secretary-General of the United Nations that they are in a position to ensure that the obligations imposed by the Covenant in respect of that territory can be fully implemented."

Upon ratification:

"Firstly, the government of the United Kingdom maintain their declaration in respect of Article 1 made at the time of signature of the Covenant.

"The Government of the United Kingdom declare that for the purposes of Article 2(3) the British Virgin Islands, the Cayman Islands, the Gilbert Islands, the Pitcairn Islands Group, St Helena and Dependencies, the Turks and Caicos Islands and Tuvalu are developing countries.

"The Government of the United Kingdom reserve the right to interpret Article 6 as not precluding the imposition of restrictions, based on place of birth or residence qualification, on the taking of employment in any particular region or territory for the purpose of safeguarding the employment opportunities of workers in that region or territory.

"The Government of the United Kingdom reserve the right to postpone the application of sub-paragraph (i) of paragraph (a) of Article 7, in so far as it concerns the provision of equal pay to men and women for equal work in the private sector in Jersey, Guernsey, the Isle of Man, Bermuda, Hong Kong and the Solomon Islands.

"The Government of the United Kingdom reserve the right not to apply sub-paragraph 1(b) of article 8 in Hong Kong.

"The Government of the United Kingdom while recognising the right of everyone to social security in accordance with Article 9 reserve the right to postpone implementation of the right in the Cayman Islands and the Falkland Islands because of shortage of resources in these territories.

"The Government of the United Kingdom reserve the right to postpone the application of paragraph 1 of article 10 in regard to a small number of customary marriages in the Solomon Islands and the application of paragraph 2 of article 10 in so far as it concerns paid maternity leave in Bermuda and the Falkland Islands.

"The Government of the United Kingdom maintain the right to postpone the application of sub-paragraph (a) of paragraph 2 of Article 13, and article 14, in so far as they require compulsory primary education, in the Gilbert Islands, the Solomon Islands and Tuvalu.

"Lastly the Government of the United Kingdom declare that the provisions of the Covenant shall not apply to Southern Rhodesia unless and until they inform the Secretary-General of the United Nations that they are in a position to ensure that the obligations imposed by the Covenant in respect of that territory can be fully implemented.

DECLARATIONS AND RESERVATIONS MADE BY THE UNITED KINGDOM IN RESPECT OF:

THE CONVENTION ON THE ELIMINATION OF ALL FORMS OF DISCRIMINATION AGAINST WOMEN (CEDAW)

Upon signature:

"The Government of the United Kingdom of Great Britain and Northern Ireland declare that it is their intention to make certain reservations and declarations upon ratification of the Convention.

Upon ratification:

"A.   On behalf of the United Kingdom of Great Britain and Northern Ireland:"

"(a)   The United Kingdom understands the main purpose of the Convention, in the light of the definition contained in Article 1, to be the reduction, in accordance with its terms, of discrimination against women, and does not therefore regard the Convention as imposing any requirement to repeal or modify any existing laws, regulations, customs or practices which provide for women to be treated more favourably then men, whether temporarily or in the longer term; the United Kingdom's undertakings under Article 4, paragraph 1, and other provisions of the Convention are to be construed accordingly.

"(c)   In the light of the definition contained in Article 1, the United Kingdom's ratification is subject to the understanding that none of its obligations under the Convention shall be treated as extending to the succession to, or possession and enjoyment of, the Throne, the peerage, titles of honour, social precedence or armorial bearings, or as extending to the affairs of religious denominations or orders or to the admission into or service in the Armed Forces of the Crown.

"(d)   The United Kingdom reserves the right to continue to apply such immigration legislation governing entry into, stay in, and departure from, the United Kingdom as it may deem necessary from time to time and, accordingly, its acceptance of Article 15(4) and of the other provisions of the Convention is subject to the provisions of any such legislation as regards persons not at the time having the right under the law of the United Kingdom to enter and remain in the United Kingdom.

"Article 9

The British Nationality Act 1981, which was brought into force with effect from January 1983, is based on principles which do not allow of any discrimination against women within the meaning of Article 1 as regards acquisition, change or retention of their nationality or as regards the nationality of their children. The United Kingdom's acceptance of Article 9 shall not, however, be taken to invalidate the continuation of certain temporary or transitional provisions which will continue in force beyond that date.

"Article 11

"The United Kingdom reserves the right to apply all United Kingdom legislation and the rules of pension schemes affecting retirement pensions, survivors' benefits and other benefits in relation to death or retirement (including retirement on grounds of redundancy), whether or not derived from a Social Security scheme.

"This reservation will apply equally to any future legislation which may modify or replace such legislation, or the rules of pension schemes, on the understanding that the terms of such legislation will be compatible with the United Kingdom's obligations under the Convention.

"The United Kingdom reserves the right to apply the following provisions of United Kingdom legislation concerning the benefits specified:

    (b)   increases of benefits for adult dependants under section 44 to 47, 49 and 66 of the Social Security Act 1975 and under sections 44 to 47, 49 and 66 of the Social Security (Northern Ireland) Act 1975;

The United Kingdom reserves the right to apply any non-discriminatory requirement for a qualifying period of employment or insurance for the application of the provisions contained in Article 11 (2).

"Article 15

"In relation to Article 15, paragraph 3, the United Kingdom understands the intention of this provision to be that only those terms or elements of a contract or other private instrument which are discriminatory in the sense described are to be deemed null and void, but not necessarily the contract or instrument as a whole.

"Article 16

As regards sub-paragraph 1 (f) of Article 16, the United Kingdom does not regard the reference to the paramountcy of the interests of the children as being directly relevant to the elimination of discrimination against women, and declares in this connection that the legislation of the United Kingdom regulating adoption, while giving a principal position to the promotion of the children's welfare, does not give to the child's interests the same paramount place as in issues concerning custody over children.

"B.   On behalf of the Isle of Man, the British Virgin Islands, the Falkland Islands, South Georgia and the South Sandwich Islands, and the Turks and Caicos Islands:

[Same reservations as the one made on behalf of the United Kingdom under paragraphs A (a), (c), and (d) except that in the case of (d) it applies to the territories and their laws).]

Article 1

[Same reservation as the one made in respect of the United Kingdom except with regard to the absence of a reference to United Kingdom legislation.]

Article 2

[Same reservation as the one made in respect of the United Kingdom except that reference is made to the laws of the territories, and not the laws of the United Kingdom.]

Article 9

[Same reservation as the one made in respect of the United Kingdom.]

Article 11

[Same reservation as those made in respect of the United Kingdom except that a reference is made to the laws of the territories, and not to the laws of the United Kingdom.]

"Also, as far as the territories are concerned, the specific benefits listed and which may be applied under the provisions of these territories' legislation are as follows:

    (a)   social security benefits for persons engaged in caring for a severely disabled person;

    (b)   increases of benefit for adult dependants;

    (c)   retirement pensions and survivors' benefits;

    (d)   family income supplements.

"This reservation will apply equally to any future legislation which may modify or replace any of the provisions specified in sub-paragraphs (a) to (d) above, on the understanding that the terms of such legislation will be compatible with the United Kingdom's obligations under the Convention.

"The United Kingdom reserves the right to apply any non-discriminatory requirement for a qualifying period of employment or insurance for the application of the provisions contained in Article 11 (2)."

Article 13, 15 and 16

[Same reservations as those made on behalf of the United Kingdom.]

DECLARATIONS AND RESERVATIONS MADE BY THE UNITED KINGDOM IN RESPECT OF:

THE CONVENTION ON THE RIGHTS OF THE CHILD (CRC)

Upon signature:

"The United Kingdom reserves the right to formulate, upon ratifying the Convention, any reservations or interpretative declarations which it might consider necessary."

Upon ratification:

Declarations:

"(a)   The United Kingdom interprets the Convention as applicable only following a live birth.

"(b)   The United Kingdom interprets the references in the Convention to 'parents' to mean only those persons who, as a matter of national law, are treated as parents. This includes cases where the law regards a child as having only one parent, for example where a child has been adopted by one person only and in certain cases where a child is conceived other than as a result of sexual intercourse by the woman who gives birth to it and she is treated as the only parent.

Reservations:

"(c)   The United Kingdom reserves the right to apply such legislation, in so far as it relates to the entry into, stay in and departure from the United Kingdom of those who do not have the right under the law of the United Kingdom to enter and remain in the United Kingdom, and to the acquisition and possession of citizenship, as it may deem necessary from time to time.

"(d)   Employment legislation in the United Kingdom does not treat persons under 18, but over the school-leaving age as children, but as 'young people'. Accordingly the United Kingdom reserves the right to continue to apply article 32 subject to such employment legislation.

"(e)   Where at any time there is a lack of suitable accommodation or adequate facilities for a particular individual in any institution in which young offenders are detained, or where the mixing of adults and children is deemed to be mutually beneficial, the United Kingdom reserves the right not to apply article 37(c) in so far as those provisions require children who are detained to be accommodated separately from adults.

Declaration:

"The United Kingdom reserves the right to extend the Convention at a later date to any territory for whose international relations the Government of the United Kingdom is responsible."

7 September 1994

Declarations:

"The United Kingdom refers to the reservations and declarations (a), (b) and (c) which accompanied its instrument of ratification and makes a similar reservation and declarations in respect to each of its dependent territories.

The United Kingdom, in respect of each of its dependent territories except Hong Kong and Pitcairn, reserves the right to apply article 32 subject to the laws of those territories which treat certain persons under 18 not as children but as 'young people'. In respect of Hong Kong, the United Kingdom reserves the right not to apply article 32 (b) in so far as it might require regulation of the hours of employment of young persons who have attained the age of fifteen years in respect of work in non-industrial establishments.

Where at any time there is a lack of suitable detention facilities or where the mixing of adults and children is deemed to be mutually beneficial, the United Kingdom, in respect of each of its dependent territories, reserves the right not to apply article 37(c) in so far as those provisions require children who are detained to be accommodated separately from adults.

The United Kingdom, in respect of Hong Kong and the Cayman Islands, will seek to apply the Convention to the fullest extent to children seeking asylum in those territories except in so far as conditions and resources make full implementation impracticable. In particular, in relation to article 22, the United Kingdom reserves the right to continue to apply any legislation in those territories governing the detention of children seeking refugee status, the determination of their status and their entry into, stay in and departure from those territories.

The Government of the United Kingdom reserves the right to extend the Convention at a later date to any other territories for whose international relations the Government of the United Kingdom is responsible."

DECLARATIONS AND RESERVATIONS MADE BY THE UNITED KINGDOM IN RESPECT OF:

THE CONVENTION ON THE ELIMINATION OF RACIAL DISCRIMINATION (CERD)

Upon signature:

Subject to the following reservation and interpretative statements:

"First, in the present circumstances deriving from the usurpation of power in Rhodesia by the illegal regime, the United Kingdom must sign subject to a reservation of the right not to apply the Convention to Rhodesia unless and until the United Kingdom informs the Secretary-General of the United Nations that it is in a position to ensure that the obligations imposed by the Convention in respect of that territory can be fully implemented.

"Secondly, the United Kingdom wishes to state its understanding of certain articles in the Convention. It interprets article 4 as requiring a party to the Convention to adopt further legislative measures in the fields covered by sub-paragraphs (a), (b) and (c) of that article only in so far as it may consider with due regard to the principles embodied in the Universal Declaration of Human Rights and the rights expressly set forth in article 5 of the Convention (in particular the right to freedom of opinion and expression and the right to freedom of peaceful assembly and association) that some legislative addition to or variation of existing law and practice in those fields is necessary for the attainment of the end specified in the earlier part of article 4. Further, the United Kingdom interprets the requirement in article 6 concerning 'reparation or satisfaction' as being fulfilled if one or other of these forms of redress is made available and interprets 'satisfaction' as including any form of redress effective to bring the discriminatory conduct to an end. In addition it interprets article 20 and the other related provisions of Part III of the Convention as meaning that if a reservation is not accepted the State making the reservation does not become a Party to the Convention.

"Lastly, the United Kingdom maintains its position in regard to article 15. In its view this article is discriminatory in that it establishes a procedure for the receipt of petitions relating to dependent territories while making no comparable provision for States without such territories. Moreover, the article purports to establish a procedure applicable to the dependent territories of States whether or not those States have become parties to the Convention. Her Majesty's Government have decided that the United Kingdom should sign the Convention, these objections notwithstanding, because of the importance they attach to the Convention as a whole."

Upon ratification:

"First, the reservation and interpretative statements made by the United Kingdom at the time of signature of the Convention are maintained.

"Secondly, the United Kingdom does not regard the Commonwealth Immigrants Acts, 1962 and 1968, or their application, as involving any racial discrimination within the meaning of paragraph 1 of article 1, or any other provision of the Convention, and fully reserves its right to continue to apply those Acts.

"Lastly, to the extent if any, that any law relating to election in Fiji may not fulfil the obligations referred to in article 5 (c), that any law relating to land in Fiji which prohibits or restricts the alienation of land by the indigenous inhabitants may not fulfil the obligations referred to in article 5 (d) (v), or that the school system of Fiji may not fulfil the obligations referred to in articles 2, 3 or 5 (e) (v), the United Kingdom reserves the right not to apply the Convention to Fiji.

DECLARATIONS AND RESERVATIONS MADE BY THE UNITED KINGDOM IN RESPECT OF:

THE CONVENTION AGAINST TORTURE (CAT)

Upon signature:

"The United Kingdom reserves the right to formulate, upon ratifying the Convention, any reservations or interpretative declarations which it might consider necessary."

Status of Ratification of the Six Core United Nations Human Rights Instruments[1]

(i)   The International Covenant on Civil and Political Rights (ICCPR).

(ii)   The International Covenant on Economic, Social and Cultural Rights (ICESCR).

(iii)   The Convention on the Elimination of all forms of Discrimination Against Women (CEDAW).

(iv)   The Convention on the Rights of the Child (CRC).

(v)   The Convention on the Elimination of Racial Discrimination (CERD).

(vi)   The Convention Against Torture (CAT).

Additional information:

(vii)   Optional Protocol to the International Covenant on Civil and Political Rights.

(viii)   Second Optional Protocol to the International Covenant on Civil and Political Rights.

International Covenant on Civil and Political Rights

Non State Parties

Country	Date of Signature (if applicable)
Andorra	
Antigua and Barbuda	
Bahamas	
Bahrain	
Bangladesh	
Bhutan	
Botswana	
Brunei Darussalam	
Burkina Faso	
China	
Comoros	
Cook Islands	
Cuba	
Djibouti	
Eritrea	
Fiji	
Ghana	
Guinea-Bissau	
Holy See	
Indonesia	
Kazakhstan	
Kiribati	
Lao People's Democratic Republic	
Liberia	18.4.67
Liechtenstein	
Malaysia	
Maldives	
Marshall Islands	
Mauritania	
Micronesia (Federated States of)	
Myanmar	
Nauru	
Niue	
Oman	
Pakistan	
Palau	
Papua New Guinea	
Qatar	
Saint Kitts and Nevis	
Saint Lucia	
Samoa	
Sao Tom and Principe	31.10.95
Saudi Arabia	

---

[1] Broken down into lists of Non State Parties and State Parties giving dates of entry into force, receipt by the United Nations of instruments of ratification and signature where applicable. **QUERY ratification and QUERY COPY NOT SUPPLIED**

Country	Date of Signature (if applicable)
Singapore	
Solomon Islands	
South Africa	31.10.94
Swaziland	
Tajikistan	
Tonga	
Turkey	
Tuvalu	
United Arab Emirates	
Vanuatu	

Source: UN High Commissioner for Human Rights Website (*www.unhchr.ch*)—
15 October 1998.

State Parties

Country	Entry into Force	Receipt of Instrument of ratification	Date of Signature
Afghanistan	24.4.83	24.1.83	
Albania	4.1.92	4.10.91	
Algeria	12.12.89	12.9.89	10.12.68
Angola	10.4.92	10.1.92	
Argentina	8.11.86	8.8.86	19.2.68
Armenia	23.9.93	23.6.93	
Australia	13.11.80	13.8.80	18.12.72
Austria	10.12.78	10.9.78	10.12.73
Azerbaijan	13.11.92	13.8.92	
Barbados	23.3.76	5.1.73	
Belarus	23.3.76	12.11.73	19.3.68
Belgium	21.7.83	21.4.83	10.12.68
Belize	10.9.96	10.6.96	
Benin	12.6.92	12.3.92	
Bolivia	12.11.82	12.8.82	
Bosnia and Herzegovina	6.3.92	1.9.93	
Brazil	24.4.92	24.1.92	
Bulgaria	23.3.76	21.9.70	8.10.68
Burundi	9.8.90	9.5.90	
Cambodia	26.8.92	26.5.92	17.10.80
Cameroon	27.9.84	27.6.84	
Canada	19.8.76	19.5.76	
Cape Verde	6.11.93	6.8.93	
Central African Republic	8.8.81	8.5.81	
Chad	9.9.95	9.6.95	
Chile	23.3.76	10.2.72	16.9.69
Colombia	23.3.76	29.10.69	21.12.66
Congo	5.1.84	5.10.83	
Costa Rica	23.3.76	29.11.68	19.12.66
Côte d'Ivoire	26.6.92	26.3.92	
Croatia	8.10.91	12.10.92	
Cyprus	23.3.76	2.4.69	19.12.66
Czech Republic	1.1.93	22.2.93	
Democratic People's Republic of Korea	14.12.81	14.9.81	
Democratic Republic of the Congo	1.2.77	1.11.76	
Denmark	23.3.76	6.1.72	20.3.68
Dominica	17.9.93	17.6.93	
Dominican Republic	4.4.78	4.1.78	
Ecuador	23.3.76	6.3.69	4.4.68
Egypt	14.4.82	14.1.82	4.8.67
El Salvador	29.2.80	30.11.79	21.9.67
Equatorial Guinea	25.12.87	25.9.87	
Estonia	21.1.92	21.10.91	
Ethiopia	11.9.93	11.6.93	
Finland	23.3.76	19.8.75	11.10.67
France	4.2.81	4.11.80	
Gabon	21.4.83	21.1.83	
Gambia	22.6.79	22.3.79	
Georgia	3.8.94	3.5.94	

Country	Entry into Force	Receipt of Instrument of ratification	Date of Signature
Germany	23.3.76	17.12.73	9.10.68
Greece	5.8.97	5.5.97	
Grenada	6.12.91	6.9.91	
Guatemala	5.8.92	6.5.92	
Guinea	24.4.78	24.1.78	28.2.67
Guyana	15.5.77	15.2.77	22.8.68
Haiti	6.5.91	6.2.91	19.12.66
Honduras	25.11.97	25.8.97	19.12.66
Hungary	23.3.76	17.1.74	25.3.69
Iceland	22.11.79	22.8.79	30.12.68
India	10.7.79	10.4.79	
Iran (Islamic Republic of)	23.3.76	24.6.75	4.4.68
Iraq	23.3.76	25.1.71	18.2.69
Ireland	8.3.90	8.12.89	1.10.73
Israel	3.1.92	3.10.91	19.12.66
Italy	15.12.78	15.9.78	18.1.67
Jamaica	23.3.76	3.10.75	19.12.66
Japan	21.9.79	21.6.79	30.5.78
Jordan	23.3.76	28.5.75	30.6.72
Kenya	23.3.76	1.5.72	
Kuwait	21.8.96	21.5.96	
Kyrgyzstan	7.1.95	7.10.94	
Latvia	14.7.92	14.4.92	
Lebanon	23.3.76	3.11.72	
Lesotho	9.12.92	9.9.92	
Libyan Arab Jamahiriya	23.3.76	15.5.70	
Lithuania	20.2.92	20.11.91	
Luxembourg	18.11.83	18.8.83	26.11.74
Madagascar	23.3.76	21.6.71	17.9.69
Malawi	22.3.94	22.12.93	
Mali	23.3.76	16.7.74	
Malta	13.12.90	13.9.90	
Mauritius	23.3.76	12.12.73	
Mexico	23.6.81	23.3.81	
Monaco	28.11.97	28.8.97	26.6.97
Mongolia	23.3.76	18.11.74	5.6.68
Morocco	3.8.79	3.5.79	19.1.77
Mozambique	21.10.93	21.7.93	
Namibia	28.2.95	28.11.94	
Nepal	14.8.91	14.5.91	
Netherlands	11.3.79	11.12.78	25.6.69
New Zealand	28.3.79	28.12.78	12.11.68
Nicaragua	12.6.80	12.3.80	
Niger	7.6.86	7.3.86	
Nigeria	29.10.93	29.7.93	
Norway	23.3.76	13.9.72	20.3.68
Panama	8.6.77	8.3.77	27.7.76
Paraguay	10.9.92	10.6.92	
Peru	28.7.78	28.4.78	11.8.77
Philippines	23.1.87	23.10.86	19.12.66
Poland	18.6.77	18.3.77	2.3.67
Portugal	15.9.78	15.6.78	7.10.76
Republic of Korea	10.7.90	10.4.90	
Republic of Moldova	26.4.93	26.1.93	
Romania	23.3.76	9.12.74	27.6.68
Russian Federation	23.3.76	16.10.73	18.3.68
Rwanda	23.3.76	16.4.75	
Saint Vincent and the Grenadines	9.2.82	9.11.81	
San Marino	18.1.86	18.10.85	
Senegal	13.5.78	13.2.78	6.7.70
Seychelles	5.8.92	5.5.92	
Sierra Leone	23.11.96	23.8.96	
Slovak Republic	1.1.93	28.5.93	
Slovenia	25.6.91	6.7.92	
Somalia	24.4.90	24.1.90	
Spain	27.7.77	27.4.77	28.9.76
Sri Lanka	11.9.80	11.6.80	
Sudan	18.6.86	18.3.76	
Suriname	28.3.77	28.12.76	

Country	Entry into Force	Receipt of Instrument of ratification	Date of Signature
Sweden	23.3.76	6.12.71	29.9.67
Switzerland	18.9.92	18.6.92	
Syrian Arab Republic	23.3.76	21.4.69	
Thailand	29.1.97	29.10.96	
The Former Yugoslav Republic of Macedonia	17.9.91	18.1.94	
Togo	24.8.84	24.5.84	
Trinidad and Tobago	21.3.79	21.12.78	
Tunisia	23.3.76	18.3.69	30.4.68
Turkmenistan	1.8.97	1.5.97	
Uganda	21.9.95	21.6.95	
Ukraine	23.3.76	12.11.73	20.3.68
United Kingdom of Great Britain and Northern Ireland	20.8.76	20.5.76	16.9.68
United Republic of Tanzania	11.9.76	11.6.76	
United States of America	8.9.92	8.6.92	5.10.77
Uruguay	23.3.76	1.4.70	21.2.67
Uzbekistan	28.12.95	28.9.95	
Venezuela	10.8.78	10.5.78	24.6.69
Viet Nam	24.12.82	24.9.82	
Yemen	9.5.87	9.2.87	
Yugoslavia	23.3.76	2.6.71	8.8.67
Zambia	10.7.84	10.4.84	
Zimbabwe	13.8.91	13.5.91	

Source: UN High Commissioner for Human Rights Website (*www.unhchr.ch*)—15 October 1998.

International Covenant on Economic, Social and Cultural Rights

Non State Parties

Country	Date of Signature (if applicable)
Andorra	
Antigua and Barbuda	
Bahamas	
Bahrain	
Bangladesh	
Belize	
Bhutan	
Botswana	
Brunei Darussalem	
Burkina Faso	
China	27.10.97
Comoros	
Cook Islands	
Cuba	
Djibouti	
Eritrea	
Fiji	
Ghana	
Haiti	
Holy See	
Indonesia	
Kazakhstan	
Kiribati	
Lao People's Democratic	
Liberia	18.4.67
Liechstenstein	
Malaysia	
Maldives	
Marshall Islands	
Mauritania	
Micronesia (Federated States of)	
Mozambique	
Myanmar	
Nauru	
Niue	
Oman	
Pakistan	

Country	Date of Signature (if applicable)
Palau	
Papua New Guinea	
Qatar	
Saint Kitts and Nevis	
Saint Lucia	
Samoa	
Sao Tom and Principe	31.10.95
Saudi Arabia	
Singapore	
South Africa	3.10.94
Swaziland	
Tajikistan	
Thailand	
Tonga	
Turkey	
Tuvalu	
United Arab Emirates	
United States of America	5.10.77
Vanuatu	

Source: UN High Commissioner for Human Rights Website (*www.unhchr.ch*)—
15 October 1998.

State Parties

Country	Entry into Force	Receipt of Instrument of ratification	Date of Signature
Afghanistan	24.4.83	24.1.83	
Albania	4.1.92	4.10.91	
Algeria	12.12.89	12.9.89	
Angola	10.4.92	10.1.92	
Argentina	8.11.86	8.8.86	
Armenia	13.12.93	13.9.93	
Australia	10.3.76	10.12.75	
Austria	10.12.78	10.9.78	
Azerbaijan	13.11.92	13.8.92	
Barbados	3.1.76	5.1.73	
Belarus	3.1.76	12.11.73	
Belguim	21.7.83	21.4.83	
Benin	12.6.92	12.3.92	
Bolivia	12.11.82	12.8.82	
Bosnia and Herzegovina	6.3.92	3.3.92	
Brazil	24.4.92	24.1.92	
Bulgaria	3.1.76	21.9.70	
Burundi	9.8.90	9.5.90	
Cambodia	26.8.92	26.5.92	
Cameroon	27.9.84	27.6.84	
Canada	19.8.76	19.5.76	
Cape Verde	6.11.93	6.8.93	
Central African Republic	8.8.81	8.5.81	
Chad	9.9.95	9.6.95	
Chile	3.1.76	10.2.72	
Colombia	3.1.76	29.10.69	
Congo	5.1.84	5.10.83	
Costa Rica	3.1.76	29.11.68	
Cote d'Ivoire	26.6.92	26.3.92	
Croatia	8.10.91	8.10.91	
Cyprus	3.1.76	2.4.69	
Czech Republic	1.1.93	1.1.93	
Democratic People's Republic of Korea	14.12.81	14.9.81	
Democratic Republic of the Congo	1.2.77	1.11.76	
Denmark	3.1.76	6.1.72	
Dominica	17.9.93	17.6.93	
Dominican Republic	4.4.78	4.1.78	
Ecuador	3.1.76	6.3.69	
Egypt	14.4.82	14.1.82	
El Salvador	29.2.80	30.11.79	
Equatorial Guinea	25.12.87	25.9.87	
Estonia	21.1.92	21.10.91	

Country	Entry into Force	Receipt of Instrument of ratification	Date of Signature
Ethiopia	11.9.93	11.6.93	
Finland	3.1.76	19.8.75	
France	4.2.81	4.11.80	
Gabon	21.4.83	21.1.83	
Gambia	29.3.79	29.12.78	
Georgia	3.8.94	3.5.94	
Germany	3.1.76	17.12.73	
Greece	16.8.85	16.5.85	
Grenada	6.12.91	6.9.91	
Guatemala	19.8.88	19.5.88	
Guinea	24.4.78	24.1.78	
Guinea-Bissau	2.10.92	2.7.92	
Guyana	15.5.77	15.2.77	
Honduras	17.5.81	17.2.81	
Hungary	3.1.76	17.1.74	
Iceland	22.8.79	22.11.79	
India	10.7.79	10.4.79	
Iran (Islamic Republic of)	3.1.76	24.6.75	
Iraq	3.1.76	25.1.71	
Ireland	8.3.90	8.12.89	
Isreal	3.1.92	3.10.91	
Italy	15.12.78	15.9.78	
Jamaica	3.1.76	3.10.75	
Japan	21.9.79	21.6.79	
Jordan	3.1.76	28.5.75	
Kenya	3.1.76	1.5.72	
Kuwait	21.8.96	21.5.96	
Kyrgyzstan	7.10.94	7.10.94	
Latvia	14.7.92	14.4.92	
Lebanon	3.1.76	3.11.72	
Lestho	9.12.92	9.9.92	
Libyan Arab Jamahiriya	3.1.76	15.5.70	
Lithuania	20.2.92	20.11.91	
Luxembourg	18.11.83	18.8.83	
Madagascar	3.1.76	22.9.71	
Malawi	22.3.94	22.12.93	
Mali	3.1.76	16.7.74	
Malta	13.12.90	13.9.90	
Mauritius	3.1.76	12.12.73	
Mexico	23.6.81	23.3.81	
Monaco	28.11.97	28.8.97	26.6.97
Mongolia	3.1.76	18.11.74	
Morocco	3.8.79	3.5.79	
Namibia	28.2.95	28.11.94	
Nepal	14.8.91	14.5.91	
Netherlands	11.3.79	11.12.78	
New Zealand	28.3.79	28.12.78	
Nicaragua	12.6.80	12.3.80	
Niger	7.6.86	7.3.86	
Nigeria	29.10.93	29.7.93	
Norway	3.1.76	13.9.72	
Panama	8.6.77	8.3.77	
Paraguay	10.9.92	10.6.92	
Peru	28.7.78	28.4.78	
Philippines	3.1.76	7.6.74	
Poland	18.6.77	18.3.77	
Portugal	31.10.78	31.7.78	
Republic of Korea	10.7.90	10.4.90	
Republic of Moldova	26.4.93	26.1.93	
Romania	3.1.76	9.12.74	
Russian Federation	3.1.76	16.10.73	
Rwanda	3.1.76	16.4.75	
Saint Vincent and the Grenadines	9.2.82	9.11.81	
San Marino	18.1.86	18.10.85	
Senegal	13.5.78	13.2.78	
Seychelles	5.8.92	5.5.92	
Sierra Leone	23.11.96	23.8.96	
Slovak Republic	28.5.93	28.5.93	
Slovenia	6.7.92	6.7.92	
Solomon Islands	17.3.82	17.3.82	
Somalia	24.4.90	24.1.90	

Country	Entry into Force	Receipt of Instrument of ratification	Date of Signature
Spain	27.7.77	27.4.77	
Sri Lanka	11.9.80	11.6.80	
Sudan	18.6.86	18.3.86	
Suriname	28.3.77	28.12.76	
Sweden	3.1.76	6.12.71	
Switzerland	18.9.92	18.6.92	
Syrian Arab Republic	3.1.76	21.4.69	
The Former Yugoslav Republic of Macedonia	18.1.94	18.1.94	
Togo	24.8.84	24.5.84	
Trinidad and Tobago	8.3.79	8.12.78	
Tunisia	3.1.76	18.3.69	
Turkmenistan	1.8.97	1.5.97	
Uganda	21.4.87	21.1.87	
Ukraine	3.1.76	12.11.73	
United Kingdom of Great Britain and Northern Ireland	20.8.76	20.5.76	
United Republic of Tanzania	11.9.76	11.6.76	
Uruguay	3.1.76	1.4.70	
Uzbekistan	28.12.95	28.9.95	
Venezuela	10.8.78	10.5.78	
Viet Nam	24.12.82	24.9.82	
Yemen	9.5.87	9.2.87	
Yugoslavia	3.1.76	2.6.71	
Zambia	10.7.84	10.4.84	
Zimbabwe	13.8.91	13.5.91	

Source: UN High Commissioner for Human Rights Website (*www.unhchr.ch*)—15 October 1998.

Convention on the Elimination of All Forms of Discrimination against Women

Non State Parties

Country	Date of Signature (if applicable)
Afgahnistan	
Bahrain	
Brunei Darussalem	
Cook Islands	
Democratic People's Republic of Korea	
Djibouti	
Holy See	
Iran (Islamic Republic of)	
Kazakhstan	
Kiribati	
Marshall Islands	
Mauritania	
Micronesia (Federated States of)	
Monaco	
Nauru	
Niger	
Niue	
Oman	
Palau	
Qatar	
San Marino	
Sao Tome and Principe	31.10.95
Saudi Arabia	
Solomon Islands	
Somalia	
Sudan	
Swaziland	
Syrian Arab Republic	
Tonga	
Tuvalu	
United Arab Emirates	
United States of America	

Source: UN High Commissioner for Human Rights Website (*www.unhchr.ch*)—
15 October 1998.

State Parties

Country	Entry into Force	Receipt of Instrument of ratification	Date of Signature
Albania	10.6.94	11.5.94	
Algeria	21.6.96	22.5.96	
Andorra	14.2.97	15.1.97	
Angola	17.10.86	17.9.86	
Antigua and Barbuda	31.8.89	1.8.89	
Argentina	14.8.85	15.7.85	
Armenia	13.10.93	13.9.93	
Australia	27.8.83	28.7.83	
Austria	30.4.82	31.3.82	
Azerbaijan	9.8.95	10.7.95	
Bahamas	5.11.93	6.10.93	
Bangladesh	6.12.84	6.11.84	
Barbados	3.9.81	16.10.80	
Belarus	3.9.81	4.2.81	
Belgium	9.8.85	10.7.85	
Belize	15.6.90	16.5.90	
Benin	11.4.92	12.3.92	
Bhutan	30.9.81	31.8.81	
Bolivia	8.7.90	8.6.90	
Bosnia and Herzegovina	1.10.93	1.9.93	
Botswana	12.9.96	13.8.96	
Brazil	2.3.84	1.2.84	
Bulgaria	10.3.82	8.2.82	
Burkina Faso	13.11.87	14.10.87	
Burundi	7.2.92	8.1.92	
Cambodia	14.11.92	15.10.92	
Cameroon	22.9.94	23.8.94	
Canada	9.1.82	10.12.81	
Cape Verde	3.9.81	5.12.80	
Central African Republic	21.7.91	21.6.91	
Chad	9.7.95	9.6.95	
Chile	6.1.90	7.12.89	
China	3.9.81	4.11.80	
Colombia	18.2.82	19.1.82	
Comoros	30.11.94	31.10.94	
Congo	25.8.82	26.7.82	
Costa Rica	4.5.86	4.4.86	
Côte d'Ivoire	17.1.96	19.12.95	
Croatia	9.10.92	9.9.92	
Cuba	3.9.81	17.7.80	
Cyprus	22.8.85	23.7.85	
Czech Republic	24.3.93	22.2.93	
Democratic Republic of the Congo	16.11.86	17.10.86	
Denmark	21.5.83	21.4.83	
Dominica	3.9.81	15.9.80	
Dominican Republic	2.10.82	2.9.82	
Ecuador	9.12.81	9.11.81	
Egypt	18.10.81	18.9.81	
El Salvador	18.9.81	19.8.81	
Equatorial Guinea	22.11.84	23.10.84	
Eritrea	5.10.95	5.9.95	
Estonia	20.11.91	21.10.91	
Ethiopia	10.10.81	10.9.81	
Fiji	27.9.95	28.8.95	
Finland	4.10.86	4.9.86	
France	13.1.84	14.12.83	
Gabon	20.2.83	21.1.83	
Gambia	16.5.93	16.4.93	
Georgia	25.11.94	26.10.94	
Germany	9.8.85	1.7.85	
Ghana	1.2.86	2.1.86	
Greece	7.7.83	7.6.83	
Grenada	29.9.90	30.8.90	
Guatemala	11.9.82	12.8.82	
Guinea	8.9.82	9.8.82	
Guinea-Bissau	22.9.85	23.8.85	
Guyana	3.9.81	17.7.80	
Haiti	3.9.81	20.7.81	

Country	Entry into Force	Receipt of Instrument of ratification	Date of Signature
Honduras	2.4.83	3.3.83	
Hungary	3.9.81	22.12.80	
Iceland	18.7.85	18.6.85	
India	8.8.93	9.7.93	
Indonesia	13.10.84	13.9.84	
Iraq	12.9.86	13.8.86	
Ireland	22.01.86	23.12.85	
Israel	2.11.91	3.10.91	
Italy	10.7.85	10.6.85	
Jamaica	18.11.84	19.10.84	
Japan	25.7.85	25.6.85	
Jordan	31.7.92	1.7.92	
Kenya	8.4.84	9.3.84	
Kuwait	2.10.94	2.9.94	
Kyrgyzstan	11.3.97	10.2.97	
Lao People's Democratic Republic	13.9.81	14.8.81	
Latvia	14.5.92	14.4.92	
Lebanon	21.5.97	21.4.97	
Lesotho	21.9.95	22.8.95	
Liberia	16.8.84	17.7.84	
Libyan Arab Jamahiriya	15.6.89	16.5.89	
Liechtenstein	21.1.96	22.12.95	
Lithuania	17.2.94	18.1.94	
Luxembourg	4.3.89	2.2.89	
Madagascar	16.4.89	17.3.89	
Malawi	11.4.87	12.3.87	
Malaysia	4.8.95	5.7.95	
Maldives	31.7.93	1.7.93	
Mali	10.10.85	10.9.85	
Malta	7.4.91	8.3.91	
Mauritius	8.8.84	9.7.84	
Mexico	3.9.81	23.3.81	
Mongolia	3.9.81	20.7.81	
Morocco	21.7.93	21.6.93	
Mozambique	16.5.97	16.4.97	
Myanmar	21.8.97	22.7.97	
Namibia	23.12.92	23.11.92	
Nepal	22.5.91	22.4.91	
Netherlands	22.8.91	23.7.91	
New Zealand	9.2.85	10.1.85	
Nicaragua	26.11.81	27.10.81	
Nigeria	13.7.85	13.6.85	
Norway	3.9.81	21.5.81	
Pakistan	11.4.96	12.3.96	
Panama	28.11.81	29.10.81	
Papua New Guinea	11.2.95	12.1.95	
Paraguay	6.5.87	6.4.87	
Peru	13.10.82	13.9.82	
Philippines	4.9.81	5.8.81	
Poland	3.9.81	30.7.80	
Portugal	3.9.81	30.7.80	
Republic of Korea	26.1.85	27.12.84	
Republic of Moldova	31.7.94	1.7.94	
Romania	6.2.82	7.1.82	
Russian Federation	3.9.81	23.1.81	
Rwanda	3.9.81	2.3.81	
Saint Kitts and Nevis	25.5.85	25.4.85	
Saint Lucia	7.11.82	8.10.82	
Saint Vincent and the Grenadines	3.9.81	4.8.81	
Samoa	25.10.92	26.9.92	
Senegal	7.3.85	5.2.85	
Seychelles	4.6.92	5.5.92	
Sierra Leone	11.12.88	11.11.88	
Singapore	5.11.95	5.10.95	
Slovak Republic	27.6.93	28.5.93	
Slovenia	5.8.92	6.7.92	
South Africa	14.1.96	15.12.95	
Spain	4.2.84	5.1.84	
Sri Lanka	4.11.81	5.10.81	

Country	Entry into Force	Receipt of Instrument of ratification	Date of Signature
Suriname	31.3.93	1.3.93	
Sweden	3.9.81	2.7.80	
Switzerland	26.4.97	27.3.97	
Tajikistan	25.11.93	26.10.93	
Thailand	8.9.85	9.8.85	
The Former Yugoslav Republic of Macedonia	17.2.94	18.1.94	
Togo	26.10.83	26.9.83	
Trinidad and Tobago	11.2.90	12.1.90	
Tunisia	20.10.85	20.9.85	
Turkey	19.1.86	20.12.85	
Turkmenistan	30.5.97	1.5.97	
Uganda	21.8.85	22.7.85	
Ukraine	3.9.81	12.3.81	
United Kingdom of Great Britain and Northern Ireland	7.5.86	7.4.86	
United Republic of Tanzania	19.9.85	20.8.85	
Uruguay	8.11.81	9.10.81	
Uzbekistan	18.8.95	19.7.95	
Vanuatu	8.10.95	8.9.95	
Venezuela	1.6.83	2.5.83	
Vietnam	19.3.82	17.2.82	
Yemen	29.6.84	30.5.84	
Yugoslavia	28.3.82	26.2.82	
Zambia	21.7.85	21.6.85	
Zimbabwe	12.6.91	13.5.91	

Source: UN High Commissioner for Human Rights Website (*www.unhchr.ch*)—15 October 1998.

Convention on the Rights of the Child

Non State Parties

Country	Date of Signature (if applicable)
Somalia	
United States of America	

State Parties

Country	Entry into Force	Receipt of Instrument of ratification	Date of Signature
Afghanistan	27.4.94	28.3.94	27.9.90
Albania	28.3.92	27.2.92	26.1.90
Algeria	16.5.93	16.4.93	26.1.90
Andorra	1.2.96	2.1.96	2.10.95
Angola	4.1.91	5.12.90	14.2.90
Antigua and Barbuda	4.11.93	5.10.93	12.3.91
Argentina	3.1.91	4.12.90	29.6.90
Armenia	22.7.93	23.6.93	
Australia	16.1.91	17.12.90	22.8.90
Austria	5.9.92	6.8.92	26.1.90
Azerbaijan	12.9.92	13.8.92	
Bahamas	22.3.91	20.2.91	30.10.90
Bahrain	14.3.92	13.2.92	
Bangladesh	2.9.90	3.8.90	26.1.90
Barbados	8.11.90	9.10.90	19.4.90
Belarus	31.10.90	1.10.90	26.1.90
Belgium	15.1.92	16.12.91	26.1.90
Belize	2.9.90	2.5.90	2.3.90
Benin	2.9.90	3.8.90	25.4.90
Bhutan	2.9.90	1.8.90	4.6.90
Bosnia and Herzegovina	6.3.92	1.9.93	
Botswana	13.4.95	14.3.95	
Brazil	24.10.90	24.9.90	26.1.90

Country	Entry into Force	Receipt of Instrument of ratification	Date of Signature
Brunei Darussalam	26.1.96	27.12.95	
Bulgaria	3.7.91	3.6.91	31.5.90
Burkina Faso	30.9.90	31.8.90	26.1.90
Burundi	18.11.90	19.10.90	8.5.90
Cambodia	14.11.92	15.10.92	22.9.92
Cameroon	10.2.93	11.1.93	25.9.90
Canada	12.1.92	13.12.91	28.5.90
Cape Verde	4.7.92	4.6.92	
Central African Republic	23.5.92	23.4.92	30.7.90
Chad	1.11.90	2.10.90	30.9.90
Chile	12.9.90	13.8.90	26.1.90
China	1.4.92	2.3.92	29.8.90
Colombia	27.2.91	28.1.91	26.1.90
Comoros	21.7.93	22.6.93	30.9.90
Congo	13.11.93	14.10.93	
Cook Islands	6.7.97	6.6.97	
Costa Rica	20.9.90	21.8.90	26.1.90
Côte d'Ivoire	6.3.91	4.2.91	26.1.90
Croatia	8.10.91	12.10.92	
Cuba	20.9.91	21.8.91	26.1.90
Cyprus	9.3.91	7.2.91	5.10.90
Czech Republic	1.1.93	22.2.93	
Democratic People's Republic of Korea	21.10.90	21.9.90	23.8.90
Democratic Republic of the Congo	27.10.90	27.9.90	20.3.90
Denmark	18.8.91	19.7.91	26.1.90
Djibouti	5.1.91	6.12.90	30.9.90
Dominica	12.4.91	13.3.91	26.1.90
Dominican Republic	11.7.91	11.6.91	8.8.90
Ecuador	2.9.90	23.3.90	26.1.90
Egypt	2.9.90	6.7.90	5.2.90
El Salvador	2.9.90	10.7.90	26.1.90
Equatorial Guinea	15.7.92	15.6.92	
Eritrea	2.9.94	3.8.94	20.12.93
Estonia	20.11.91	21.10.91	
Ethiopia	13.6.91	14.5.91	
Fiji	12.9.93	13.8.93	2.7.93
Finland	20.7.91	20.6.91	26.1.90
France	6.9.90	7.8.90	26.1.90
Gabon	11.3.94	9.2.94	26.1.90
Gambia	7.9.90	8.8.90	5.2.90
Georgia	2.7.94	2.6.94	
Germany	5.4.92	6.3.92	26.1.90
Ghana	2.9.90	5.2.90	29.1.90
Greece	10.6.93	11.5.93	26.1.90
Grenada	5.12.90	5.11.90	21.2.90
Guatemala	2.9.90	6.6.90	26.1.90
Guinea	2.9.90	13.7.90	
Guinea-Bissau	19.9.90	20.8.90	26.1.90
Guyana	13.2.91	14.1.91	30.9.90
Haiti	8.7.95	8.6.95	20.1.90
Holy See	2.9.90	20.4.90	20.4.90
Honduras	9.9.90	10.8.90	31.5.90
Hungary	6.11.91	7.10.91	14.3.90
Iceland	27.11.92	28.10.92	26.1.90
India	11.1.93	11.12.92	
Indonesia	5.10.90	5.9.90	26.1.90
Iran (Islamic Republic of)	12.8.94	13.7.94	5.9.91
Iraq	15.7.94	15.6.94	
Ireland	28.10.92	28.9.92	30.9.90
Isreal	2.11.91	3.10.91	3.7.90
Italy	5.10.91	5.9.91	26.1.90
Jamaica	13.6.91	14.5.91	26.1.90
Japan	22.5.94	22.4.94	21.9.90
Jordan	23.6.91	24.5.91	29.8.90
Kazakhstan	11.9.94	12.8.94	16.2.94
Kenya	2.9.90	30.7.90	26.1.90
Kiribati	10.1.96	11.12.95	
Kuwait	20.11.91	21.10.91	7.6.90
Kyrgyzstan	6.11.94	7.10.94	

Country	Entry into Force	Receipt of Instrument of ratification	Date of Signature
Lao People's Democratic Republic	7.6.91	8.5.91	
Latvia	14.5.92	14.4.92	
Lebanon	13.6.91	14.5.91	26.1.90
Lesotho	9.4.92	10.3.92	21.8.90
Liberia	4.7.93	4.6.93	26.4.90
Libyan Arab Jamahiriya	15.5.93	15.4.93	
Liechtenstein	21.1.96	22.12.95	30.9.90
Lithuania	1.3.92	31.1.92	
Luxembourg	6.4.94	7.3.94	21.3.90
Madagascar	18.4.91	19.3.91	19.4.90
Malawi	1.2.91	2.1.91	
Malaysia	19.3.95	17.2.95	
Maldives	13.3.91	11.2.91	21.8.90
Mali	20.10.90	20.9.90	26.1.90
Malta	30.10.90	30.9.90	26.1.90
Marshall Islands	3.11.93	4.10.93	14.4.93
Mauritania	15.6.91	16.5.91	26.1.90
Mauritius	2.9.90	26.7.90	
Mexico	21.10.90	21.9.90	26.1.90
Micronesia (Federated States of)	4.6.93	5.5.93	
Monaco	21.7.93	21.6.93	
Mongolia	2.9.90	5.7.90	26.1.90
Morocco	21.7.93	21.6.93	26.1.90
Mozambique	26.5.94	26.4.94	30.9.90
Myanmar	14.8.91	15.7.91	
Namibia	30.10.90	30.9.90	26.9.90
Nauru	26.8.94	27.7.94	
Nepal	14.10.90	14.9.90	26.1.90
Netherlands	7.3.95	6.2.95	26.1.90
New Zealand	6.5.93	6.4.93	1.10.90
Nicaragua	4.11.90	5.10.90	6.2.90
Niger	30.10.90	30.9.90	26.1.90
Nigeria	19.5.91	19.4.91	26.1.90
Niue	19.1.96	20.12.95	
Norway	7.2.91	8.1.91	26.1.90
Oman	8.1.97	9.12.96	
Pakistan	12.12.90	12.11.90	20.9.90
Palau	3.9.95	4.8.95	
Panama	11.1.91	12.12.90	26.1.90
Papua New Guinea	31.3.93	1.3.93	30.9.90
Paraguay	25.10.90	25.9.90	4.4.90
Peru	4.10.90	4.9.90	26.1.90
Philippines	20.9.90	21.8.90	26.1.90
Poland	7.7.91	7.6.91	26.1.90
Portugal	21.10.90	21.9.90	26.1.90
Qatar	3.5.95	3.4.95	8.12.92
Republic of Korea	20.12.91	20.11.91	25.9.90
Republic of Moldova	25.2.93	26.1.93	
Romania	28.10.90	28.9.90	26.1.90
Russian Federation	15.9.90	16.8.90	26.1.90
Rwanda	23.2.91	24.1.91	26.1.90
Saint Kitts and Nevis	2.9.90	24.7.90	26.1.90
Saint Lucia	16.7.93	16.6.93	
Saint Vincent and the Grenadines	25.11.93	26.10.93	20.9.93
Samoa	29.12.94	29.11.94	30.9.90
San Marino	25.12.91	25.11.91	
Sao Tome and Principe	13.6.91	14.5.91	
Saudi Arabia	25.2.96	26.1.96	
Senegal	2.9.90	31.7.90	26.1.90
Seychelles	7.10.90	7.9.90	
Sierra Leone	2.9.90	18.6.90	13.2.90
Singapore	4.11.95	5.10.95	
Slovak Republic	1.1.93	28.5.93	
Slovenia	25.6.91	6.7.92	
Solomon Islands	9.5.95	10.4.95	
South Africa	16.7.95	16.6.95	29.1.93
Spain	5.1.91	6.12.90	26.1.90
Sri Lanka	11.8.91	12.7.91	26.1.90
Sudan	2.9.90	3.8.90	24.7.90

Country	Entry into Force	Receipt of Instrument of ratification	Date of Signature
Suriname	31.3.93	1.3.93	26.1.90
Swaziland	6.10.95	7.9.95	22.8.90
Sweden	2.9.90	29.6.90	26.1.90
Switzerland	26.3.97	24.2.97	1.5.91
Syrian Arab Republic	14.8.93	15.7.93	18.9.90
Tajikistan	25.11.93	26.10.93	
Thailand	26.04.92	27.3.92	
The Former Yugoslav Republic of Macedonia	17.9.91	2.12.93	
Togo	2.9.90	1.8.90	26.1.90
Tonga	6.12.95	6.11.95	
Trinidad and Tobago	4.1.92	5.12.91	30.9.90
Tunisia	29.2.92	30.1.92	26.2.90
Turkey	4.5.95	4.4.95	14.9.90
Turkmenistan	19.10.93	20.9.93	
Tuvalu	22.10.95	22.9.95	
Uganda	16.9.90	17.8.90	17.8.90
Ukraine	27.9.91	28.8.91	21.2.91
United Arab Emirates	2.2.97	3.1.97	
United Kingdom of Great Britain and Northern Ireland	15.1.92	16.12.91	19.4.90
United Republic of Tanzania	10.7.91	10.6.91	1.6.90
Uruguay	20.12.90	20.11.90	26.01.90
Uzbekistan	29.7.94	29.6.94	
Vanuatu	6.8.93	7.7.93	30.9.90
Venuzuela	13.10.90	13.9.90	26.1.90
Viet Nam	2.9.90	28.2.90	26.1.90
Yemen	31.5.91	1.5.91	13.2.90
Yugoslavia	2.2.91	3.1.91	26.1.90
Zambia	5.1.92	5.12.91	30.9.90
Zimbabwe	11.10.90	11.9.90	8.3.90

Source: UN High Commissioner for Human Rights Website (*www.unhchr.ch*)–15 October 1998.

Convention on the Elimination of All Forms of Racial Discrimination

Non-State Parties

Country	Date of Signature (if applicable)
Andorra	
Angola	
Belize	
Benin	2.2.67
Bhutan	
Brunei Darussalem	
Comoros	
Cook Islands	
Democratic People's Republic of Korea	
Djibouti	
Dominica	
Equatorial Guinea	
Eritrea	
Georgia	
Grenada	
Guinea-Bissau	
Honduras	
Indonesia	
Ireland	21.3.78
Kazakhstan	
Kenya	
Kiribati	
Liechtenstein	
Lithuania	8.6.98
Malaysia	
Marshall Islands	
Micronesia (Federated States of)	
Myanmar	
Nauru	

Country		Date of Signature (if applicable)
Niue		
Oman		
Palau		
Paraguay		
Saint Kitts and Nevis		
Samoa		
San Marino		
Sao Tom and Principe		
Singapore		
South Africa		3.10.94
Thailand		
Turkey		13.10.72
Tuvalu		
Vanuatu		

Source: UN High Commissioner for Human Rights Website (*www.unhchr.ch*)— 15 October 1998.

State Parties

Country	Entry into Force	Receipt of Instrument of ratification	Date of Signature
Afghanistan	5.8.83	6.7.83	
Albania	10.6.94	11.5.94	
Algeria	15.3.72	14.2.72	
Antigua and Barbuda	25.10.88	25.10.88	
Argentina	4.1.69	2.10.68	
Armenia	23.7.93	23.6.93	
Australia	30.10.75	30.9.75	
Austria	8.6.72	9.5.72	
Azerbaijan	15.9.96	16.8.96	
Bahamas	5.8.75	5.8.75	
Bahrain	26.4.90	27.3.90	
Bangladesh	11.7.79	11.6.79	
Barbados	8.12.72	8.11.72	
Belarus	8.5.69	8.4.69	
Belgium	6.9.75	7.8.75	
Bolivia	22.10.70	22.9.70	
Bosnia and Herzegovina	16.7.93	16.7.93	
Botswana	22.3.74	20.2.74	
Brazil	4.1.69	27.3.68	
Bulgaria	4.1.69	8.8.66	
Burkina Faso	17.8.74	18.7.74	
Burundi	26.11.77	27.10.77	
Cambodia	28.12.86	28.11.83	
Cameroon	24.7.71	24.6.71	
Canada	15.11.70	14.10.70	
Cape Verde	2.11.79	3.10.79	
Central African Republic	15.4.71	16.3.71	
Chad	16.9.77	17.8.77	
Chile	19.11.71	20.10.71	
China	28.1.82	29.12.81	
Colombia	2.10.81	2.9.81	
Congo	10.8.88	11.7.88	
Costa Rica	4.1.69	16.1.67	
Côte d'Ivoire	3.2.73	4.1.73	
Croatia	8.10.91	12.10.92	
Cuba	16.3.72	15.2.72	
Cyprus	4.1.69	21.4.67	
Czech Republic	1.1.93	22.2.93	
Democratic Republic of the Congo	21.5.76	21.4.76	
Denmark	8.1.72	9.12.71	
Dominican Republic	24.6.83	25.5.83	
Ecuador	4.1.69	22.9.66	
Egypt	4.1.69	1.5.67	
El Salvador	31.12.79	30.11.79	
Estonia	20.11.91	21.10.91	
Ethiopia	23.7.76	23.6.76	
Fiji	11.1.73	11.1.73	

Country	Entry into Force	Receipt of Instrument of ratification	Date of Signature
Finland	13.8.70	14.7.70	
France	27.8.71	28.7.71	
Gabon	30.3.80	29.2.80	
Gambia	28.1.79	29.12.78	
Germany	15.6.69	16.5.69	
Ghana	4.1.69	8.9.66	
Greece	18.7.70	18.6.70	
Guatemala	17.2.83	18.1.83	
Guinea	13.4.77	14.3.77	
Guyana	17.3.77	15.2.77	
Haiti	18.1.73	19.12.72	
Holy See	31.5.69	1.5.69	
Hungary	4.1.69	1.5.67	
Iceland	4.1.69	13.3.67	
India	4.1.69	3.12.68	
Iran (Islamic Republic of)	4.1.69	29.8.68	
Iraq	13.2.70	14.1.70	
Israel	2.2.79	3.1.79	
Italy	4.2.76	5.1.76	
Jamaica	4.7.71	4.6.71	
Japan	14.1.96	15.12.95	
Jordan	29.6.74	30.5.74	
Kuwait	4.1.69	15.10.68	
Kyrgyzstan	5.10.97	5.9.97	
Lao People's Democratic Republic	24.3.74	22.2.74	
Latvia	14.5.92	14.4.92	
Lebanon	12.12.71	12.11.71	
Lesotho	4.12.71	4.11.71	
Liberia	5.12.76	5.11.76	
Libyan Arab Jamahiriya	4.1.69	3.7.68	
Luxembourg	31.5.78	1.5.78	
Madagascar	9.3.69	7.2.69	
Malawi	11.7.96	11.6.96	
Maldives	24.5.84	24.4.84	
Mali	15.8.74	16.7.74	
Malta	26.6.71	27.5.71	
Mauritania	12.1.89	13.12.88	
Mauritius	29.6.72	30.5.72	
Mexico	22.3.75	20.2.75	
Monaco	27.10.95	27.9.95	
Mongolia	5.9.69	6.8.69	
Morocco	17.1.71	18.12.70	
Mozambique	18.5.83	18.4.83	
Namibia	11.12.82	11.11.82	
Nepal	1.3.71	30.1.71	
Netherlands	9.1.72	10.12.71	
New Zealand	22.12.72	22.11.72	
Nicaragua	17.3.78	15.2.78	
Niger	4.1.69	27.4.67	
Nigeria	4.1.69	16.10.67	
Norway	5.9.70	6.8.70	
Pakistan	4.1.69	21.9.66	
Panama	4.1.69	16.8.67	
Papua New Guinea	26.2.82	27.1.82	
Peru	29.10.71	29.9.71	
Philippines	4.1.69	15.9.67	
Poland	4.1.69	5.12.68	
Portugal	23.9.82	24.8.82	
Qatar	21.8.76	22.7.76	
Republic of Korea	4.1.79	5.12.78	
Republic of Moldova	25.2.93	26.1.93	
Romania	15.10.70	15.9.70	
Russian Federation	6.3.69	4.2.69	
Rwanda	16.5.75	16.4.75	
Saint Lucia	14.2.90	14.2.90	
Saint Vincent and the Grenadines	9.12.81	9.11.81	
Saudi Arabia	23.10.97	23.9.97	
Senegal	19.5.72	19.4.72	
Seychelles	6.4.78	7.3.78	

Country	Entry into Force	Receipt of Instrument of ratification	Date of Signature
Sierra Leone	4.1.69	2.8.67	
Slovak Republic	28.5.93	28.5.93	
Slovenia	6.7.92	6.7.92	
Solomon Islands	17.3.82	17.3.82	
Somalia	25.9.75	26.8.75	
Spain	4.1.69	13.9.68	
Sri Lanka	20.3.82	18.2.82	
Sudan	20.4.77	21.3.77	
Suriname	15.3.84	15.3.84	
Swaziland	7.5.69	7.4.69	
Sweden	5.1.72	6.12.71	
Switzerland	29.12.94	29.11.94	
Syrian Arab Republic	21.5.69	21.4.69	
Tajikistan	10.2.95	11.1.95	
The Former Yugoslav Republic of Macedonia	17.9.91	18.1.94	
Togo	1.10.72	1.9.72	
Tonga	17.3.72	16.2.72	
Trinidad and Tobago	3.11.73	4.10.73	
Tunisia	4.1.69	13.1.67	
Turkmenistan	29.10.94	29.9.94	
Uganda	21.12.80	21.11.80	
Ukraine	6.4.69	7.3.69	
United Arab Emirates	20.7.74	20.6.74	
United Kingdom of Great Britain and Northern Ireland	6.4.69	7.3.69	
United Republic of Tanzania	26.11.72	27.10.72	
United States of America	20.11.94	21.10.94	
Uruguay	4.1.69	30.8.68	
Uzbekistan	28.10.95	28.9.95	
Venezuela	4.1.69	10.10.67	
Viet Nam	9.7.82	9.6.82	
Yemen	17.11.72	18.10.72	
Yugoslavia	4.1.69	2.10.67	
Zambia	5.3.72	4.2.72	
Zimbabwe	12.6.91	13.5.91	

Source: UN High Commissioner for Human Rights Website *(www.unhchr.ch)*—15 October 1998.

Convention Against Torture and Other Cruel Inhuman or Degrading Treatment or Punishment

Non State Parties

Country	Date of Signature (if applicable)
Andorra	
Angola	
Bahamas	
Bangladesh	
Barbados	
Belgium	4.2.85
Bhutan	
Bolivia	4.2.85
Botswana	
Brunei Darussalam	
Burkina Faso	
Central African Republic	
Comoros	
Congo	
Cook Islands	
Democratic People's Republic of Korea	
Djibouti	
Dominica	
Dominican Republic	4.2.85
Equatorial Guinea	
Eritrea	
Fiji	
Gabon	21.1.86
Gambia	23.10.85

Country	Date of Signature (if applicable)
Ghana	
Grenada	
Guinea-Bissau	
Haiti	
Holy See	
India	14.10.97
Indonesia	23.10.85
Iran (Islamic Republic of)	
Iraq	
Ireland	28.9.92
Jamaica	
Japan	
Kazakhstan	
Kiribati	
Lao People's Democratic Republic	
Lebanon	
Lesotho	
Liberia	
Madagascar	
Malaysia	
Maldives	
Mali	
Marshall Islands	
Mauritania	
Micronesia (Federated States of)	
Mongolia	
Mozambique	
Myanmar	
Nauru	
Nicaragua	15.4.85
Niger	
Nigeria	28.7.88
Niue	
Oman	
Pakistan	
Palau	
Papua New Guinea	
Qatar	
Rwanda	
Saint Kitts and Nevis	
Saint Lucia	
Saint Vincent and the Grenadines	
Samoa	
San Marino	
Sao Tom and Principe	
Sierra Leone	18.3.85
Singapore	
Solomon Islands	
South Africa	29.1.93
Sudan	4.6.86
Suriname	
Swaziland	
Syrian Arab Republic	
Thailand	
Tonga	
Trinidad and Tobago	
Turkmenistan	
Tuvalu	
United Arab Emirates	
United Republic of Tanzania	
Vanuatu	
Vietnam	
Zambia	
Zimbabwe	

Source: UN High Commissioner for Human Rights Website (*www.unhchr.ch*)—
15 October 1998.

State Parties

Country	Entry into Force	Receipt of Instrument of ratification	Date of Signature
Afghanistan	26.6.87	1.4.87	4.2.85
Albania	10.6.94	11.5.94	
Algeria	12.10.89	12.9.89	26.11.85
Antigua and Barbuda	18.8.93	19.7.93	
Argentina	26.6.87	24.9.86	4.2.85
Armenia	13.10.93	13.9.93	
Australia	7.9.89	8.8.89	10.12.85
Austria	28.8.87	29.7.87	14.3.85
Azerbaijan	15.9.96	16.8.96	
Bahrain	5.4.98	6.3.98	
Belarus	26.6.87	13.3.87	19.12.85
Belize	26.6.87	17.3.86	
Benin	11.4.92	12.3.92	
Bosnia and Herzegovina	6.3.92	1.9.93	
Brazil	28.10.89	28.9.89	23.9.85
Bulgaria	26.6.87	16.12.86	10.6.86
Burundi	20.3.93	18.2.93	
Cambodia	14.11.92	15.10.92	
Cameroon	26.6.87	19.12.86	
Canada	24.7.87	24.6.87	23.8.85
Cape Verde	4.7.92	4.6.92	
Chad	9.7.95	9.6.95	
Chile	30.10.88	30.9.88	23.9.87
China	3.11.88	4.10.88	12.12.86
Colombia	7.1.88	8.12.87	10.4.85
Costa Rica	11.12.93	11.11.93	4.2.85
Côte d'Ivoire	17.1.96	18.12.95	
Croatia	8.10.91	12.10.92	
Cuba	16.6.95	17.5.95	27.1.86
Cyprus	17.8.91	18.7.91	9.10.85
Czech Republic	1.1.93	1.1.93	
Democratic Republic of the Congo	17.4.96	18.3.96	
Denmark	26.6.87	27.5.87	4.2.85
Ecuador	29.4.88	30.3.88	4.2.85
Egypt	26.6.87	25.6.86	
El Salvador	17.7.96	17.6.96	
Estonia	20.11.91	21.10.91	
Ethiopia	13.4.94	13.3.94	
Finland	29.9.89	30.8.89	4.2.85
France	26.6.87	18.2.86	4.2.85
Georgia	25.11.94	26.10.94	
Germany	31.10.90	1.10.90	13.10.86
Greece	5.11.88	6.10.88	4.2.85
Guatemala	4.2.90	5.1.90	
Guinea	9.11.89	10.10.89	30.5.86
Guyana	18.6.88	19.5.88	25.1.88
Honduras	4.1.97	5.12.96	
Hungary	26.6.87	15.4.87	28.11.86
Iceland	22.11.96	23.10.96	4.2.85
Israel	2.11.91	3.10.91	22.10.86
Italy	11.2.89	12.1.89	4.2.85
Jordan	13.12.91	13.11.91	
Kenya	23.3.97	21.2.97	
Kuwait	7.4.96	8.3.96	
Kyrgyzstan	5.10.97	5.9.97	
Latvia	14.5.92	14.4.92	
Libyan Arab Jamahiriya	15.6.89	16.5.89	
Liechtenstein	2.12.90	2.11.90	27.6.85
Lithuania	2.3.96	1.2.96	
Luxembourg	29.10.87	29.9.87	22.2.85
Malawi	11.7.97	11.6.96	
Malta	13.10.90	13.9.90	
Mauritius	8.1.93	9.12.92	
Mexico	26.6.87	23.1.86	18.3.85
Monaco	5.1.92	6.12.91	
Morocco	21.7.93	21.6.93	8.1.86
Namibia	28.12.94	28.11.94	
Nepal	13.6.91	14.5.91	

Country	Entry into Force	Receipt of Instrument of ratification	Date of Signature
Netherlands	20.10.89	21.12.88	4.2.85
New Zealand	9.1.90	10.12.89	14.1.86
Norway	26.6.87	9.7.86	4.2.85
Panama	23.9.87	24.8.87	22.2.85
Paraguay	11.4.90	12.3.90	23.10.89
Peru	6.8.88	7.7.88	29.5.85
Philippines	26.6.87	18.6.86	
Poland	25.8.89	26.7.89	13.1.86
Portugal	11.3.89	9.2.89	4.2.85
Republic of Korea	8.2.95	9.1.95	
Republic of Moldova	28.12.95	28.11.95	
Romania	17.1.91	18.12.90	
Russian Federation	26.6.87	3.3.87	10.12.85
Saudi Arabia	23.10.97	23.9.97	
Senegal	26.6.87	21.8.86	4.2.85
Seychelles	4.6.92	5.5.92	
Slovak Republic	28.5.93	28.5.93	
Slovenia	15.8.93	16.7.93	
Somalia	23.2.90	24.1.90	
Spain	20.11.87	21.10.87	4.2.85
Sri Lanka	2.2.94	3.1.94	
Sweden	26.6.87	8.1.86	4.2.85
Switzerland	26.6.87	2.12.86	4.2.85
Tajikistan	10.2.95	11.1.95	
The Former Yugoslav Republic of Macedonia	12.12.94	12.12.94	
Togo	18.12.87	18.11.87	25.3.87
Tunisia	23.10.88	23.9.88	26.8.87
Turkey	1.9.88	2.8.88	25.1.88
Uganda	26.6.87	3.11.86	
Ukraine	26.6.87	24.2.87	27.2.86
United Kingdom of Great Britain and Northern Ireland	7.1.89	8.12.88	15.3.85
United States of America	20.11.94	21.10.94	18.4.88
Uruguay	26.6.87	24.10.86	4.2.85
Uzbekistan	28.10.95	28.9.95	
Venezuela	28.8.91	29.7.91	15.2.85
Yemen	5.12.91	5.11.91	
Yugoslavia	10.10.91	10.9.91	18.4.89

Source: UN High Commissioner for Human Rights Website (*www.unhchr.ch*)—15 October 1998.

Optional Protocol to the International Covenant on Civil and Political Rights

Non State Parties

Country	Date of Signature (if applicable)
Afghanistan	
Albania	
Andorra	14.3.98
Andorra	
Antigua and Barbuda	
Azerbaijan	
Bahamas	
Bahrain	
Bangladesh	
Belize	
Bhutan	
Botswana	
Brazil	
Brunei Darussalam	
Burkina Faso	
Burundi	
Cambodia	
Cape Verde	
China	
Comoros	
Cook Islands	
Cuba	

Country	Date of Signature (if applicable)
Democratic People's Republic of Korea	
Djibouti	
Dominica	
Egypt	
Eritrea	
Ethiopia	
Fiji	
Gabon	
Ghana	
Grenada	
Guatemala	
Guinea-Bissau	
Haiti	
Holy See	
Honduras	19.12.66
India	
Indonesia	
Iran (Islamic Republic of)	
Iraq	
Israel	
Jamaica	
Japan	
Jordan	
Kazakhstan	
Kiribati	
Kuwait	
Lao People's Democratic Republic	
Lebanon	
Lesotho	
Liberia	
Leichtenstein	
Malaysia	
Maldives	
Mali	
Marshall Islands	
Mauritania	
Mexico	
Micronesia (Federated States of)	
Monaco	
Morocco	
Mozambique	
Myanmar	
Nauru	
Nigeria	
Niue	
Oman	
Pakistan	
Palau	
Papua New Guinea	
Qatar	
Republic of Moldova	
Rwanda	
Saint Kitts and Nevis	
Saint Lucia	
Samoa	
Sao Tom and Principe	
Saudi Arabia	
Singapore	
Solomon Islands	
South Africa	
Sudan	
Swaziland	
Switzerland	
Syrian Arab Republic	
Tajikistan	
Thailand	
Tonga	
Tunisia	
Turkey	
Tuvalu	

Country	Date of Signature (if applicable)
United Arab Emirates	
United Kingdom of Great Britain and Northern Ireland	
United States of America	
Vanuatu	
Viet Nam	
Yemen	
Yugoslavia	14.3.90
Zimbabwe	

Source: UN High Commissioner for Human Rights Website *(www.unhchr.ch)*– 15 October 1998.

State Parties

Country	Entry into Force	Receipt of Instrument of ratification	Date of Signature
Algeria	12.12.89	12.9.89	
Angola	10.4.92	10.1.92	
Argentina	8.11.86	8.8.86	
Armenia	23.9.93	23.6.93	
Australia	25.12.91	25.9.91	
Austria	10.3.88	10.12.87	10.12.73
Barbados	23.3.76	5.1.73	
Belarus	30.12.92	30.9.92	
Belgium	17.8.94	17.5.94	
Benin	12.6.92	12.3.92	
Bolivia	12.11.82	12.8.82	
Bosnia and Herzegovina	1.6.95	1.3.95	
Bulgaria	26.6.92	26.3.92	
Cameroon	27.9.84	27.6.84	
Canada	19.8.76	19.5.76	
Central African Republic	8.8.81	8.5.81	
Chad	9.9.95	9.6.95	
Chile	28.8.92	28.5.92	
Colombia	23.3.76	29.10.69	21.12.66
Congo	5.1.84	5.10.83	
Costa Rica	23.3.76	29.11.68	9.12.66
Côte d'Ivoire	5.6.97	5.3.97	
Croatia	12.1.96	12.10.95	
Cyprus	15.7.92	15.4.92	19.12.66
Czech Republic	1.1.93	22.2.93	
Democratic Republic of the Congo	1.2.77	1.11.76	
Denmark	23.3.76	6.1.72	20.3.68
Dominican Republic	4.4.78	4.1.78	
Ecuador	23.3.76	6.3.69	4.4.68
El Salvador	6.9.95	6.6.95	21.9.67
Equatorial Guinea	25.12.87	25.9.87	
Estonia	21.1.92	21.10.91	
Finland	23.3.76	19.8.75	11.12.67
France	17.5.84	17.2.84	
Gambia	9.9.88	9.6.88	
Georgia	3.8.94	3.5.94	
Germany	25.11.93	25.8.93	
Greece	5.8.97	5.5.97	
Guinea	17.9.93	17.6.93	19.3.75
Guyana	10.8.93	10.5.93	
Hungary	7.12.88	7.9.88	
Iceland	22.11.79	22.8.79	
Ireland	8.3.90	8.12.89	
Italy	15.12.78	15.9.78	30.4.76
Kyrgyzstan	7.1.94	7.10.95	
Latvia	22.9.94	22.6.94	
Libyan Arab Jamahiriya	16.8.89	16.5.89	
Lithuania	20.2.92	20.11.91	
Luxembourg	18.11.83	18.8.83	
Madagascar	23.3.76	21.6.71	17.9.69
Malawi	11.9.96	11.6.96	
Malta	13.12.90	13.9.90	

Country	Entry into Force	Receipt of Instrument of ratification	Date of Signature
Mauritius	23.3.76	12.12.73	
Mongolia	16.7.91	16.4.91	
Namibia	28.2.95	28.11.94	
Nepal	14.8.91	14.5.91	
Netherlands	11.3.79	11.12.78	25.6.69
New Zealand	26.8.89	26.5.89	
Nicaragua	12.6.80	12.3.80	
Niger	7.6.86	7.3.86	
Norway	23.3.76	13.9.72	20.3.68
Panama	8.6.77	8.3.77	27.7.76
Paraguay	10.4.95	10.1.95	
Peru	3.1.81	3.10.80	11.8.77
Philippines	22.11.89	22.8.89	19.12.66
Poland	7.2.92	7.11.91	
Portugal	3.8.83	3.5.83	1.8.78
Republic of Korea	10.7.90	10.4.90	
Romania	20.10.93	20.7.93	
Russian Federation	1.1.92	1.10.91	
Saint Vincent and the Grenadines	9.2.82	9.11.81	
San Marino	18.1.86	18.10.85	
Senegal	13.5.78	13.2.78	6.7.70
Seychelles	5.8.92	5.5.92	
Sierra Leone	23.8.96	23.8.96	
Slovak Republic	1.1.93	28.5.93	
Slovenia	16.10.93	16.7.93	
Somalia	24.4.90	24.1.90	
Spain	25.4.85	25.1.85	
Sri Lanka	3.1.98	3.10.97	
Suriname	28.3.77	28.12.76	
Sweden	23.3.76	6.12.71	29.9.67
The Former Yugoslav Republic of Macedonia	12.3.95	12.12.94	
Togo	30.6.88	30.3.88	
Trinidad and Tobago	14.2.81	14.11.80	
Turkmenistan	1.8.97	1.5.97	
Uganda	14.2.96	14.11.95	
Ukraine	25.10.91	25.7.91	
Uruguay	23.3.76	1.4.70	21.2.67
Uzbekistan	28.12.95	28.9.95	
Venezuela	10.8.78	10.5.78	15.11.76
Zambia	10.7.84	10.4.84	

Source: UN High Commissioner for Human Rights Website *(www.unhchr.ch)*—15 October 1998.

Second Optional Protocol to the International Covenant on Civil and Political Rights

Non State Parties

Country	Date of Signature (if applicable)
Afghanistan	
Albania	
Algeria	
Angola	
Antigua and Barbuda	
Argentina	
Armenia	
Azerbaijan	
Bahamas	
Bahrain	
Bangladesh	
Barbados	
Belarus	
Belgium	12.7.90
Belize	
Benin	
Bhutan	

Country	Date of Signature (if applicable)
Bolivia	
Bosnia and Herzegovina	
Botswana	
Brazil	
Brunei	
Darussalam	
Bulgaria	
Burkina Faso	
Burundi	
Cambodia	
Cameroon	
Canada	
Cape Verde	
Central African Republic	
Chad	
Chile	
China	
Comoros	
Congo	
Cook Islands	
Cote d'Ivoire	
Cuba	
Cyprus	
Czech Republic	
Democratic People's Republic of Korea	
Democratic Republic of the Congo	
Djibouti	
Dominica	
Dominican Republic	
Egypt	
Equatorial Guinea	
Eritrea	
Estonia	
Ethiopia	
Fiji	
France	
Gabon	
Gambia	
Georgia	
Ghana	
Grenada	
Guatemala	
Guinea	
Guinea-Bissau	
Guyana	
Haiti	
Holy See	
Honduras	10.5.90
India	
Indonesia	
Iran (Islamic Republic of)	
Iraq	
Israel	
Jamaica	
Japan	
Jordan	
Kazakhstan	
Kenya	
Kiribati	
Kuwait	
Kyrgyzstan	
Lao People's Democratic Republic	
Latvia	
Lebanon	
Lesotho	
Liberia	
Libyan Arab Jamahiriya	
Liechtenstein	

Country	Date of Signature (if applicable)
Lithuania	
Madagascar	
Malawi	
Malaysia	
Maldives	
Mali	
Marshall Islands	
Mauritania	
Mauritius	
Mexico	
Micronesia (Federated States of)	
Monaco	
Mongolia	
Morocco	
Myanmar	
Nauru	
Nicaragua	21.2.90
Niger	
Nigeria	
Niue	
Oman	
Pakistan	
Palau	
Papua New Guinea	
Paraguay	
Peru	
Philippines	
Poland	
Qatar	
Republic of Korea	
Republic of Moldova	
Russian Federation	
Rwanda	
Saint Kitts and Nevis	
Saint Lucia	
Saint Vincent and the Grenadines	
Samoa	
San Marino	
Sao Tom and Principe	
Saudi Arabia	
Senegal	
Sierra Leone	
Singapore	
Slovak Republic	
Solomon Islands	
Somalia	
South Africa	
Sri Lanka	
Sudan	
Suriname	
Swaziland	
Syrian Arab Republic	
Tajikistan	
Thailand	
Togo	
Tonga	
Trinidad and Tobago	
Tunisia	
Turkey	
Turkmenistan	
Tuvalu	
Uganda	
Ukraine	
United Arab Emirates	
United Kingdom of Great Britain and Northern Ireland	
United Republic of Tanzania	
United States of America	
Uzbekistan	

Country	Date of Signature (if applicable)
Vanuatu	
Vietnam	
Yemen	
Yugoslavia	
Zambia	
Zimbabwe	

Source: UN High Commissioner for Human Rights Website (*www.unhchr.ch*)—15 October 1998.

State Parties

Country	Entry into Force	Receipt of Instrument of ratification	Date of Signature
Australia	11.7.91	2.10.90	
Austria	2.6.93	2.3.93	8.4.91
Colombia	4.11.97	5.8.97	
Costa Rica	5.6.98	5.6.98	14.2.90
Croatia	12.1.96	12.10.95	
Denmark	24.5.94	24.2.94	13.2.90
Ecuador	23.5.93	23.2.93	
Finland	11.7.91	4.4.91	13.2.90
Germany	18.11.92	18.8.92	13.2.90
Greece	5.8.97	5.5.97	
Hungary	24.5.94	24.2.94	
Iceland	11.7.91	2.4.91	30.1.91
Ireland	18.9.93	18.6.93	
Italy	14.5.95	14.2.95	13.2.90
Luxembourg	12.5.92	12.2.92	13.2.90
Malta	29.3.95	29.12.94	
Mozambique	21.10.93	21.7.93	
Namibia	28.2.95	28.11.94	
Nepal	4.6.98	4.3.98	
Netherlands	11.7.91	26.3.91	9.8.90
New Zealand	11.7.91	22.2.90	22.2.90
Norway	5.12.91	5.9.91	13.2.90
Panama	21.4.93	21.1.93	
Portugal	11.7.91	17.10.90	13.2.90
Romania	11.7.91	27.2.91	15.3.90
Seychelles	15.3.95	15.12.94	
Slovenia	10.6.94	10.3.94	14.9.93
Spain	11.7.91	11.4.91	23.2.90
Sweden	11.7.91	11.5.90	13.2.90
Switzerland	16.9.94	16.6.94	
The Former Yugoslav Republic of Macedonia	26.4.95	26.1.95	
Uruguay	21.4.93	21.1.93	13.2.90
Venezuela	22.5.93	22.2.93	7.6.90

Source: UN High Commissioner for Human Rights Website (*www.unhchr.ch*)—15 October 1998.

ANNEX C

United Nations List of Human Rights Instruments

International Covenant on Civil and Political Rights (ICCPR);

International Covenant on Economic, Social and Cultural Rights (ICESCR);

Optional Protocol to the International Covenant on Civil and Political Rights;

Second Optional Protocol to the International Covenant on Civil and Political Rights;

International Convention on the Elimination of All Forms of Racial Discrimination;

International Convention on the Suppression and Punishment of the Crime of Apartheid;

International Convention Against Apartheid in Sport;

Convention on the Prevention and Punishment of the Crime of Genocide;

Convention on the Non-Applicability of Statutory Limitations to War Crimes and Crimes Against Humanity;

Convention on the Rights of the Child;

Convention on the Elimination of all Forms of Discrimination Against Women;

Convention on the Political Rights of Women;

Convention on the Nationality of Married Women;

Convention on Consent to Marriage, Minimum Age for Marriage and Registration of Marriages;

Convention against Torture and Other Cruel, Inhuman or Degrading Treatment or Punishment;

Slavery Convention of 1926;

1953 Protocol amending the 1926 Convention;

Slavery Convention of 1926 as amended;

Supplementary Convention on the Abolition of Slavery, the Slave Trade, and Institutions and Practices Similar to Slavery;

Convention on the Suppression of the Traffic in Persons and of the Exploitation of the Prostitution of Others;

Convention on the Reduction of Statelessness;

Convention Relating to the Status of Stateless Persons;

Convention Relating to the Status of Refugees;

Protocol Relating to the Status of Refugees;

Convention on the Rights of Migrant Workers and the Members of their Families.

Source: United Nations Chart of Ratifications as at *31 December 1997* ST/HR/4/Rev.16

ANNEX D

Full list of International Labour Organisation (ILO) Conventions

List as shown in the ILO "List of Ratifications by Convention and by country". The Conventions which the UK has ratified are shown in bold type.

LIST OF CONVENTIONS ADOPTED, BY SESSION

First Session (Washington) 1919

    C. 1   Hours of Work (Industry) Convention, 1919

    C. 2   Unemployment Convention, 1919

    ¹C. 3   Maternity Protection Convention, 1919

    ¹**C. 4   Night Work (Women) Convention, 1919**

    ¹**C. 5   Minimum Age (Industry) Convention, 1919**

    ¹**C. 6   Night Work of Young Persons (Industry) Convention, 1919**

Second Session (Genoa) 1920

    ¹**C. 7   Minimum Age (Sea) Convention, 1920**

    C. 8   Unemployment Indemnity (Shipwreck) Convention, 1920

    C. 9   Placing of Seamen Convention, 1920

Third Session (Geneva) 1921

    ¹**C. 10   Minimum Age (Agriculture) Convention, 1921**

    C. 11   Rights of Association (Agriculture) Convention, 1921

    ¹**C. 12   Workmen's Compensation (Agriculture) Convention, 1921**

    C. 13   White Lead (Painting) Convention, 1921

    C. 14   Weekly Rest (Industry) Convention, 1921

    ¹**C. 15   Minimum Age (Trimmers and Stokers) Convention, 1921**

    C. 16   Medical Examination of Young Persons (Sea) Convention, 1921

Seventh Session (Geneva) 1925

    ¹**C. 17   Workmen's Compensation (Accidents) Convention, 1925**

    ¹**C. 18   Workmen's Compensation (Occupational Diseases) Convention, 1925**

    C. 19   Equality of Treatment (Accident Compensation) Convention, 1925

    C. 20   Night Work (Bakeries) Convention, 1925

Eighth Session (Geneva) 1926

    C. 21   Inspection of Emigrants Convention, 1926

Ninth Session (Geneva) 1926

   C. 22   Seamen's Articles of Agreement Convention, 1926
   ¹**C. 23   Repatriation of Seamen Convention, 1926**

Tenth Session (Geneva) 1927

   ¹**C. 24   Sickness Insurance (Industry) Convention, 1927**
   ¹**C. 25   Sickness Insurance (Agriculture) Convention, 1927**

Eleventh Session (Geneva) 1928

   C. 26   Minimum Wage-Fixing Machinery Convention, 1928

Twelfth Session (Geneva) 1929

   C. 27   Marking of Weight (Packages Transported by Vessels) Convention, 1929
   ^{1,2}C. 28   Protection against Accidents (Dockers) Convention, 1929

Fourteenth Session (Geneva) 1930

   C. 29   Forced Labour Convention, 1930
   C. 30   Hours of Work (Commerce and Offices) Convention, 1930

Fifteenth Session (Geneva) 1931

   ^{1,2,3}C. 31   Hours of Work (Coal Mines) Convention, 1931

Sixteenth Session (Geneva) 1932

   ^{1,2}**C. 32   Protection against Accidents (Dockers) Convention (Revised), 1932**
   ^{1,2}C. 33   Minimum Age (Non-Industrial Employment) Convention, 1932

Seventeenth Session (Geneva) 1933

   ^{1,2}C. 34   Fee-Charging Employment Agencies Convention, 1933
   ^{1,2}**C. 35   Old-Age Insurance (Industry, etc.) Convention, 1933**
   ^{1,2}**C. 36   Old-Age Insurance (Agriculture) Convention, 1933**
   ^{1,2}**C. 37   Invalidity Insurance (Industry, etc.) Convention, 1933**
   ^{1,2}**C. 38   Invalidity Insurance (Agriculture) Convention, 1933**
   ^{1,2}**C. 39   Survivors' Insurance (Industry, etc.) Convention, 1933**
   ^{1,2}**C. 40   Survivors' Insurance (Agriculture) Convention, 1933**

Eighteenth Session (Geneva) 1934

   ^{1,2}**C. 41   Night Work (Women) Convention (Revised), 1934**
   ¹**C. 42   Workmen's Compensation (Occupational Diseases) Convention (Revised), 1934**
   C. 43   Sheet-Glass Works Convention, 1934
   ^{1,2}**C. 44   Unemployment Provision Convention, 1934**

Nineteenth Session (Geneva) 1935

   C. 45   Underground Work (Women) Convention, 1935
   ³C. 46   Hours of Work (Coal Mines) Convention (Revised), 1935
   C. 47   Forty-Hour Week Convention, 1935
   ^{1,2}C. 48   Maintenance of Migrants' Pension Rights Convention, 1935
   C. 49   Reduction of Hours of Work (Glass-Bottle Works) Convention, 1935

Twentieth Session (Geneva) 1936

   C. 50   Recruiting of Indigenous Workers Convention, 1936
   ⁴C. 51   Reduction of Hours of Work (Public Works) Convention, 1936
   ^{1,2}C. 52   Holidays with Pay Convention, 1936

Twenty-first Session (Geneva) 1936

   C. 53   Officers' Competency Certificates Convention, 1936
   ^{1,2,3}C. 54   Holidays with Pay (Sea) Convention, 1936
   C. 55   Shipowners' Liability (Sick and Injured Seamen) Convention, 1936
   ^{1,2}**C. 56   Sickness Insurance (Sea) Convention, 1936**
   ^{1,3}C. 57   Hours of Work and Manning (Sea) Convention, 1936

Twenty-second Session (Geneva) 1936

   ¹C. 58   Minimum Age (Sea) Convention (Revised), 1936

Twenty-third Session (Geneva) 1937

   ¹C. 59   Minimum Age (Industry) Convention (Revised), 1937
   ¹C. 60   Minimum Age (Non-Industrial Employment) Convention (Revised), 1937
   ⁴C. 61   Reduction of Hours of Work (Textiles) Convention, 1937
   ^{1,2}C. 62   Safety Provisions (Building) Convention, 1937

Twenty-fourth Session (Geneva) 1938

[1,2]**C. 63   Convention concerning Statistics of Wages and Hours of Work, 1938**

Twenty-fifth Session (Geneva) 1939

C. 64   Contracts of Employment (Indigenous Workers) Convention, 1939

C. 65   Penal Sanctions (Indigenous Workers) Convention, 1939

[2,4]C. 66   Migration for Employment Convention, 1939

[1,2]C. 67   Hours of Work and Rest Periods (Road Transport) Convention, 1939

Twenty-eighth Session (Seattle) 1946

C. 68   Food and Catering (Ships' Crews) Convention, 1946

C. 69   Certification of Ships Cooks Convention, 1946

[1,2,3]**C. 70   Social Security (Seafarers) Convention, 1946**

C. 71   Seafarers' Pensions Convention, 1946

[1,2,3]**C. 72   Paid Vacations (Seafarers) Convention, 1946**

C. 73   Medical Examination (Seafarers) Convention, 1946

C. 74   Certification of Able Seamen Convention, 1946

[1,2,3]C. 75   Accommodation of Crews Convention, 1946

[1,3]C. 76   Wages, Hours of work and Manning (Sea) Convention, 1946

Twenty-ninth Session (Montreal) 1946

C. 77   Medical Examination of Young Persons (Industry) Convention, 1946

C. 78   Medical Examination of young Persons (Non-Industrial Occupations) Convention, 1946

C. 79   Night Work of Young Persons (Non-Industrial Occupations) Convention, 1946

C. 80   Final Articles Revision Convention, 1946

Thirtieth Session (Geneva) 1947

C. 81   Labour Inspection Convention, 1947 [and Protocol, 1995]

[1]**C. 82   Social Policy (Non-Metropolitan Territories) Convention, 1947**

C. 83   Labour Standards (Non-Metropolitan Territories) Convention, 1947

C. 84   Right of Association (Non-Metropolitan Territories) Convention, 1947

C. 85   Labour Inspectorates (Non-Metropolitan Territories) Convention, 1947

C. 86   Contracts of Employment (Indigenous Workers) Convention, 1947

Thirty-first Session (San Francisco) 1948

C. 87   Freedom of Association and Protection of the Right to Organise Convention, 1948

C. 88   Employment Service Convention, 1948

C. 89   Night Work (Women) Convention (Revised), 1948 [and Protocol, 1990]

C. 90   Night Work of Young Persons (Industry) Convention (Revised), 1948

Thirty-second Session (Geneva) 1949

[1,2]C. 91   Paid Vacations (Seafarers) Convention (Revised), 1949

C. 92   Accommodation of Crews Convention (Revised), 1949

[1,3]C. 93   Wages, Hours of Work and Manning (Sea) Convention (Revised), 1949

C. 94   Labour Clauses (Public Contracts) Convention, 1949

[1]**C. 95   Protection of Wages Convention, 1949**

C. 96   Fee-Charging Employment Agencies Convention (Revised), 1949

C. 97   Migration for Employment Convention (Revised), 1949

C. 98   Right to Organize and Collective Bargaining Convention, 1949

Thirty-fourth Session (Geneva) 1951

C. 99   Minimum Wage Fixing Machinery (Agriculture) Convention, 1951

C. 100   Equal Remuneration Convention, 1951

Thirty-fifth Session (Geneva) 1952

[1]**C. 101   Holidays with Pay (Agriculture) Convention, 1952**

C. 102   Social Security (Minimum Standards) Convention, 1952

C. 103   Maternity Protection Convention (Revised), 1952

Thirty-eighth Session (Geneva) 1955

C. 104   Abolition of Penal Sanctions (Indigenous Workers) Convention, 1955

Fortieth Session (Geneva) 1957

C. 105   Abolition of Forced Labour Convention, 1957

C. 106   Weekly Rest (Commerce and Offices) Convention, 1957

[1,2]C. 107   Indigenous and Tribal Populations Convention, 1957

Forty-first Session (Geneva) 1958

   C. 108 Seafarers' Identity Documents Convention, 1958

   ³C. 109 Wages, Hours of work and Manning (Sea) Convention (Revised), 1958

Forty-second Session (Geneva) 1958

   C. 110 Plantations Conventions, 1958 [and Protocol, 1982]

   C. 111 Discrimination (Employment and Occupation) Convention, 1958

Forty-third Session (Geneva) 1959

   ¹C. 112 Minimum Age (Fishermen) Convention, 1959

   C. 113 Medical Examination (Fishermen) Convention, 1959

   C. 114 Fishermen's Articles of Agreement Convention, 1959

Forty-fourth Session (Geneva) 1960

   C. 115 Radiation Protection Convention, 1960

Forty-fifth Session (Geneva) 1961

   C. 116 Final Articles Revision Convention, 1961

Forty-sixth Session (Geneva) 1962

   C. 117 Social Policy (Basic Aims and Standards) Convention, 1962

   C. 118 Equality of Treatment (Social Security) Convention, 1962

Forty-seventh Session (Geneva) 1963

   C. 119 Guarding of Machinery Convention, 1963

Forty-eighth Session (Geneva) 1964

   C. 120 Hygiene (Commerce and Offices) Convention, 1964

   C. 121 Employment Injury Benefits Convention, 1964 [Schedule I amended in 1980]

   ¹**C. 122 Employment Policy Convention, 1964**

Forty-ninth Session (Geneva) 1965

   ¹C. 123 Minimum Age (Underground Work) Convention, 1965

   C. 124 Medical Examination of Young Persons (Underground Work) Convention 1965

Fiftieth Session (Geneva)

   C. 125 Fishermen's Competency Certificates Convention, 1966

   C. 126 Accommodation of Crews (Fishermen) Convention, 1966

Fifty-first Session (Geneva) 1967

   C. 127 Maximum Weight Convention, 1967

   C. 128 Invalidity, Old-Age and Survivors' Benefits Convention, 1967

Fifty-third Session (Geneva) 1969

   C. 129 Labour Inspection (Agriculture) Convention, 1969

   C. 130 Medical Care and Sickness Benefits Convention, 1969

Fifty-fourth Session (Geneva) 1970

   C. 131 Minimum Wage Fixing Convention, 1970

   C. 132 Holidays with Pay Convention (Revised), 1970

Fifty-fifth Session (Geneva) 1970

   C. 133 Accommodation of Crews (Supplementary Provisions) Convention, 1970

   C. 134 Prevention of Accidents (Seafarers) Convention, 1970

Fifty-sixth Session (Geneva) 1971

   C. 135 Workers' Representatives Convention, 1971

   C. 136 Benzene Convention, 1971

Fifty-eighth Session (Geneva) 1973

   C. 137 Dock Work Convention, 1973

   C. 138 Minimum Age Convention, 1973

Fifty-ninth Session (Geneva) 1974

   C. 139 Occupational Cancer Convention, 1974

   C. 140 Paid Educational Leave Convention, 1974

Sixtieth Session (Geneva) 1975

   C. 141 Rural Workers' Organisations Convention, 1975

   C. 142 Human Resources Development Convention, 1975

   C. 143 Migrant Workers (Supplementary Provisions) Convention, 1975

Sixty-first Session (Geneva) 1976

   C. 144 Tripartite Consultation (International Labour Standards) Convention, 1976

Sixty-second Session (Geneva) 1976

C. 145   Continuity of Employment (Seafarers) Convention, 1976

C. 146   Seafarers' Annual Leave with Pay Convention, 1976

C. 147   Merchant Shipping (Minimum Standards) Convention, 1976 [and Protocol, 1996]

Sixty-third Session (Geneva) 1977

C. 148   Working Environments (Air Pollution, Noise and Vibration) Convention, 1977

C. 149   Nursing Personnel Convention, 1977

Sixty-fourth Session (Geneva) 1978

C. 150   Labour Administration Convention, 1978

C. 151   Labour Relations (Public Service) Convention, 1978

Sixty-fifth Session (Geneva) 1979

C. 152   Occupational Safety and Health (Dock Work) Convention, 1979

C. 153   Hours of Work and Rest Periods (Road Transport) Convention, 1979

Sixty-seventh Session (Geneva) 1981

C. 154   Collective Bargaining Convention, 1981

C. 155   Occupational Safety and Health Convention, 1981

C. 156   Workers with Family Responsibilties Convention, 1981

Sixty-eighth Session (Geneva) 1982

C. 157   Maintenance of Social Security Rights Convention, 1982

C. 158   Termination of Employment Convention, 1982

Sixty-ninth Session (Geneva) 1983

C. 159   Vocational Rehabilitation and Employment (Disabled Persons) Convention, 1983

Seventy-first Session (Geneva) 1985

C. 160   Labour Statistics Convention, 1985

C. 161   Occupational Health Services Convention, 1985

Seventy-second Session (Geneva) 1986

C. 162   Asbestos Convention, 1986

Seventy-fourth Session (Geneva) 1987

C. 163   Seafarers Welfare Convention, 1987

C. 164   Health Protection and Medical Care (Seafarers) Convention, 1987

C. 165   Social Security (Seafarers) Convention, (Revised), 1987

C. 166   Repatriation of Seafarers Convention (Revised), 1987

Seventy-fifth Session (Geneva) 1988

C. 167   Safety and Health in Construction Convention, 1988

C. 168   Employment Promotion and Protection against Unemployment Convention, 1988

Seventy-sixth Session (Geneva) 1989

C. 169   Indigenous and Tribal Peoples Convention, 1989

Seventy-seventh Session (Geneva) 1990

C. 170   Chemicals Convention, 1990

C. 171   Night Work Convention, 1990

Seventy-eighth Session (Geneva) 1991

C. 172   Working Conditions (Hotels and Restaurants) Convention, 1991

Seventy-ninth Session (Geneva) 1992

C. 173   Protection of Workers' Claims (Employer's Insolvency) Convention 1992

Eightieth Session (Geneva) 1993

C. 174   Prevention of Major Industrial Accidents Convention 1993

Eighty-first Session (Geneva) 1994

[3]C. 175   Part-Time Work Convention 1994

Eighty-second Session (Geneva) 1995

[4]C. 176   Safety and Health in Mines Convention, 1995

Eighty-third Session (Geneva) 1996

C. 177   Home Work Convention, 1996

Eighty-third Session (Geneva) 1996

⁴C. 178　Inspection of Seafarers' Working and Living Conditions Convention, 1996

⁴C. 179　Recruitment and Placement of Seafarers Convention 1996

⁴C. 180　Seafarers' Hours of Work and the Manning of Ships Convention, 1996

Total number of ratifications of international labour Conventions as at 31 December 1996: 6,390

¹ Convention revised by a subsequent Convention (not counting Final Articles revisions made by Conventions Nos. 80 and 116).

² Convention no longer open to ratification as a result of the entry into force of a revising Convention.

³ Convention which had not received the required number of ratifications for entry into force.

⁴ Convention which had not yet received any ratification.

APPENDIX 31

Memorandum submitted by Rights and Accountability in Development (RAID), Queen Elizabeth House, Oxford University

We would like to submit information on the following areas for the Committee's consideration:

1. *Ratification of International Human Rights Treaties*

    (a)　The ratification of the Revised Social Charter of the Council of Europe.

    (b)　The ratification of the Additional Protocol to the Revised Social Charter.

    (c)　Support the drafting of an Optional Protocol to the International Covenant on Economic, Social and Cultural Rights.

2. *Promotion of a Human Rights Agenda for the European Union*

3. *Establishment of a Permanent Human Rights body in Parliament*

RAID is a specialist research and advocacy agency working on the relationship between human rights and development. It is based in Queen Elizabeth House, Oxford University. It works closely with Oxfam, Human Rights Watch, and the UK Coalition Against Poverty. It produces case studies and analytical reports to help promote wider recognition for and understanding of social, economic and cultural rights. It makes recommendations to multilateral and bilateral donor institutions, such as the World Bank, the European Commission and DFID and it submits reports and complaints to relevant international human rights treaty monitoring bodies. Over the past year it has worked closely with the European Ombudsman.

SUMMARY RECOMMENDATIONS

As a fitting tribute to the 50th anniversary of the Universal Declaration of Human Rights RAID would like to propose a number of specific measures that could be taken by the British Government which show its commitment to the principles of universality, indivisibility and interdependence of all human rights. The incorporation of the European Convention of Human Rights into British law is an important first step towards full recognition of the European Bill of Human Rights.

There is a need to display a consistency in our approach to human rights at home and abroad. A credible external human rights policy depends on our willingness to apply the same standards internally.

I.　RATIFICATION

RAID and the UK Coalition Against Poverty recommend that the following specific measures be taken to signal the UK Government's commitment to the fundamental, indivisible and equal nature of all human rights, including those in the sphere of social protection:

    (a)　The United Kingdom should move to ratification of a comprehensive, renewed version of the Social Charter—the Revised European Social Charter. The UK Government signed this instrument in

November 1997, indicating the UK's endorsement of the rights it protects. Moving to is full ratification would greatly enhance the social protection afforded to all members of society, but especially to those living in poverty or suffering the effects of social exclusion.

(b) It is recommended that the UK ratifies the Additional Protocol to the European Social Charter providing for a system of collective complaints (1995). Ratification of this Protocol will allow trade unions, international non-governmental organisations and national NGOs to file *bona fide* complaints alleging unsatisfactory application of the Charter. The complaints Protocol has recently entered into force in seven Member States and RAID and the UK Coalition Against Poverty strongly advocate that access to the same mechanism be accorded to UK-based NGOs.

(c) Members of the Commission on Human Rights have been invited to comment on a proposal for an Optional Protocol for the International Covenant on Economic, Social and Cultural Rights (IESCR). Such a protocol, which would allow for a complaints mechanism, is long overdue. It is important that preliminary work on drafting a protocol should proceed. The current system, whereby we have an Optional Protocol allowing for complaints under the International Covenant on Civil and Political Rights only, is unbalanced and helps perpetuate an out-dated and hierarchical view of human rights. This is then easily characterised by developing country governments (who may not always be acting in good faith) as Northern hypocrisy. The British Government should make a statement of principle at the Commission on Human Rights of support for the start of work on the drafting of an Optional Protocol to the IESCR. It is then up to those who draft the protocol to ensure that they produce a text which will be acceptable to a number of governments.

II. THE PROMOTION OF A HUMAN RIGHTS AGENDA FOR THE EU

The human rights policies of the European Union are beset by a paradox. On the one hand, the Union is a staunch defender of human rights in both its internal and external affairs. On the other hand, it lacks a comprehensive or coherent policy at either level and fundamental doubts persist as to whether the institutions of the Union possess adequate legal competence in relation to a wide range of human rights issues arising within the framework of Community policies.

(a) That the British Government should encourage the Council of Ministers to adopt a solemn statement confirming the Union's commitments to a human rights policy based on the recognition of the universality, indivisibility and interdependence of all human rights.

(b) Call for the appointment of a Human Rights Commissioner in the next Commission.

(c) Request the Commission to prepare a detailed study on the proposal to establish a fully fledged European Union Human Rights Monitoring Agency.

(d) The expansion of the human rights aspects of the Commission's development and co-operation programmes (in particular, to give emphasis to the promotion of economic and social rights). The Union should also investigate allegations that specific development co-operation projects have had a negative human rights impact.

(e) Promote the accession by the Community to the European Social Charter of the Council of Europe, the sister instrument to the European Convention on Human Rights.

III. PROMOTE THE UN PARIS PRINCIPLES FOR THE ESTABLISHMENT OF HUMAN RIGHTS COMMISSIONS

(a) The British Government through the Department for International Development has a commitment to promoting good governance, democracy and respect for human rights. In its work in support of National Human Rights Commissions the British Government should do all in its power to ensure that the principles agreed by the United Nations for the creation of human rights commissions are enhanced and promoted.

(b) Building on the debates with Northern Ireland and Scotland we would hope that should there be agreement for the establishment of a sub-committee to work on human rights issues, that one item for its consideration would be how to promote human rights protection nationally, by for example creating a National Human Rights Commission.

ADDENDA

Background on the European Social Charter

Alongside the more widely known European Convention on Human Rights, the European Social Charter is the other central pillar of human rights protection in the Council of Europe. It has the potential to safeguard human rights in the social field across the 40 Member States of the Council of Europe. Yet, after the influx of new Member States to the Council of Europe in the late 1980s and 1990s, the number of ratifications of the Social Charter has not increased accordingly and remains at 22. While this situation persists, meaningful recognition of half the agreed content of human rights is denied and a lacuna lies at the heart of human rights protection in Europe.

The Member States of the Council of Europe identified the need, at the Ministerial conference held in Rome on 5 November 1990, to emphasise the indivisible nature of all human rights and give the European Social Charter new impetus. This culminated in the Revised European Social Charter, opened for signature on 3 May 1996, which better reflects the range of social rights which modern European governments agree as warranting protection. These include the right to protection against poverty and social exclusion, the right to decent housing, the right to protection against sexual harassment and victimisation, and the right of workers with family responsibilities to equal opportunities and equal treatment.

The United Kingdom was the first Member State of the Council of Europe to sign and ratify the original (1961) European Social Charter. By being among the first in line to move to ratification of the Revised European Social Charter, the United Kingdom would impress upon the other 40 Member States of the Council of Europe that it recognises the fundamental, indivisible and equal nature of all human rights, to include the social rights which the Revised European Social Charter protects. Its ratification, together with the adoption of a new complaints Protocol to improve supervision of the Charter, would send a clear message that the United Kingdom is prepared to stand by its record in ensuring that social rights, and the opportunities they afford, are enjoyed in full.

So far, 17 Member States have signed the Revised European Social Charter, including the UK which did so on 7 November 1997; yet only one State, Sweden, has moved to ratification. If the impetus and credibility of the Revised European Social Charter is to be maintained, its swift ratification by all signatories must follow.

Endorsement of the European Social Charter by NGOs in civil society

The ground-swell of opinion from civil society for the adoption of the Revised Social Charter is compelling at both the domestic and European levels.

Non-governmental organisations across Europe are actively supporting the Social Charter relaunch. A letter calling on all Members States to complete the process of ratification was presented to the Heads of State and Government of the Council of Europe at the intergovernmental colloquy, *The Social Charter of the 21st century*, held in Strasboug in May 1997. This was the first time that a colloquy had been dedicated to the Social Charter. The Parliamentary Assembly of the Council of Europe has also been active. It passed a recommendation in January 1998 to lend its support to a campaign for ratification. It also called for greater transparency and accessibility and for improvements in the Charter's enforcement.

Ratification of the Revised European Social Charter is viewed as a balance to the welcome incorporation of the European Convention on Human Rights into domestic law in the UK. Following a series of regional meetings organised in the UK by the National Council for Voluntary Organisations in March 1997, and attended by several hundred British agencies, a key recommendation was to endorse the call for ratification of the Revised Social Charter. In November 1997, a coalition of 15 prominent UK NGOs submitted a joint report on social and economic rights in the UK to the UN Committee on Economic, Social and Cultural Rights.[1] This is the first time that such co-ordinated action on social rights has been taken in the UK. The same coalition is actively seeking to engage with the European Social Charter.

In order to facilitate an open exchange between the British government and the corpus of non-governmental organisations in the UK active in the field of social rights, and in order to improve the effective enforcement of the social rights guaranteed by the Charter, it is deemed essential that the UK ratifies the Additional Protocol to the European Social Charter providing for a system of collective complaints (1995).

Ratification of this complaints Protocol will allow effective, independent scrutiny when a *bona fide* allegation of unsatisfactory application of the Charter is made by any party entitled to submit complaints. This includes trade unions, international NGOs and, provided a supporting declaration has been made, national non-governmental organisations. So far, seven Member States have ratified the complaints Protocol which thereby entered into force on 1 July. It is the strongly held view of RAID and the UK Coalition Against Poverty that it is appropriate for the UK to join their ranks and afford civil society organisations working in the UK the same powers of complaint.

A HUMAN RIGHTS AGENDA FOR THE EUROPEAN UNION FOR THE YEAR 2000

The human rights policies of the European Union are beset by a paradox. On the one hand, the Union is a staunch defender of human rights in both its internal and external affairs. On the other hand, it lacks a comprehensive or coherent policy at either level and fundamental doubts persist as to whether the institutions

---

[1] The Children's Rights Office; The Disability Alliance Educational and Research Association; Disability Awareness in Action; The European Anti-Poverty network; JUSTICE; Low Pay Unit; National Council for One Parent Families; The 1990 Trust; Oxfam UK/I; Parity; The Refugee Council; The Runnymede Trust; and Shelter.

of the Union possess adequate legal competence in relation to a wide range of human rights issues arising within the framework of Community policies.

Human rights are all too often assumed to be primarily matters arising in the context of external relations rather than internal affairs. But it is apparent that the internal and external dimensions of human rights policy can never be kept separate: they are two sides of the same coin.

A credible human rights policy must avoid unilateralism and double standards and that can only be done by ensuring reciprocity and consistency. Leading by example should become the leitmotif of a new European Union human rights policy.

The European Union is a key player in world affairs. It has close to 7 per cent of the world's population and almost as many people as the USA and Japan combined. It accounts for 27 per cent of the world's Gross Domestic Product, almost one-fifth of its trade flows and well over half of the total official development assistance flows to developing countries. Along with the power and influence that these statistics represent comes responsibility. The Union cannot be a credible defender of human rights in multilateral fora and in other countries while insisting that it has no general competence of its own in relation to those same rights.

The increasing incidence of racism, xenophobia and ethnic hatred within Europe is a matter of deep concern. The quality of justice within the EU is inevitably judged in part by our response to the plight of refugees fleeing persecution. Yet, within Europe we see pressures to shape asylum policy to accommodate nationalism and to weaken accepted international protection standards in the name of greater "efficiency" or the need to meet "new challenges".

There is concern about the inadequate institutional arrangements made by the Community in order to implement its numerous human rights policies in both internal and external matters. The current arrangements have led to an over-complicated and fragmented system.

[see *Leading by Example. A Human Rights Agenda for the European Union for the Year 2000*, Executive Summary of the Report by the Comité des Sages].

October 1998

APPENDIX 32

Letter from the Chairman of the Committee to the Foreign Secretary, 5 November 1998

On 16 September you issued a statement to the effect that all flights by Yugoslav carriers to the United Kingdom were to be banned with immediate effect, consequent upon the Common Position (98/426/CFSP) adopted by the European Council on 29 June and the subsequent Council Regulation no. 1901/98, which entered into force on 8 September 1998. I understand that the prohibition was given effect in United Kingdom law by the Yugoslavia (Prohibition of Flights) Regulations 1998, which came into force on 18 September.

The Committee was concerned to read reports in mid-September which indicated that the Government had considered delaying implementation of the prohibition order until after the expiry of the twelve-month notice period stipulated in the UK/Yugoslavia Air Services Agreement of 1959, a position which your statement happily reversed.

I should be grateful if you could indicate to the Committee on what legal grounds the 1959 agreement had been deemed to take precedence over the Council Regulation; why the notice of the ban was not served upon the Yugoslavian Government until 9 September; and the reason for the review of the timing of the ban's implementation.

Letter to the Chairman of the Committee from the Foreign Secretary, 30 November 1998

YUGOSLAVIA FLIGHT BAN

Thank you for your letter of 5 November about the EU flight ban on Yugoslav carriers. You asked three specific questions.

First, the relationship between our obligations under the 1959 UK/Yugoslavia Air Services Agreement (ASA) and the EC Regulation. Article 234 of the EC Treaty sets out the principle that a pre-accession agreement between a Member State and a third country is not affected by the provisions of the EC Treaty or by subsidiary Community legislation.

Second, the timing of serving notice on the FRY Government. The EU adopted a Common Position on the flight ban on 29 June. It was generally accepted that EU Member States would only take action once the implementing Regulation was adopted. The Commission then invited Member States to submit details of their air services arrangements. The Commission produced a draft Regulation at the end of July. It was eventually adopted on 8 September. Our Embassy in Belgrade handed over a Note Verbale to the FRY authorities the following day giving notice of termination of the ASA.

Third, the timing of implementation of the flight ban. There was always a balance to be struck between our legal obligation under the 1959 ASA (which was not overridden by the EC Regulation) and the need to bring Milosevic to comply with his obligations. That balance had tilted sharply by September given the worsening humanitarian situation on the ground in Kosovo, and in particular the reports of serious human rights abuses committed by the FRY and Serbian security forces. As my statement of 16 September makes clear, I concluded that, on moral and political grounds, Milosevic had forfeited the right to the 12 months' notice period which would normally apply under the terms of the ASA.

There is an implication in your letter that we were more reluctant than EU partners to implement the flight ban. This is not the case. The decision to press forward with a flight ban and other sanctions against Yugoslavia was taken under our Presidency. In addition, no Member State took action before the Regulation came into effect on 8 September. For practical and administrative reasons, most took a day or two to impose the flight ban: and Greece has still not implemented the ban. The UK gave notice of termination of the ASA on 9 September (the day after the Regulation came into effect). We implemented the flight ban a week later on 16 September.

————————